The Word

JOHN BARTON

The Word

On the Translation of the Bible

ALLEN LANE
an imprint of
PENGUIN BOOKS

ALLEN LANE

UK | USA | Canada | Ireland | Australia
India | New Zealand | South Africa

Penguin Books is part of the Penguin Random House group of companies
whose addresses can be found at global.penguinrandomhouse.com

First published by Allen Lane 2022

001

Copyright © John Barton, 2022

The moral right of the author has been asserted

Set in 10.5/14pt Sabon LT Std
Typeset by Jouve (UK), Milton Keynes
Printed and bound in Great Britain by Clays Ltd, Elcograf S.p.A.

The authorized representative in the EEA is Penguin Random House Ireland,
Morrison Chambers, 32 Nassau Street, Dublin D02 YH68

A CIP catalogue record for this book is available from the British Library

ISBN: 978-0-241-44881-6

For all members of Campion Hall

Contents

'If every man's humour were to be followed, there would be no end of translating'

Bishop Bancroft at the Hampton Court Conference, 1604

Foreword

Two books above all others stimulated me to write this one. The first was George Steiner's now classic *After Babel*, which I read with enthusiasm when it was first published in 1975 and have never stopped reflecting on. More recently, David Bellos's *Is That a Fish in Your Ear?* (2011) showed me that it is possible to write accessibly on translation even for readers unfamiliar with the languages discussed. I have myself found wide and encouraging interest in the topic as it pertains to the Bible, and have benefited from a lot of excellent feedback on various talks I have given – much of it from those with no specialist knowledge of either translation or the Bible. A number of friends and colleagues advised me along the way, and I must single out Nicholas King, SJ, himself the translator of the entire Greek Bible, for his sage assessment on both the practical and the theoretical issues the biblical translator faces.

This is not a handbook on how to translate the Bible, however, nor a reflection on a personal attempt to do so. It does not chronicle the history of different versions either, but analyses how translators over the centuries have approached the Bible – and what this means for everyone else. In mapping the field it draws on some recent contributions to translation studies, but it is not intended to be of interest only to theorists and practitioners of the discipline but rather to everyone with a stake in the Bible, whether as a document of faith or landmark of culture.

The modern translations cited are principally in English, but some examples are taken from other languages I know. Writing this book, I often wished I had command of some of the non-European languages into which the Bible is regularly translated by dedicated linguists seeking to spread the Christian gospel, but I am necessarily restricted to those I can read with understanding. Fortunately, that does include the ancient Hebrew, Aramaic and Greek in which the Bible was first written. I draw on dozens of translations, but biblical quotations are from the New Revised Standard Version, Anglicized Edition, unless otherwise noted. This has become the default version for much biblical study today.

My work on this project has all been conducted after 2014, when I retired as Oriel and Laing Professor of the Interpretation of Holy Scripture at Oxford. I have since been a Senior Research Fellow at Campion Hall, Oxford, which has proved the perfect base for thinking and writing about the Bible. It has been a privilege to be part of such a stimulating, warm and tolerant community. The book is dedicated to all my friends at the Hall with great affection and gratitude.

I am grateful to my agent, Felicity Bryan, who so sadly died while the book was in preparation. Felicity was an inspiration and the provider of endless encouragement to me, as to so many others. Warmest thanks now to Catherine Clarke, who continues her work for all of us represented by Felicity Bryan Associates. I'm delighted to benefit again from the expert and meticulous copy-editing of Linden Lawson and the insight of my editor at Penguin, Ben Sinyor. With this book, as with my previous one, *A History of the Bible: The Book and Its Faiths*, he has worked through every line of the text and made detailed suggestions that helped me to articulate implications of my arguments I was barely aware of myself. It is said, with a nod to Schleiermacher, that good interpreters understand their authors better than the authors understand themselves; and this has proved true of Ben.

Campion Hall, Oxford
April 2022

Glossary of English Editions

ASV   American Standard Version (1900–1901)
CEV   Contemporary English Version (1991–9)
ESV   English Standard Version (2001)
GNB   Good News Bible (1966–76)
JB   Jerusalem Bible (1966)
KJV   King James Version (1611)
NEB   New English Bible (1961–70)
NET   Christian Standard Bible/New English Translation (2001)
NETS   New English Translation of the Septuagint (2000–2007)
NIV   New International Version (1973–8)
NJB   New Jerusalem Bible (1985)
NRSV   New Revised Standard Version (1989)
REB   Revised English Bible (1989)
RNJB   Revised New Jerusalem Bible (2018–19)
RSV   Revised Standard Version (1946–52)
RV   Revised Version (1881–5)
TNIV   Today's New International Version (2002–5)

Introduction

Almost everyone who reads the Bible today reads it in translation. There are Jews who can read the Hebrew Bible (what Christians call the Old Testament) in the original languages, Hebrew and Aramaic; and Greek Orthodox Christians can understand the New Testament in the language it was written in, even though Greek is now very different from that used by its writers. Otherwise, however, it is only scholars and students of the Bible who learn the Bible's original languages. Everyone else depends on translations.

The Protestant Reformation of the sixteenth century is widely seen as the time when the Bible began to be translated into vernacular languages. But the use of a translated Bible goes back much further. In western Europe vernacular versions came in to replace not the original texts, but the Latin Bible, which was itself a translation. Where the Old Testament is concerned, the Latin Bible in turn rested only partly on the Hebrew and Aramaic. It was a rendering made largely in the fifth century CE by St Jerome (d. 420 CE), who did use the original Hebrew and Aramaic, but also earlier Latin translations that rested on a previous Greek version. That Greek text, now often known as the Septuagint, had been produced in the third century BCE for Jews who could no longer read Hebrew fluently. As we shall see, most Christians from the New Testament writers until the Reformation knew the Old Testament only in its Greek or Latin guise. Very few Christians after the age of the apostles knew any Hebrew. And by the time that vernacular translations of the New Testament were being made in Europe, few there could still read either Testament in Greek. The Latin Bible was 'The Bible', just as for generations of Anglophone readers the King James (or 'Authorized') Version has been 'The Bible', and remains so to an extent that is striking, though not unique to the English language. Most clergy will claim to have heard someone say, 'If the King James Bible was good enough for St Paul, it's good enough for me.' When I told a colleague some years ago that I was writing a history of the Bible, he replied: 'Presumably starting with the King James Version?', and was surprised to learn that I was beginning in the tenth century BCE, the era preceding Homer, rather than the seventeenth century of our era, the time of Shakespeare and the production of the King James Version.

So translation of the Bible is not a new phenomenon, even relatively speaking. Down the centuries, ever since there was a complete Bible, those who could read it in its original languages have formed a minority, and translation has been the primary medium through which Scripture has been manifest and understood. It is easy to miss just how remarkable this is. In Islam, which is the stereotypical 'religion of the book', translation of the Qur'an is frowned upon. Translations are described as paraphrases or guides to the holy text, aids to those who are learning to read it in Arabic, and it is only in its original form that it is authoritative. But Judaism, and even more so Christianity, are not quite so defined by the exact wording of a holy book in a language that many believers do not know: they allow, and in the Christian case positively encourage, translation, so that the meaning of their Scriptures can be understood by all.

Translating the Bible has often been seen, indeed, as a sacred task. Not only is it important in itself, so that the truth revealed in Scripture can be known; it is also crucial that it is undertaken with a properly reverent attitude. The translators of the King James Bible saw their work as a sacred trust. Translating the Bible was not, as they saw it, just like translating any other book, but demanded a particular kind of care and exactness. People's salvation depended on getting the wording right. Biblical translation for most practitioners has not been a hobby, nor even a serious literary endeavour, but a contribution to human salvation and perseverance. Translators have been persecuted and executed for renderings of the Bible deemed heretical, while in the modern world large sums have been poured into the manufacture of new versions because they were deemed essential – especially in cultures never before possessing a vernacular Bible – that it is difficult to imagine being spent on any other book.

Yet biblical translation cannot be wholly distinguished from translation in general. Indeed, translating the Bible has often been the paradigm case of translation, not only because it has been translated more often and widely than any other book, but also because theories about how it should be rendered into other languages have been the framework for thinking about the work of 'secular' translation. Attention to the wording of the original (the 'source') text, yet also to the intended readership in the language the text is being translated into (the 'target'), is present in every act of translation, not only with the Bible. The assembly of flat-pack furniture is rarely a religious experience, but anyone who has tried to match badly rendered Chinese to equally bad diagrams is familiar with the practical effects of poor translation. At a more critical level, the work of interpreters can aid or sabotage international agreements. In all spheres translation matters, and many of the principles involved are common to both biblical and secular contexts.

This book is about how translators negotiate the difficult task of producing usable versions of the Bible in the language of their own day, while remaining true to the original. It is a task that raises issues of faith and interpretation, as well as the obvious technical requirements, such as an intimate knowledge of the languages in which the Bible was written. This is not intended primarily as a history of biblical translation, though examples of different types will be taken from past practice, but is rather a discussion of what translation means for readers of the Bible, whether they are religious or not.

We will begin, though, with a brief history of biblical translation (Chapter 1), and with a special emphasis on translation into English. I then move on to detail the two main possibilities in rendering the Bible as set out by Eugene Nida, the father of modern biblical translation, usually known respectively as formal and functional equivalence – what most people would call literal versus free translation (Chapter 2). In reality, there is a spectrum of possibilities. Nida can be needlessly Procrustean, and I try to develop a new map of various kinds of translation, suggesting that the most interesting cases fall between Nida's two types (Chapter 3). The pursuit of a 'really accurate' translation is something of a red herring: all types have their place and none is suitable in all contexts. While there can be translations that are simply wrong, there cannot be one that is uniquely right. Nevertheless, it seems irrefutable that some are particularly ingenious or brilliant. Following George Steiner, I argue that good translation involves a kind of equilibrium between source and target (Chapter 4).

From here the book spills outwards to address matters the translator must consider but which are rarely discussed – and the significance of these for all those who rely upon their labour. Should the style be modern or 'traditional' (Chapter 5)? Should the development of Hebrew over time, or the New Testament's occasional use of archaizing Greek, be indicated in the translation? How far can differences of register be identified, and how should any that are identified be conveyed to a modern reader? Should occasional examples of 'bad' Greek in the New Testament be rendered in bad English? How much should the demands of liturgical use weigh with translators – and should this incline the translator in the direction of 'inclusive' language (Chapter 6)? Should translations register or elide the difference in meaning between Hebrew words in the Old Testament and their Greek 'equivalents' in the New – 'soul', for example, or 'salvation' (Chapter 7)? Are critical issues about the possibly composite nature of some texts to be taken account of in translation, or do they belong to a different sphere in which the translator should not interfere? Is the whole Bible to be treated as a single work, in which 'intertextual' links are to be noted and marked in the translation, or should each biblical book be regarded as a separate task, a self-contained entity (Chapter 8)? Should the original text be emended where it appears corrupt or mistaken, before it is translated (Chapter 9)? And finally, in the case of the Old Testament, which canon should be the basis for translation: the original Hebrew, or the Greek or Latin versions that have had an official status in respectively the Eastern Orthodox and Roman Catholic Churches (Chapter 10)?

These questions may seem a luxury to the practical demands made on modern translators, many of whom work in faith to provide the first Bible ever in a language for which they had also to devise the first writing system. In much of the world, it is demanding enough to give the sense of the Bible as accurately as possible, for those who have never heard its message before. According to the United Bible

Societies (UBS), the Bible now exists in some 700 languages – more than ten times the number for J. K. Rowling's *Harry Potter* series, the only widely translated work of comparable length – and in nearly every case in only one version. Translators employed by the UBS, and by Wycliffe Bible Translators, work tirelessly to increase their coverage: there are, after all, something like 7,000 living languages in the world.[1]

One language stands apart from this. There is a huge number of English translations, with new ones appearing every year. It means that those with no Hebrew or Greek can compare different versions and at least see some of the possibilities for what the text might mean, and – I suspect – encourages other would-be translators to try their own hand at the difficult but rewarding task of capturing the biblical messages in English. And because there evidently isn't only one 'correct' translation of any text, it challenges readers to be open to ambiguity and nuance in the text when they see just how differently various interpreters tackle the same book. It enables, in sum, the kind of work this book undertakes. And given this, it makes sense to ask searching questions about the theoretical basis of the entire enterprise, and the significance of its practice for the religions which hold the Bible sacred. On the whole, as Robert Alter argues, translating the Bible into English has been thought to depend on expertise in the biblical languages, but little reflection on the nature and practice of translation as such, and not always much literary talent. Consequently biblical translation is not highly 'theorized', whereas translation studies is now a growing field for other kinds of translation (and Nida's ideas in particular have been assimilated into it, even though they were originally developed for the sake of Bible translation).[2] There are theoretical questions that are not asked insistently enough.[3]

Theoretical does not mean abstract, however, and it is all too easy to underestimate the importance and the power of translating the Bible, as though it were a side issue in the history of religion and theology. The great religious awakening we associate with the Reformation is often thought to have caused great numbers of Christians who previously only had access to the Latin Bible to want to read the Scriptures themselves, and therefore to have provided the impetus for vernacular translation across Europe. Diarmaid MacCulloch has argued, conversely, that the surge of translations of the Bible made in the fifteenth and early sixteenth centuries – before Luther's ninety-five theses and what is usually reckoned to be the onset of the Reformation – was a major factor in bringing about reform. Reading the Bible in their own language led Christians to see that many of the religious customs and ideas they knew from the Church were not attested in Scripture, and therefore to question them. That realization was a significant cause of reform, rather than merely one of its consequences.

Translating the Bible thus drove religious change – and not only in early modern Europe. A millennium and a half earlier Christians scattered around the coast of the Mediterranean overwhelmingly used the Old Testament in its Greek translation as they defined their new religion, and we shall see how features particular to the Septuagint came to shape their ideas about the identity and nature of Jesus. Greek renderings of titles for the God of the Hebrew Bible, especially 'Lord', came to be applied also to Jesus, as we can see in the New Testament, suggesting a degree of contiguity between him and God that the Hebrew could not. This is not to say that Christians would not otherwise have come to regard Jesus as divine; but at the birth of Christianity, when his relation to God was not yet settled, the precise terms used to name him were certainly significant. Had the Hebrew Bible remained untranslated, it is difficult to imagine the development of Christianity in late antiquity following the course it did.

Translators have more power than they often realize, therefore. They are not mere conduits between an original text and a vernacular version, and translation is not simply the transferring of a body of information out of one language and into another. What is said is not separable from how it is said, and sentences expressing what we might call the same thoughts expressed in different languages are never exact equivalents. Translated texts that are purely informative – instruction manuals, for example – can sometimes match the original very closely indeed, but this is precisely because they lack metaphysical significance. Literature, however – and for believers the Bible may be more than literature, but it certainly isn't less – is imprinted by the particular linguistic culture that gave rise to it, and its passage to and setting in another can be far from straightforward.

For the majority of its history, Scripture has been encountered almost entirely in languages other than those in which it was written. Its translators have been among the principal agents in mediating the Bible's message to readers and hearers, even in shaping what that message is. Our picture of Christianity in particular – a religion formed in dialogue with translated Scripture – is incomplete without taking in the history, practice and theoretical underpinning of their endeavours.

I

A Brief History of Biblical Translation[1]

The books of the Old Testament were for the most part written in Hebrew, though there are a few sections in Aramaic,[2] an equally ancient relation – about as close as Dutch is to German, or Spanish to Italian. The New Testament was all composed in Greek. Sometimes it is possible to tell, from a syntactic or lexical feature, that the authors of the Gospels spoke and thought in Aramaic, which had become the normal language of everyday speech in Palestine by the first century CE. None of the books of the New Testament is a translation from that language, however, and some of its authors may well have spoken only Greek, such as the writer of the Letter to the Hebrews, and perhaps also Luke. Occasionally it has been suggested that one or other of the Gospels is a translation from some lost Aramaic original, but the idea has never gained much traction.[3] By the time the first Gospel (probably Mark) was written, perhaps around 70 CE, Greek was already the main language of Christians, and it remained so for several centuries. In the 50s and 60s CE Paul was already writing in Greek to the Churches he had founded (and to the Church in Rome), in which no one, evidently, spoke Aramaic.

GREEK VERSIONS

Even before its latest books, such as (probably) Ecclesiastes and Daniel, were being written, the bulk of the Hebrew Bible had already been translated into Greek. Such translation began in the third century BCE.[4] It was undertaken not by Christians (who did not yet exist), but by Jews wanting to help fellow Jews who no longer understood

Hebrew with any fluency because they lived in Egypt, where Greek was the normal language of everyday life. At first the Pentateuch (the five 'Books of Moses', Genesis, Exodus, Leviticus, Numbers and Deuteronomy) was translated into Greek, with the rest of the Hebrew Bible following not long after. A legend arose that the initial translation had been requested by the Egyptian ruler Ptolemy II Philadelphus (r. 285–246 BCE). This story is preserved in *The Letter of Aristeas to Philocrates*,[5] dating from the second century BCE, which maintains that the translation was prompted by Ptolemy's desire to gather copies of all the greatest books in the world into the great library at Alexandria (which did indeed come, in time, to be one of the wonders of the world, a kind of research university).[6] He asked the high priest in Jerusalem to send learned men to make a translation of the Pentateuch, six from each of the twelve tribes of Israel, and these seventy-two scholars finished their work, with complete agreement, in seventy-two days. For that reason their version is called the Septuagint, from the Latin for 'seventy', abbreviated in Roman numerals as LXX.[7] *Aristeas* does not claim that they were divinely inspired but probably implies it, and a later addition to the text says that each man translated the whole Pentateuch and every version was found to be the same, a feat which surely would have required divine intervention of some kind.[8]

Though the account is legendary, it is no doubt correct in implying that the Septuagint, and Greek translations of other scriptural books that followed, were made for the community of Jews in Alexandria. This community came to revere the translation as highly as the original Hebrew, and a sense that it had been made through divine providence passed into the Christian Church. It is normally this version that New Testament writers cite, and in later times even the theologians of Antioch in Syria, although this was a Semitic-speaking area, treat it as absolutely authoritative, just as the Greek Orthodox Church still does today. Though the name Septuagint properly refers to the translation of the Pentateuch alone, the term is nowadays commonly used to designate the whole Old Testament in the Greek Bible.

Once Christians adopted the Greek Bible, Jews started to suspect that they might have tampered with it and distorted the original Hebrew – introducing changes that gave more support to Christian ideas such as the divinity of Christ. (As we shall see, the Septuagint offered the first Christians things the underlying Hebrew could not, though this was a product of developments in theological thinking between the composition of the Hebrew Bible and its translation as well as linguistic features of Greek and Hebrew themselves, rather than the result of Christian interference with the text after the fact.) In the second century CE there were at least three attempts to improve the translation, by three Jewish scholars traditionally called Aquila, Symmachus and Theodotion (clearly not their Hebrew names). They tried to make the Greek a more literal version of the Hebrew, Aquila to such an extent that some of his translations are almost incomprehensible, as we shall see later (see Chapter 3). Symmachus produced a new translation, in more stylish Greek. Theodotion's version is closer to a Greek text found at Nahal Hever near the Dead Sea, containing the Twelve Minor Prophets, probably from the first century BCE – which may show that correction of the Septuagint in a more literal direction was already under way even before the suspicion arose that Christians had altered the text. Eventually, agreed versions of the Greek Bible established themselves, in three different editions (usually called 'recensions') used by Christians in different areas: in Alexandria and the rest of Egypt an edition produced by Hesychius, a bishop martyred in 312 CE; in Constantinople and Antioch that of Lucian, and, in between, the version recorded by Origen (d. 254 CE) in his Hexapla, a collation of six different texts of the Bible in parallel columns.

The Greek Bible as it has come down to us includes more books than the Hebrew Bible. These are the books known usually as the Apocrypha, though Catholics and Orthodox Christians describe them as 'deuterocanonical', that is, belonging to a second (Greek *deuteros*) level within the biblical canon. From early in the Christian era these books were known only in Greek, though some of them were originally written in Hebrew or Aramaic. The Hebrew text of Sirach and Tobit is now partly known thanks to recent archaeological finds. Some books, notably Wisdom of Solomon, were clearly written in Greek from the beginning. The deuterocanonical books were produced later than most books in the Hebrew Bible, mainly in the last two centuries BCE. Though they continued to be read by Jews, the Jewish canon of Scripture eventually excluded them, and they came to be revered only by Christians. The Greek Bible itself does not distinguish them from the books that also occur in the Hebrew Bible, and they are interspersed among the books of that Bible without any distinction – narrative books (such as Tobit and Judith) next to other narratives (Chronicles, Esther), and 'wisdom' books (Wisdom of Solomon, Sirach) next to other wisdom books (Proverbs, Job). This arrangement can be seen in a modern Catholic Bible such as the Jerusalem Bible or the Revised New Jerusalem Bible. Although it is a translation, the Greek Bible is regarded as the canonical text in the Greek Orthodox Church, in preference to the Hebrew. Whether the Greek Bible, as the Bible of the early Church, should be authoritative for other Christians too is a point we shall return to in Chapter 10.

ARAMAIC RENDERINGS

Jews in Egypt, living in a Greek culture, could not always cope with Hebrew; but in Palestine and Babylonia too Hebrew could be a problem, since Aramaic was the common tongue, and Hebrew was the language only of the learned. So Aramaic translations began to appear. Some think that Nehemiah 8:8 refers to this activity: when the Torah was read to Jewish exiles newly returned from Babylonia in the fifth century BCE, the Levites 'gave the sense', which may mean that they translated it into Aramaic. (The Torah is a Hebrew name for the Pentateuch, but it can also mean all authoritative forms of divine instruction, and in this case we do not know whether what was read was the whole Pentateuch, a selection from it, or other laws and directives that had not yet been canonized.) For a long time Aramaic renderings were oral in character. Indeed, well into the Christian era it was held that the Aramaic version, the *targum*, should not be written down but produced ad hoc after the scriptural reading in Hebrew in the synagogue, and must not be made by the same person, so as to avoid any impression that the targum was itself inspired or authoritative. Nevertheless, targums did come to be written down. Examples are Targum Onkelos on the Pentateuch, which had become the official version by the third century CE, and Targum Jonathan, a translation of the prophetic books, from about the same period. The targums offer quite 'loose' translations, sometimes even radically changing the meaning of the Hebrew text. Indeed, sometimes they offer what are politely called 'converse' translations, which give the opposite sense from the original. Thus God's threat to the Israelites in Exodus 33:3, 'I will not go up among you', is rendered in Targum Neofiti 'I will not remove the glory of my presence from among you'.[9]

A dialect of Aramaic spoken in Edessa (now Urfa, in south-east Turkey) also acquired its own Christian version of both Testaments, known as the Peshitta, probably in the second or third century CE: the dialect is normally known as Syriac. The Old Testament translation is thought to have been the work of Jewish converts to Christianity. The Peshitta survives as the Bible of the Syriac-speaking Churches (the Church of the East, the Syrian Orthodox Church and the Maronite Church in Lebanon).

LATIN TRANSLATIONS

Greek was the common language of the whole Mediterranean world and of the Middle East from the late fourth century BCE, when Alexander the Great created his empire, until the beginning of the Roman Empire 300 years later. Educated Romans were expected to know Greek. Christian worship was conducted in Greek, even in Rome itself – hence the fragments of Greek that persist in the Western liturgy such as *kyrie eleison*, 'Lord, have mercy'. But Latin did eventually take over, and Christians, probably in the Roman territories along the northern coast of Africa, began to make Latin versions of the Bible, normally known as the Old Latin (*Vetus Latina*). These were not made from the Hebrew, but from the Greek of the Septuagint; so the Old Latin Old Testament was a translation of a translation. (The New Testament was of course in Greek anyway, so there we have a Latin translation of a Greek original.)

The first person to translate the Old Testament into Latin directly from Hebrew and Aramaic was Jerome (347–420 CE). The Pope, Damasus, had asked him to revise the Latin of the New Testament in the light of the best manuscripts available, but Jerome decided to go further and revise the whole Bible; and he took the major step of learning some Hebrew. Settling in Bethlehem in 386, he found a Christian convert from Judaism who was able to teach him the language, and he consulted other Jewish scholars, as well as using Origen's Hexapla in the library at Caesarea. He produced a nearly complete translation of both Testaments.

Jerome's version was not received very well at first: believers predictably preferred the translation they already knew. Augustine tells us that, when it was first used in what is now Tripoli, the congregation objected so strongly to hearing that Jonah was sheltered by ivy rather than a gourd (as in the Old Latin) that a riot ensued. Eventually, however, Jerome's translation established itself, especially in Italy and in northern Europe, as the standard, or *biblia vulgata* – hence the English term Vulgate, though that was earlier applied to the Old Latin and only became attached to Jerome's Bible in the sixteenth century. Jerome personally translated the whole New Testament, but in the Latin Old Testament to this day some books still appear in the Old Latin where he did not get around to them, notably Daniel, Maccabees and Sirach (traditionally known in Latin as Ecclesiasticus – not to be confused with Ecclesiastes).

OTHER TRANSLATIONS

During the Middle Ages there were translations of all or parts of the Bible into various languages, often as aids to study. The Hebrew Bible was translated into Arabic, though probably written in Hebrew script, by Saadia Gaon, a leader of the Jewish community in Babylonia in the tenth century CE. His version is still used by some Jews in Yemen, though there are more up-to-date Arabic versions available. Medieval Christian translations also survive in Ethiopic, and in many European languages. The Psalms are often to be found in translation, usually as aids to monks learning to recite them in the liturgy, and normally rendered from the Latin. There are fragments of Psalters, written in German, dating back to the ninth century and associated with the abbey of Reichenau on Lake Constance. From the fourteenth we have a translation of the entire Bible by Marchwart Biberli (1265–1330), a Dominican from Zurich. There are the remains of a Bible in Gothic, an East Germanic language (now extinct), which is almost the only evidence for that language, along with a biblical commentary in Gothic known as *Skeireins*, the Gothic for 'commentary'. The translation, by the missionary bishop Wulfila (311–83 CE), dates to the fourth century, remarkably early for a rendering into a language of northern Europe – though Gothic was widespread at the time and spoken in parts of Italy and France as well as the traditional Germanic lands. Prefiguring the work of so many translators of the Bible for cultures in the modern world with no tradition of writing, Wulfila invented an alphabet for Gothic, based on the Roman alphabet but incorporating letters modelled on runes as well.

In England, Bede is said to have been working on an English translation of St John's Gospel at the time of his death in 735, and King Alfred (849–99) apparently translated the Psalms, or more likely patronized their translation. Aelfric of Winchester in 1010 seems to have succinctly paraphrased, rather than exactly translated, some of the narrative books of the Old Testament, but wrote that he was hesitant about rendering Scripture in the common tongue because of the danger that the ignorant might misunderstand it – an attitude which hardened in the later Middle Ages into a reluctance to allow lay people to read the Bible at all, and which attracted the anger of the Reformers. A real translation of the Gospels can be found in the Northumbrian Lindisfarne Gospels, where the Latin text is glossed with an interlinear, word-by-word translation in the local dialect of English.

The Bible was also translated into Slavic languages, following the missionary activity of Cyril (826–69) and Methodius (815–85) in the ninth century: this was used in the liturgy rather than for private study, as with most western European versions. Once again an alphabet was produced especially for the purpose – now known as Cyrillic. According to the posthumous *Life of Methodius* he translated the entire Bible into Slavonic – what is now called Church Slavonic – in six months in 884. This extraordinary feat may be an exaggeration – he may have translated only the liturgical readings. But there is a manuscript from the following century, the Codex Zographensis, that does contain all four Gospels in their entirety in a Slavonic version. A complete Slavonic Bible was not produced until the fifteenth century.

THE EARLY MODERN PERIOD

It is clear, from all the translations surveyed so far, that translating the Bible was by no means a novelty by the sixteenth century and the time of the Reformation. The practice had continued in the years before Martin Luther's ninety-five theses of 1517: the Bible was translated into various forms of German between 1466 and 1522, into Dutch in 1477, into Spanish and Czech in 1478 and into Catalan in 1492. It was Johannes Gutenberg's invention of the printing press in 1439 that facilitated such ventures – as mentioned, it has been argued that the rise in biblical translations made possible by the press helped to prepare the ground for the Reformation, rather than being a product of it.[10]

Even so, the drive to translate the Bible into various vernaculars gained a fresh impetus from the emphasis placed by the great Reformers, Luther, Calvin and Zwingli, on access to the Bible for all Christians in their own language. A translation of the Bible into Middle German had been made as early as 1350 and was printed in 1466, but it was naturally a translation from the Vulgate, and the translators had no knowledge of Greek or Hebrew. Luther, on the other hand, worked on the New Testament from the Greek of Desiderius Erasmus's edition and produced a German version in 1522, with the Old Testament, direct from the Hebrew, following in 1534. By then his New Testament had already been translated in its turn into Dutch, Danish and Swedish. Part of his genius was to forge a kind of standard German comprehensible to speakers of the many regional varieties of the language, which was far more varied than English in the late Middle Ages – though for the benefit of readers in the north a translation was made into Low German, with a glossary of unusual words.

Catholics responded by producing versions of their own. The first, by Hieronymus Emser (1477–1527), adapted an early version of Luther's New Testament to bring it closer to the Vulgate, and survived in use among Catholics in German-speaking areas into the eighteenth century. Even subsequent Catholic Bibles in German tended to adhere quite closely to Luther, demonstrating a point we shall return to (see Chapter 5): the difficulty of deviating from the classic translation of a text. This is the problem that has beset all translations into English since the King James Version (KJV).

There were Bibles in Middle English, the language of Chaucer, in the late fourteenth century – so-called Wycliffite Bibles, associated with John Wyclif though probably not made by him.[11] Being tainted with Lollardy, a sort of proto-Protestant movement critical of the Church's structures, and of which Wyclif was a leader, these were opposed by the Church hierarchy, as was also the significant translation into modern English by William Tyndale (1494–1536), who had produced his own rendering of the Greek New Testament, inspired by Luther's, by 1526. Like so many translators in this period he added his own notes, and translated many terms in a way that was tendentious: thus 'penance' was rendered 'repentance', undermining the medieval system of penitential practices, including indulgences, which were to be such a major negative theme in Luther's teaching. Many copies of Tyndale's New Testament were burnt, and Thomas More wrote a refutation in 1529, describing it as heretical; Tyndale himself was arrested and executed in 1536 when he was halfway through translating the Old Testament from Hebrew.

Yet only a year later Tyndale's version was completed by John Rogers, his associate, and published for the English market as the Matthew Bible, and it was licensed by Henry VIII. By the end of 1539 England had the Great Bible, edited by Miles Coverdale (who had produced a translation of his own in 1535), the first official English Bible. The king directed a copy to be placed in all churches in the land, and it was also a success in Scotland. The Great Bible was essentially a revision of Tyndale as completed in the Matthew Bible, but where Tyndale had not finished the translation Coverdale worked from the Vulgate and from Luther's German. The year 1560 saw another milestone, the Geneva Bible, produced by the exiles in Geneva who had fled the persecution of the Catholic Queen Mary. In private and domestic use this supplanted previous versions, and it is the Bible of Shakespeare, John Donne and George Herbert, as well as of Oliver Cromwell, John Bunyan and indeed of King James himself; it was also the first vernacular Bible to be printed in Scotland.[12] In 1568 there followed the Bishops' Bible, an official attempt at a compromise between the Great Bible and the Geneva Bible. It did not become popular despite official instruction that it be read in churches, but it was the immediate basis for the King James Version of 1611. Bruce M. Metzger, an expert on biblical translations, comments that 'for the idiom and vocabulary, Tyndale deserves the greatest credit; for the melody and harmony, Coverdale; for scholarship and accuracy, the Geneva version'.[13]

Catholics also produced Bibles in English: the Rheims-Douai New Testament appeared in 1582, with the Old Testament following in 1609–10. This was a translation of the Vulgate and used a lot of Latinate terms, at which the King James translators had an enjoyable tilt: 'we have shunned the obscuritie of the papists ... of purpose to darken the sence, that since they must needs translate the Bible, yet by the language thereof, it may be kept from being understood'.[14] Soon there were Bibles in almost all the languages of Europe, in both Protestant and Catholic countries. Even though the liturgy remained in Latin until the 1960s, many Catholics around the world have used vernacular Bibles for study, and to refute Protestants.

THE KING JAMES VERSION

In 1604 the Puritan party in the Church of England petitioned the King (James I of England, James VI of Scotland) to commission a new translation to improve on both the Bishops' and the Geneva Bible. Rather than work in haste, as previous translators had done, the six 'companies' based in Westminster, Oxford and Cambridge were allowed to take their time, and to take account of improved knowledge of Hebrew, Aramaic and Greek. So it was six years before publication of the 'Authorized Version' – though it was never actually authorized, despite the fact that the king had commissioned the translators. These included some of the best scholars of the day, overseen by Lancelot Andrewes, successively Bishop of Chichester, Ely and Winchester, and a great prose stylist as well as a formidable scholar.

The KJV was not a new translation. As the Preface puts it,

Truly, good Christian Reader, we never thought from the beginning, that we should neede to make a new Translation, nor yet to make of a bad one a good one . . . but to make a good one better, or out of many good ones, one principall good one, not justly to be excepted against; that hath bene our endeavour, that our marke.[15]

It is a statement enthusiasts of the KJV would do well to reflect upon: many of the striking phrases for which it is justly famous go back to the Bishops' Bible, to the Geneva or Great Bible, and even to Tyndale. The KJV was slightly old-fashioned in its language for the time, just as is the Book of Common Prayer, using Tudor rather than Jacobean English. This is partly the result of its dependence on older models, but partly also deliberate, giving it a certain patina of venerability: we shall look at this device in Chapter 5.

TRANSLATION IN MODERN TIMES

The KJV held sway in the English-speaking world for several centuries, with occasional light revisions. It was not until the late nineteenth century that there was a serious drive to revise it thoroughly, resulting in the Revised Version (RV) of 1885 (the New Testament part appeared in 1881). One of the revisers' principles was to use the same English word for the same Hebrew, Aramaic or Greek word, so far as possible – an important qualification, since languages do not work in such a way that it is always feasible to be so literal. The RV is thus a 'formal-equivalence' version, a type discussed in Chapter 3. The translators were assisted by an American panel, and the wrangling between the two groups poisoned relations in the world of transatlantic biblical studies for a generation.[16] The American panel eventually published its own version as the American Standard Version (ASV) in 1901, and it became the preferred Bible for many in North America who were not firmly wedded to the KJV.

In the twentieth century translations of the Bible into English proliferated, and the flood continues to this day. In most other languages they have been less numerous, but the global reach of English has meant that publishers have always seen a market for new English versions. But the energies of translators have often also been directed to producing versions in languages that till now had lacked any translation at all. Indeed, biblical translators have often been at the forefront of recording and analysing languages previously without a writing system, in order to go on to produce a version of the Scriptures. This work is carried on by the United Bible Societies, the overarching organization that includes 146 national Bible societies in some 200 countries. Included is the British and Foreign Bible Society (now known simply as the Bible Society), founded in 1805. There are also independent translation bodies in many countries, such as Wycliffe Bible Translators, who have a clear evangelical allegiance. The linguistic skill and knowledge of these biblical translators is usually enormously high.

Modern translations into English are of two kinds. First, there are revisions of older versions, principally of the KJV. Once the RV had begun this process, it continued throughout the twentieth century and into the twenty-first. In 1936 the Churches of the USA and Canada resolved to prepare a fresh revision of the KJV to replace the ASV but to stay as close to the KJV tradition as might be feasible, given the (once again) improved state of knowledge of biblical languages and culture. This Revised Standard Version (RSV) of the Old and New Testaments was published in 1952, the RSV Apocrypha following in 1957.[17] The RSV was a sober and sound revision of the KJV, and soon established itself as useful alike for study and for worship: it sounds like the KJV, but makes sense in places where its predecessor is obscure or even meaningless. Catholics and Eastern Orthodox Christians came to see the value of the RSV, and in 1973 the Common Bible appeared, an ecumenical edition of the RSV containing all the books regarded by Protestants as the Apocrypha and by Catholics as 'deuterocanonical', such as Wisdom, Sirach, Tobit. In the following year it was expanded to include the three additional books treated as canonical by the Eastern Orthodox Churches alone (Psalm 151 and 3 and 4 Maccabees).

The RSV was itself revised in the 1980s to produce the New Revised Standard Version (NRSV), published in 1989. This differs from the RSV in no longer using the old second-person singular forms 'thou', 'thee' and 'thine' in passages addressing God, and in opting for 'inclusive language', in which there is an avoidance of exclusively male language in places where women may be included. Thus Paul now addresses his readers as 'brothers and sisters' rather than simply as 'brothers', and many passages are pluralized: 'Blessed is the man who ...' (Psalm 1) becomes 'Happy are those who . . . '. These changes will be discussed in Chapter 6. The NRSV has appealed to many mainstream congregations in the UK and North America, supplanting the RSV.

Another and more recent revision of the RSV is the English Standard Version, which appeared in 2001. This was produced by conservative evangelical scholars, using the RSV as their starting point; but a Catholic edition, including the deuterocanonical books, was published in 2018, and then in 2019 as the Augustine Bible. It is more conservative than the NRSV, adhering more closely to a 'literal' rendering while introducing some inclusive language. There are signs that it is attracting followers in the Catholic Church among those who find the Jerusalem Bible (see below) too 'modern' in tone. As I write, it is likely to be adopted by the Catholic bishops in England and Wales for readings at Mass.

New editions of translations in other languages have also proliferated. In German, the latest Luther Bible appeared in 2016, in time for the celebration of the five-hundredth anniversary of the beginning of the Reformation the following year. This is a more conservative revision than the NRSV but takes account of much recent work on the biblical text. Also in German is the new Zürcher Bibel of 2007, technically a revision of the version published in 1531 by Huldrych Zwingli and Leo Jud, but made on the basis of a completely new study of the original texts, and among the best of modern versions.

The second type of modern translations begins from scratch, without reference to any traditional renderings. Early examples by individuals were the work of James Moffatt (1870–1944) in Britain, who published a New Testament translation in 1913 and an Old Testament in 1924, and in the USA of Edgar J. Goodspeed (1871–1962), in 1923. These completely abandon KJV style and attempt to translate the Bible as though it had never been translated before. Goodspeed in particular aims to give each book a distinctive flavour, which has seldom been attempted. The same is true of the later J. B. Phillips (1906–1982), a British scholar of the post-war period who published *The New Testament in Modern English* in 1958.[18] Phillips, to acclaim from C. S. Lewis, translated New Testament idioms in terms of modern customs, so that Paul's instruction that believers should greet each other with 'a holy kiss' becomes 'a hearty handshake all round' (Romans 16:16). Moffatt, meanwhile, was often very successful in conveying the tone of the original, as in his rendering of the famous passage on love at 1 Corinthians 13:

> Love is very patient, very kind. Love knows no jealousy; love makes no parade, gives itself no airs, is never rude, never selfish, never irritated, never resentful; love is never glad when others go wrong, love is gladdened by goodness, always slow to expose, always eager to believe the best, always hopeful, always patient.

Another important solo translation, in this case of the Gospels only, was by E. V. Rieu (1887–1972), in the Penguin Classics series of which he was the editor. In a radio discussion Rieu and Phillips agreed that they approached the translation of the New Testament from similar angles, both producing what would now be called 'functional-equivalence' translations (see Chapter 2).[19]

In the twentieth century both English and French had significant from-scratch translations made by committees. The Church of Scotland initiated a new ecumenical version, published as the New English Bible (NEB) in 1961 (New Testament) and 1970 (Old Testament and Apocrypha). This avoided archaisms, used 'you' rather than 'thou', and printed the text in paragraphs instead of verse by verse, though it did not yet use inclusive language. The style was thoroughly modern, though felt by some to be rather academic, and the scholarship behind at least the Old Testament was sometimes idiosyncratic. A revision appeared in 1989, the Revised English Bible (REB), and did take inclusivity seriously, as well as curing some of the idiosyncrasies; but superior publicity for the NRSV has meant that the REB has not had the impact that might have been expected for such an excellent translation. The REB returned to setting the translation out in double columns, which gives it a slightly archaic appearance that (in my view) detracts from its novelty.

In French there was also a highly innovative translation, produced in the Dominican École Biblique in Jerusalem and published in sections in 1948–54 as the *Bible de Jérusalem*, with a one-volume edition following in 1956. For this, the help of poets and literary scholars was enlisted. Verse texts, such as the Psalms, are rendered in metrical lines, while the underlying scholarship – as befits the place of origin – is of an extremely high standard, expressed in invaluable notes and introductions to the various biblical books. No attention at all is paid to earlier French versions, which was perhaps easier than with English, as there is no classic French rendering that might resonate behind the new one as the KJV does in English. In 1966 an English translation of this Bible, the Jerusalem Bible (JB), was produced, and it was quickly adopted liturgically by the Catholic Church in Britain and other English-speaking countries, and widely used by students of the Bible. Its achievement was that it not only used contemporary speech, like the NEB, but also tried to imitate the rhythms and tone of the original, rendering the Gospel of John, for example, in a rather more stately style than the other Gospels, Paul in colloquial English, and passages of the prophets in a broken and breathless idiom where the original conveys urgency and fear. The Jerusalem Bible was thoroughly revised in 1985 as the New Jerusalem Bible (NJB). It remains in many ways the most innovative biblical translation in common use. In 2019 a Revised New Jerusalem Bible (RNJB) appeared: this, as we shall see in Chapter 3, tended to row back more in the direction of literalism.

Jewish readers who wanted an English version of the Hebrew Bible were content for many years to use the KJV or lightly revised versions of it. In the twentieth century, however, a new translation was produced by the Jewish Publication Society in the USA in 1917, called simply Tanakh, the traditional acronymic Jewish name for the Scriptures ('Law, Prophets, Writings' = Torah, Nevi'im, Ketuvim). A second, revised edition appeared in 1985. It uses fairly modern English, but adheres very closely to the Hebrew and Aramaic. This makes it particularly useful for study purposes by those with no Hebrew or Aramaic, since it gives exactly the sense of the traditional, unamended text – especially if it is used with a commentary such as that in the excellent Jewish Study Bible.[20]

There have also been a number of translations of the Hebrew Bible by individual Jewish scholars: Martin Buber and Franz Rosenzweig, Henri Meschonnic, André Chouraqui and Everett Fox. All these are what I call 'imitative' translations, in that they try, as few Christian versions do, to capture the flavour of the Hebrew original by using unusual forms of English, German or French. Most recently there is also a translation by Robert Alter, which does not distort the English yet still tries to be to some extent imitative of the original text. All these approaches raise issues that will be discussed in Chapters 3 and 4, but they need only be registered here as further from-scratch versions. A Christian translation that pursues the opposite course by assimilating the biblical message extensively to modern idioms, and would be regarded by most as a paraphrase, is Eugene Peterson's *The Message*, published in 2002. As we shall see, the tendency of Christian translators towards paraphrase and of Jewish ones towards literalism is an important phenomenon, related to and reflecting the two religions' differing attitudes towards what is meant by the authority of the Bible.

There is another translation that is used worldwide by evangelical Christians in preference to all others: the New International Version (NIV), published in 1978 ('international' in Bibles, dictionaries and encyclopaedias usually signifies 'evangelical'). It is rather a mixed case in terms of the classification I am using, since it has a certain KJV flavour and is quite close to the RSV/NRSV, even though it was a new translation rather than a revision of an earlier version. It has its own distinctive rendering in places that are doctrinally important for evangelical Christians. As the Preface puts it, the translators believe 'that the Bible is God's word in written form'. They claim that the NIV is interdenominational, which is true though slightly disingenuous, in that those who worked on it, whatever Church they belonged to, were all committed evangelicals. No Catholics or 'liberals' were involved, so the claim that it has no 'sectarian bias' is not quite accurate. It attributes the worldwide success of the NIV to the grace of God – a high claim for any translation. Only occasionally, however, does any particular bias appear. For example, at Romans 3:25 we read that 'God presented Christ as a sacrifice of atonement', which not all New Testament scholars would agree with, but which is an important formulation for those who believe that Jesus' death was a substitutionary sacrifice, as many evangelical Christians do – and which they believe Paul taught. And at Isaiah 7:14 the main text has 'the virgin will conceive', as quoted in Matthew 1:23, though here the more probable rendering 'young woman' is given in a footnote. (The issue raised by these translations is discussed in Chapter 10.) Second Timothy 3:16 becomes 'all Scripture is God-breathed' – this is an important statement for an evangelical doctrine of the inspiration of Scripture, and a rendering entirely defensible, though again not agreed on by all. Overall, however, the NIV is a mainstream modern translation, neither particularly innovative nor overly conservative. An inclusive-language edition of it appeared in 2005 as Today's New International Version (TNIV). It is the known evangelical provenance of the NIV, rather than the very few arguably tendentious renderings of the text, that makes evangelicals trust it.

Evangelicalism has produced many more versions of the Bible, often not differing very much from each other. We have already noted the English Standard Version (ESV), published in 2001, in effect a slightly more gender-neutral RSV, and there is the Christian Standard Bible of 2004 (the New English Translation or NET), which proclaims that it has an inerrantist agenda, though it is not clear how this is manifested in the actual translation. Very different is *The Bible for Everyone*, by two prominent evangelical scholars, John Goldingay and Tom Wright, published in 2018, where the Old and New Testaments (there is no Apocrypha) follow somewhat different approaches, each marked by a clearly individual style, and unmistakably the work of one person rather than a committee. A New Testament translation in a style contrasting with Wright's is David Bentley Hart, *The New Testament: A Translation.*[21] Wright's version will be discussed in Chapter 2, Hart's in Chapter 3.

The needs of people with a restricted vocabulary are met by the Contemporary English Version (CEV), produced by the American Bible Society (New Testament 1991, Old Testament 1995, Apocrypha 1999). The Good News Bible (GNB) had this market at least partly in its sights, but the CEV presupposes a still lower reading level, and cleverly gets around technical terms in the biblical text with modern paraphrases. There is a New Testament with an even slimmer vocabulary, which will be examined in Chapter 2.

THE FUTURE OF BIBLICAL TRANSLATION

For as long as Christianity and Judaism exist there will be room for further translations made by committees, a tradition in Britain since the KJV. Such collaboration is an effective way of maximizing the use of the work of many scholars and stylists, and producing a consensus version. On the other hand, it does not encourage bold new approaches. For that, translation by one or two individuals with a distinctive attitude to the task seems better suited. Bibles made by individuals, such as those by Robert Alter, or by Goldingay and Wright, invariably have a particular flavour: some may like it, some may hate it, but it is rarely bland. Provided the underlying scholarship is sound, the result challenges the reader in a way that committee work is unlikely to do. We should remember too that the KJV, though produced by a committee, rests substantially on the work of an individual, Tyndale, for much of its style, while the Luther Bible was a solo effort in origin, even if subsequent revisions have involved many hands. It is to be hoped, therefore, that individual translators will go on tackling either the whole Bible or parts of it, even as committees continue to produce mainstream renderings.

As we have seen, however, the challenges they will face are often perennial. In English, the KJV looms over all attempts to produce fresh versions of the Bible (see Chapter 5). It is deeply embedded in our culture and speech, and readers familiar with it cannot avoid seeing any new translation, however hard it tries to begin from scratch, as deliberately either imitating or avoiding well-known words and phrases that the KJV canonized – many going back to Tyndale or beyond. Yet for all the apparent timelessness of the Bible, especially as captured in traditional renderings, each age looks for something different from it, and translators inevitably respond to this – indeed, their efforts are a partial record of the exigencies and shifts of the history of religion and interpretation of Scripture. During and in the wake of the Reformation, translators had to render in new ways words that had been appropriated for the medieval ecclesiastical system they disavowed – so that 'penance' became 'repentance'. The vocabulary of Church order likewise became an issue of central importance, making the decision whether to translate the titles for Church leaders as 'bishops' or 'overseers' sometimes literally a matter of life and death.

Translators today do not have to worry much for their personal safety, yet they too are obliged to engage with the concerns of their time. They need, for example, to think about expressions that now seem unacceptably male-centred, and to consider ways of producing an 'inclusive' Bible (see Chapter 6) – an issue that didn't trouble even their recent predecessors. At the time of the Reformation, as now, the Bible was held as an indispensable authority on matters of faith and action important to the faithful. How it is to be translated when it deals with the roles of men and women in Church and society more generally is no more indifferent now than was the translation of terms to do with hierarchies in the Church in the sixteenth century. The Bible and the contemporary scene interact for believers, and translators are among the doorkeepers of this interaction.

Yet the Bible is not a single book speaking with one accent or style, like a kind of Highway Code for the two religions that appeal to it for wisdom and guidance. It is a conglomeration of many individual texts from which no unified system of thought or doctrine can be derived. The content of the Bible both informs and reflects both Judaism and Christianity, but it is not an exact account of either: the two religions overlap considerably with the Bible, but neither is coterminous with it. To translate the Bible, therefore, is not to spell out in our own language a kind of digest of official teaching, but to present to the reader narratives, poetry, proverbial wisdom, letters and prophetic pronouncements. All of these texts are related to the faiths that acknowledge the Bible as an authority, yet they are not identical with them. Translation is one of the most important places where this relation, between the Scriptures and the religions they belong to, is negotiated. Different renderings of scriptural books show different ideas about the nature of this interplay in action.

Translation entails nothing less than the assimilation of the original text in its own context, and its re-expression within the linguistic, intellectual and spiritual culture of the translator. Neither is left unchanged by the process. It is, as we shall see, a complex and inherently difficult task, inevitably involving some judgement as to what the Bible really is, as well as contact with texts that will at times be at odds with this, and at times even with each other. Translation, like all other forms of interpretation, is a subtle art.

2

Bringing the Bible to the Reader

A MIDDLE WAY

'Translating means serving two masters. It follows that no one can do it,' wrote Franz Rosenzweig – in partnership with Martin Buber one of the most important of twentieth-century biblical translators.[1] All translation has to mediate between the source language and the target language, and be faithful, in some sense, to both. Translators must, as a bare minimum, both render the text before them without distorting it and produce something new that is comprehensible to the vernacular reader. Many believe that this involves finding a middle way between two extremes: a word-for-word rendering (which is really barely possible) at one end and a completely free paraphrase at the other. The distinction between word-for-word and sense-for-sense translation goes back to Cicero (106–43 BCE), Horace (65–8 BCE) and Jerome, and was widely recognized in the Middle Ages.[2] As Richard Hooker put it in the late sixteenth century:

> Touching translations of holy scripture, albeit we may not disallow of their painful travails herein who strictly have tied themselves to the very original letter, yet the judgement of the Church, as we see by the practice of all nations, Greeks, Latins, Persians, Syrians, Ethiopians, Arabs, hath been ever that the fittest for public audience are such as following a middle course between the rigour of literal translators and the liberty of paraphrasts, do with greatest shortness and plainness deliver the meaning of the holy Ghost. Which being a labour of such difficulty, the exact performance thereof we may rather wish than look for.[3]

John Dryden (1631–1700) classically proposed a similar map of the translator's art, presenting the ideal translation as the mean between 'metaphrase' (word-for-word rendering) and 'imitation' (a very free version): he called this mean, confusingly for us, 'paraphrase', a term which nowadays tends to imply more looseness in translation than Dryden intended by it, and to be closer to what he called 'imitation'. He described paraphrase as 'translation with latitude', in which 'the author is kept in view by the translator, so as never to be lost, but his words are not so strictly followed as his sense; and that too is admitted to be amplified but not altered'.[4] At the same time, his own translations of classical texts, like those of Alexander Pope (1688–1744), do tend to be looser than would nowadays be regarded as hitting the mean: Pope's Homer has been described as 'Homer in a powdered wig declaiming in a baroque theatre'.[5] The 'latitude' is considerable.

'Metaphrase' or literal translation is also a somewhat protean term, ranging all the way from an interlinear key for a foreign text to something many would see as a genuine translation, if rather wooden:

> 'Literal' is an unfortunate term: for some it means 'word for word' and therefore ungrammatical, like a linguist's gloss; for others it means 'the closest possible grammatical translation, probably not sounding very natural'.[6]

In practice most of those who have written about translation, as we shall see, have been averse to literal translation, but have defined 'literal', rather circularly, as the style of translation of which they disapprove: a 'word-for-word' rendering of which a critic approves is generally said not to be literal, but close or accurate.[7]

The threefold classification of translation operates with the idea that there is an ideal – Dryden's 'paraphrase' – middle ground between slavishly following the original on the one hand, and going off into one's own flights of fancy in a very loose connection with the source text on the other. The problem with this way of thinking about translation is that it really rules out two theoretical, extreme positions that hardly any practical translator is likely to adopt anyway, and leaves us with just one acceptable model, but one that does not discriminate between types that any reader can see do not rest on the same assumptions about what makes a good translation. No one supports a translation so literal that it does not observe the natural word order and syntax of the target language, and equally no one favours a version that makes hardly any contact with the source text at all, simply using it to make a work of one's own in what amounts almost to parody. The interesting cases all lie in between, which suggests that the mean position itself needs subdividing.

TWO MODELS

In modern times this subdivision has worked mainly along lines set out most simply by F. D. E. Schleiermacher (1768–1834), who in a lecture in Berlin on 24 June 1813 divided acceptable translations into two types. He wrote:

> Either the translator leaves the writer as far as possible in peace, and moves the reader towards him; or else he leaves the reader as far as possible in peace, and moves the writer towards him.[8]

In the twentieth century a much more clear-cut distinction came to be made, in the spirit of Schleiermacher, between 'formal' equivalence – translations that adhere closely to the wording and structures of the source text even when it sounds somewhat alien to a modern reader – and 'dynamic' (later 'functional') equivalence, where the translator 'moves the writer towards the reader' by adapting the source text to make it conform to the reader's cultural expectations and conditions. The originator of this terminology was Eugene Nida (1914–2011), who developed the distinction precisely so that he could analyse types of biblical translation. He went on to commend the second, 'functional equivalence', as the best way to convey the meaning of the Bible to modern readers, and especially to those in developing countries or with only basic skills in English.

Nida was an evangelical scholar and expert linguist who never produced any biblical translations himself but inspired generations of those who did, especially those who worked to make the Bible available to speakers of non-Western languages in which no Bible translation yet existed.[9] For such speakers, Nida argued, what was necessary was to convey the *message* of the Bible rather than the fine detail of its original wording. 'Translation consists in reproducing in the receptor language the closest natural equivalent of the source-language message, first in terms of meaning and secondly in terms of style.'[10] He was not interested in 'literary' translation, which he characterized as the province of those 'with time on their hands' rather than of those 'with the urgent task of translating God's word'.[11]

In this Nida was to some extent attacking a straw man. For one thing, most biblical translators have had exactly the same goal, and for another most of those who had written about translation of any sort before the twentieth century had tended to favour something very like functional equivalence anyway. Nida wrote:

> ... all translating, whether of poetry or prose, must be concerned ...
> with the response of the receptor; hence the ultimate purpose of the
> translation, in terms of its impact upon its intended audience, is a fun-
> damental factor in any evaluation of translations. This reason underlies
> Leonard Forster's definition of a good translation as 'one which fulfils
> the same purpose in the new language as the original did in the lan-
> guage in which it was written'.[12]

This is very like what Hilaire Belloc wrote in 1931: 'any hint of foreignness in the translated version is a blemish; I should keep to my canon that the translated thing should read like a first-class native thing'.[13] Dryden had made the same point, saying that the translator's aim should be 'to produce the text which the foreign poet would have written had he been composing in one's own tongue'.[14]

In practice this does not mean merely using properly idiomatic English (or whatever the target language may be), but changing idioms when necessary to fit the target audience's understanding. The Roman historian Tacitus famously described the emperor Galba as *capax imperii nisi imperasset*. Prioritizing formal equivalence, we could say: 'Galba was capable of imperial rule, if he had not ruled', which captures the sense at a basic level but not the sarcasm. In functional-equivalence mode we might prefer 'As emperor, Galba had a great future behind him', which recasts the entire sentence and does not use the English equivalents of any one of the Latin words, yet captures the emotional force of what Tacitus was saying in a modern English idiom. Nida encouraged translators writing for cultures remote from that of the

Bible to make similar substitutions. 'White as snow' might in some equatorial cultures need to be 'white as a cockatoo's feathers', for example.[15] And language-specific features such as the tendency in Biblical Hebrew for each new sentence in a narrative to begin with 'And', so familiar from the King James Version of the Old Testament, may need to be adjusted to make more normal sentences in many languages, including English, by rendering 'Then', 'Next', 'But', 'So', and so on to bring out the logical structure of the story, or simply by omitting 'and' altogether. Some have gone even further: in translations meant for some cultures, 'figs' might confuse if the fruit is unknown to them, so the figs might need to become bananas.[16]

Thus a typical functional-equivalence translation of an Old Testament narrative might be as follows (this is the story of Balaam and his talking donkey, from Numbers 22:22–31 in the New English Bible):

> But God was angry because Balaam was going, and as he came riding on his ass, accompanied by his two servants, the angel of the LORD took his stand in the road to bar his way. When the ass saw the angel standing in the road with his sword drawn, she turned off the road into the fields, and Balaam beat the ass to bring her back on to the road. Then the angel of the LORD stood where the road ran through a hollow, with fenced vineyards on either side. The ass saw the angel and, crushing herself against the wall, crushed Balaam's foot against it, and he beat her again. The angel of the LORD moved on further and stood in a narrow place where there was no room to turn either to right or left. When the ass saw the angel, she lay down under Balaam. At that Balaam lost his temper and beat the ass with his stick. The LORD then made the ass speak, and she said to Balaam, 'What have I done? This is the third time you have beaten me.' Balaam answered the ass, 'You have been making a fool of me. If I had had a sword here, I should have killed you on the spot.' But the ass answered, 'Am I not still the ass which you have ridden all your life? Have I ever taken such a liberty with you before?' He said, 'No.' Then the LORD opened Balaam's eyes: he saw the angel of the LORD standing in the road with his sword drawn, and he bowed down and fell flat on his face before him.

Compare this with the much more literal King James Version:

And God's anger was kindled because he went; and the angel of the LORD stood in the way for an adversary against him. Now he was riding upon his ass, and his two servants were with him. And the ass saw the angel of the LORD standing in the way, and his sword drawn in his hand; and the ass turned aside out of the way, and went into the field; and Balaam smote the ass, to turn her into the way. But the angel of the LORD stood in a path of the vineyards, a wall being on this side, and a wall on that side. And when the ass saw the angel of the LORD, she thrust herself unto the wall, and crushed Balaam's foot against the wall: and he smote her again. And the angel of the LORD went further, and stood in a narrow place, where was no way to turn either to the right hand or to the left. And when the ass saw the angel of the LORD, she fell down under Balaam: and Balaam's anger was kindled, and he smote the ass with a staff. And the LORD opened the mouth of the ass, and she said unto Balaam, What have I done unto thee, that thou hast smitten me these three times? And Balaam said unto the ass, Because thou hast mocked me; I would there were a sword in my hand, for now would I kill thee. And the ass said unto Balaam, Am not I thine ass, upon which thou hast ridden ever since I was thine unto this day? was I ever wont to do so unto thee? And he said, Nay. Then the LORD opened the eyes of Balaam, and he saw the angel of the LORD standing in the way, and his sword drawn in his hand; and he bowed down his head, and fell flat on his face.

Apart from the elimination of much repetition of 'and', the NEB also tends to use more up-to-date phrases – 'making a fool of me', 'on the spot', 'on either side', 'taken such a liberty' – in a way that gives the story a more idiomatic quality, and suggests that it is being narrated orally to a less-than-formal audience. 'With his stick' sounds less impressive than 'with a staff'. It is not simply that the KJV deploys archaism in places, but that it is also more formal in register and style. NEB aims not to be so literary, but more anecdotal. It is an account of this incident as someone today might retell it.

Naturally there are losses as well as gains in this. Stories with talking animals are usually legends or fairy tales in Anglophone culture, and in such tales neither characters nor creatures say things such as 'on the spot' or 'take a liberty'. The informalizing of the language in NEB introduces an odd clash between style and substance, as though such a story were a rather matter-of-fact narrative one might report in a casual way to friends and neighbours, when in fact its content is fantastic and a matter of high drama. '[Balaam] saw the angel of the LORD' comes out as mundane, something rather like 'Balaam met the postman'. Yet if the aim is to engage with modern readers and convince them that the events really happened – which would certainly have been Nida's wish, though it may not have been so much in the thoughts of the NEB panel – then the more informal style, and the use of subordinate clauses and variants on the ever-repeated 'and', does bring the story much closer. It would have seemed simply common sense to the NEB translators to aim for smooth modern English of the kind in everyday usage, not anything high-flown or portentous. Like the Penguin Classics series, the NEB uses standard educated English from the post-Second World War period, as the register that will speak most clearly to the modern reader.

In the New Testament similar effects can be seen in functional-equivalence translations.[17] Here is the Good News Bible (first edition 1976), which was strongly supported by Nida,[18] at 2 Corinthians 5:17–21:

> Anyone who is joined to Christ is a new being; the old is gone, the new has come. All this is done by God, who through Christ changed us from enemies into his friends and gave us the task of making others his friends also. Our message is that God was making the whole human race his friends through Christ. God did not keep an account of their sins, and he has given us the message which tells how he makes them his friends.
>
> Here we are then, speaking for Christ, as though God himself were making his appeal through us. We plead on Christ's behalf: let God change you from enemies into his friends! Christ was without sin, but for our sake God made him share our sin in order that in union with him we might share the righteousness of God.

Compare the Revised Standard Version:

> Therefore, if anyone is in Christ, he is a new creation; the old has passed away, behold, the new has come. All this is from God, who through Christ reconciled us to himself and gave us the ministry of reconciliation; that is, in Christ God was reconciling the world to himself, not

counting their trespasses against them, and entrusting to us the message of reconciliation. So we are ambassadors for Christ, God making his appeal through us. We beseech you on behalf of Christ, be reconciled to God. For our sake he made him to be sin who knew no sin, so that in him we might become the righteousness of God.

In the GNB more everyday language here replaces the technical terms in the Greek that RSV renders with the language of 'reconciliation', speaking instead of God making us 'into his friends'. And the difficult sentence about God '[making Christ] to be sin' becomes his '[sharing] our sin' – which does not resolve the theological difficulty but does at least tone down the language of Christ 'becoming' sin. At the same time the 'ambassador' metaphor is resolved into simply 'speaking for Christ', possibly on the basis that 'ambassador' is a term that may not be well known to the intended readership. 'The world' is, probably rightly, translated 'the whole human race', though some might think that Paul is referring to the cosmos here and not just to human beings. At any rate the essential message of Paul's teaching comes across well, without using the technical vocabulary of theology. The GNB in general succeeds in doing this, and has been a useful tool, especially in ministering to new Christians and groups with a more restricted vocabulary, from children to people learning English, and in explaining complex religious ideas in a comprehensible way.

The Contemporary English Version, as we saw in Chapter 1, is intended for those with still less reading ability than the GNB, and sometimes produces really ingenious renderings of difficult passages:

Dead to Sin but Alive because of Christ

What should we say? Should we keep on sinning, so that God's gift of undeserved grace will show up even better? No, we should not! If we are dead to sin, how can we go on sinning? Don't you know that all who share in Christ Jesus by being baptized also share in his death? When we were baptized, we died and were buried with Christ. We were baptized, so we would live a new life, as Christ was raised to life by the glory of God the Father. If we shared in Jesus' death by being baptized, we will be raised to life with him. We know that the persons we used to be were nailed to the cross with Jesus. This was done, so our sinful bodies would no longer be the slaves of sin. We know sin doesn't have power over dead people.

(Romans 6:1–7)

This does not make the thought any easier to believe in, or destroy its theological sophistication, but it inarguably makes it easier to follow.

Going further still in the direction of simplification, Anna Wierzbicka's *What Christians Believe: The Story of God and People in Minimal English*[19] operates with a vocabulary of just 400 words, which, she claims, are translatable into virtually all the languages of the world – a very useful linguistic armoury. This produces such passages as the following:

> When Caiaphas with the other men brought Jesus to the 'Praetorium', they didn't want to go inside, they wanted Pilate to speak to them outside. Many people were with them there. When Pilate was outside, he said to them, 'What do you want to say about this man? What did he do?' They said to him: 'We know well what he did. Because of this we want you to say: "This man has to die."' Pilate said to them: 'You want *me* to say this? *You* can do to him as you want, as your law says.' They said to him: 'Our law says: this man has to die. At the same time we can't kill anyone. *You* can say to the soldiers: "Kill this man." *We* can't say this to anyone.'

(John 18:28–31)

Again there can be problems. For example, like many modern translations the GNB often solves the problem of masculine language by using the word 'Christian', which is very rare in the New Testament and entirely absent from Paul's original Greek. Doing so arguably gives the impression that the followers of Christ in Paul's day were already seen as forming a group that needed a title – an overstatement, at the very least. (The New Revised Standard Version and the Revised English Bible do the same, often again to avoid gendered expressions.) And it can be argued that Paul deliberately uses technical language, so that the GNB's eschewal of jargon often results in something closer to an explanation or interpretation than a translation. But the value of such a rendering is undoubted.

The 'Christian' issue arises sharply with the Revised English Bible version of the first letter of John, which in Greek constantly uses the word *adelphos*, 'brother'. The translators are surely right in thinking that this does not mean either a literal brother or 'fellow human being', but a member of the Christian community (whether male or female). 'Let us love one another' correspondingly means 'let all members of the community love each other', not (as readers tend to think) 'let all human beings love each other'. First John is in fact one of the most sectarian and least outward-looking books in the New Testament. And here again, using 'fellow Christian' for 'brother', while correct on functional-equivalence principles, gives the false impression that the word 'Christian' was already in common use.[20]

J. B. Moffatt's masterly functional-equivalence translation of 1 Corinthians 13, quoted in Chapter 1, similarly paraphrases, but surely to good effect. It is hard not to think that Paul would have written something like this, had he been composing in modern English.

An important aspect of functional-equivalent renderings is that they pay attention to conveying what may be called the 'force' of the source text: not simply its meaning in a narrow philological sense, but what it is trying to convey. One sees this, for example, in how weights and measures are translated. Distances in the Bible are nowadays normally rendered in metres or yards: thus in the story of the miraculous catch of fish in John 21:8 the boat was 'about 100 metres' away from land (GNB) rather than 'two hundred cubits' (KJV, following the Greek closely). Money is less straightforward, however. In Matthew's version of the parable of the talents (Matthew 25:14–30) GNB renders a 'talent' as 1,000 'coins' rather than leaving the Greek word, as has been usual, and in the story of the feeding of the 5,000 (Mark 6: 30–44) 'two hundred denarii' become 'two hundred silver coins'. This is clearly preferable to trying to find a monetary equivalent, as in KJV 'two hundred pennyworth', because the value of specific monetary units changes so much over time. Already in 1789, George Campbell in the Introduction to his translation of the Gospels pointed out that looking for exact equivalents can be comic in its effect:

Nothing can be more natural than the expression 'Two hundred denarii would not purchase bread enough to afford every one of them a little' ... whereas nothing can be more unnatural than, in such a case, to descend to fractional parts and say 'Six pounds, five shillings' would not purchase ... '[21]

– which would be absurd. Campbell distinguishes 'situations where the properties of the original thing designated are essential to the functional sense' from 'situations where it is of no importance'.[22] (This may be the earliest use of 'functional' in a discussion of translation.) The point being made by the disciples is that even a considerable sum of money would not be enough, and this is not properly conveyed if one tries to provide a 'literal' rendering in modern coinage. A functional equivalent such as 'a large sum' would be a *more accurate* translation of the passage's force than an attempt to perform a currency conversion.

PARAPHRASE

Functional equivalence may, however, go much further than this, especially if the genre of the source text is attended to closely. David Bellos gives an example in the translation of headlines from English to French. In 2008 Sarah Palin was chosen as running-mate by the Republican candidate for the American presidency, to the great displeasure of the Democrats. *The Wall Street Journal* broke the news with the headline GOP VEEP PICK ROILS DEMS, which for a British audience would perhaps need to be REPUBLICAN VICE-PRESIDENTIAL CHOICE RILES DEMOCRATS. Bellos speculates how it would run in a French newspaper, where there is no tradition of punning or acronymic headlines, but information is conveyed more straightforwardly, and suggests something like *Le choix de Madame Palin comme candidate républicaine à la vice-présidence des États-Unis choque le parti démocrate* ('The choice of Mrs Palin as US Republican Vice-Presidential candidate shocks the Democratic Party'). Only so would it conform to the conventions for headlines in Francophone culture. To say that the French version is 'not a translation' of the English is surely a misunderstanding. It is certainly a departure from the original phrasing, but, like my rendering of Tacitus' comment on Galba, it is also a translation, in functional-equivalence mode. It conveys exactly the same information to the target audience as the original does to its target.

According to the Skopos Theory of Katharina Reiß and Hans Vermeer, to which we shall return in the Conclusion, one should always ask about the *purpose* of a given translation. The purpose may be to give the reader a detailed sense of the words of the source text, and in that case a good deal of literalness is needed. But the purpose may be to convey the same effect in the target language as in the source, and that is the case here, with an approximation to the norms of the target culture. This distinction is familiar from prosaic, low-level translations, such as finding equivalents for jokes or proverbs: for example, one would translate the German '*Sicher ist sicher*' as 'Better safe than sorry' rather than the literal 'Sure is sure'.[23]

Some biblical translators have attempted this kind of cultural approximation. The idea of translating the Bible into colloquial speech was not original to the NEB panels or to Nida, but had been pioneered by a number of individuals earlier in the twentieth century. Among the most successful of these were the versions of the New Testament by Moffatt, Goodspeed and J. B. Phillips, discussed in Chapter 1. Phillips tried to render idioms in a style appropriate to the cultural mores of his time: as we saw in his rendering of the holy kiss as a robust handshake. Similarly, 'Friend, go up higher' (Luke 14:10 KJV) is translated, 'My dear fellow, we have a much better seat for you' – a warning that translations can age rather fast, and are not immune to influence by the translator's social class.

Eugene Peterson's *The Message* not only translates into colloquial English, but also expands the text to help explain it. For example, here is Luke 2:8–12:

> There were sheepherders camping in the neighbourhood. They had set night watches over their sheep. Suddenly, God's angel stood among them and God's glory blazed around them. They were terrified. The angel said, 'Don't be afraid. I'm here to announce a great and joyful event that is meant for everybody, worldwide: A Saviour has just been born in David's town, a Saviour who is Messiah and Master. This is what you're to look for: a baby wrapped in a blanket and lying in a manger.'

Or this, from the Song of Solomon 7:1–5:

> Shapely and graceful your sandaled feet, and queenly your movement –
> your limbs are lithe and elegant, the work of a master artist. Your body
> is a chalice, wine-filled. Your skin is silken and tawny like a field of
> wheat touched by the breeze. Your breasts are like fawns, twins of a
> gazelle. Your neck is carved ivory, curved and slender. Your eyes are
> wells of light, deep with mystery. Quintessentially feminine! Your pro-
> file turns all heads, commanding attention. The feelings I get when I see
> the high mountain ranges – stirrings of desire, longings for the heights –
> remind me of you, and I'm spoiled for anyone else!

Most scholars would struggle to translate 'quintessentially feminine'
into Biblical Hebrew, even if they wished to do so, but Peterson cannot exactly be said to have falsified this erotic passage. His aim is to
bring the Bible to life, both for new readers who think it distant and
for old ones jaded by traditional versions, and in this he has succeeded, even though many will dismiss his version as too paraphrastic.
The language throughout is colloquial and modern:

> First this: God created the Heavens and Earth – all you see, all you don't
> see. Earth was a soup of nothingness, a bottomless emptiness, an inky
> blackness.

This rendering of Genesis 1:1–2 changes the original considerably,
perhaps borrowing 'visible and invisible' from the Christian creeds,
since it is not there in the biblical text. The evocative Hebrew phrase
tohu wabohu ('without form and void', KJV), together with 'and
darkness was upon the face of the deep' is translated with three
phrases ('a soup of nothingness, a bottomless emptiness, an inky
blackness'). It is far from literal; yet it does convey the atmosphere of
the Hebrew.

Some may question whether these are translations at all, and not
rather paraphrases of the kind deplored by Richard Hooker earlier:
not functional-equivalence renderings, but something further off the
map, even illegitimate. This is essentially a matter of definition. If functional equivalence is allowed at all, then I cannot see how Phillips's,
Peterson's and the others' versions do not qualify as translation – loose,

certainly, but intended precisely to give the reader the same experience as the original audience.

Going further still down the functional path we come into the realm of acknowledged paraphrase, which I believe can often still count as translation. Metrical psalms, for example, and hymns based on biblical passages would not usually be called translations, yet they can powerfully convey the sense of the original. A number of hymns written by Timothy Dudley-Smith come into this category. Take for instance, his 1962 reworking of the Magnificat in the NEB version (Luke 1:46–55):

> Tell out, my soul, the greatness of the Lord!
>> Unnumbered blessings, give my spirit voice;
> tender to me the promise of his word;
>> in God my Saviour shall my heart rejoice.
>
> Tell out, my soul, the greatness of his Name!
>> Make known his might, the deeds his arm has done;
> his mercy sure, from age to age the same;
>> his holy Name, the Lord, the Mighty One.
>
> Tell out, my soul, the greatness of his might!
>> Powers and dominions lay their glory by.
> Proud hearts and stubborn wills are put to flight,
>> the hungry fed, the humble lifted high.
>
> Tell out, my soul, the glories of his word!
>> Firm is his promise, and his mercy sure.
> Tell out, my soul, the greatness of the Lord
>> to children's children and for evermore![24]

Here is the NEB:

> 'Tell out, my soul, the greatness of the Lord,
> rejoice, rejoice, my spirit, in God my saviour;
> so tenderly has he looked upon his servant,
> humble as she is.
> For, from this day forth,
> all generations will count me blessed,

so wonderfully has he dealt with me,
the Lord, the Mighty One.

His name is Holy;
his mercy sure from generation to generation
toward those who fear him;
the deeds his own right arm has done disclose his might:
the arrogant of heart and mind he has put to rout,
he has brought down monarchs from their thrones,
but the humble have been lifted high.
The hungry he has satisfied with good things,
the rich sent empty away.

He has ranged himself at the side of Israel his servant;
firm in his promise to our forefathers,
he has not forgotten to show mercy to Abraham
and his children's children, for ever.'

Very little of the source text remains unrendered, and very little is added to it. Is it a translation, or a paraphrase? Does it matter? Following the principles of Reiß' and Vermeer's Skopos Theory, then, if the aim of the translator is to produce a version of the text specifically for use in worship, this is a successful translation – of course it would not be, if the intention were to provide an interlinear 'crib' for someone learning New Testament Greek.

Those who made use of metrical psalms, in the Church of Scotland and the English Free Churches in the seventeenth and eighteenth centuries, and before and after the formal service in the Church of England, probably did not feel that they were using anything but *translations* of the Psalms, even though these were often explicitly Christianized. These texts illustrate where functional equivalence can lead us, and show that it can be highly fruitful. Such versions take contemporary patterns of hymnody and poetry and accommodate the words of the source text to them. Here is an example, Psalm 84 in the version used in the Church of England's Book of Common Prayer, which is taken from Coverdale's translation of 1535 – well before the King James Version – followed by a paraphrase by the Congregationalist minister Isaac Watts (1674–1748):

O how amiable are thy dwellings: thou Lord of hosts!

My soul hath a desire and longing to enter into the courts of the Lord: my heart and my flesh rejoice in the living God.

Yea, the sparrow hath found her an house, and the swallow a nest where she may lay her young: even thy altars, O Lord of hosts, my King and my God.

Blessed are they that dwell in thy house: they will be alway praising thee.

Blessed is the man whose strength is in thee: in whose heart are thy ways.

Who going through the vale of misery use it for a well: and the pools are filled with water.

They will go from strength to strength: and unto the God of gods appeareth every one of them in Sion.

O Lord God of hosts, hear my prayer: hearken, O God of Jacob.

Behold, O God our defender: and look upon the face of thine Anointed.

For one day in thy courts: is better than a thousand.

I had rather be a door-keeper in the house of my God: than to dwell in the tents of ungodliness.

For the Lord God is a light and defence: the Lord will give grace and worship, and no good thing shall he withhold from them that live a godly life.

O Lord God of hosts: blessed is the man that putteth his trust in thee.

> Lord of the worlds above,
> How pleasant and how fair
> The dwellings of Thy love,
> Thine earthly temples are!
> To Thine abode
> My heart aspires
> With warm desires
> To see my God.
>
> The sparrow, for her young,
> With pleasure seeks her nest,

And wandering swallows long
To find their wonted rest.
My spirit faints
With equal zeal
To rise and dwell
Among Thy saints.

Oh, happy souls who pray
Where God appoints to hear!
Oh, happy men who pay
Their constant service there!
They praise Thee still;
And happy they
Who love the way
To Zion's hill.

They go from strength to strength
Through this dark vale of tears
Till each arrives at length,
Till each in heaven appears,
Oh, glorious seat
When God, our King,
Shall thither bring
Our willing feet!

Here again very little is left out; but what may have been a text about a literal pilgrimage to Jerusalem is interpreted allegorically, as the journey of life from earth to heaven. That is probably already implicit in Coverdale's version, where 'the valley of Baca', a place on the pilgrims' route, becomes 'the vale of misery'. Indeed, it may be that the original writer was punning on *bakha'*, 'weeping', in referring to this place and already had a metaphorical meaning in mind.

Watts used verse forms familiar from secular poetry and hymns of his own day; and translations such as his raise the question of whether a modern translator of the Bible should use some contemporary writer as a model. Psalms in the style of T. S. Eliot, perhaps? Most would think this going too far. Yet one must have some model in mind when translating. In the eighteenth century translators regularly used their peers (and even themselves) as models: Pope's Homer is in the same manner as Pope's original works.

RELIGIOUS IMPLICATIONS

It might be thought that a strong attachment to the authority and inspiration of the Bible would lead in the direction of more 'literal' translations, changing the text as little as possible in rendering it into another language. As we shall see, this is more or less the case in the King James Version, where the translators even mark words 'added' to the text for the sake of intelligibility by printing them in a different font – nowadays signalled by italics – even though the additions may be essential for the translation to make sense. The effect, to our eyes, can be unintentionally comic:

> And he spake to his sons, saying, Saddle me the ass. And they saddled *him*.
>
> (1 Kings 13:27)

It may come as a surprise, therefore, that functional equivalence often goes hand in hand with a high view of the inspiration of the Bible. The logic of this is as follows. The Bible contains an essential message, or gospel – good news for humanity. The essential task in and reason for translating it is to convey this message, not so much the exact words in which it is couched. Especially in versions intended for cultures that are unfamiliar with the Christian message, functional equivalence is not only permissible but actually imperative if people are to hear the gospel in ways they can assimilate. Thus Nida, an evangelical Christian with a concern for mission, developed his theory of functional equivalence as a tool for evangelism,[25] and his ideas lie behind the Good News Bible, as we have seen. For him sense-for-sense rather than word-for-word translation of the Bible was an essential evangelistic tool. (This is very different, as we shall see in the next chapter, from a Jewish perception of the nature of the biblical text, as pointed out by Naomi Seidman.[26]) The idea that the Bible has a gist, which though certainly communicated *through* its words yet is not to be identified with them, goes back at least to Luther, who spoke of the *res scripturae*, the 'matter' of Scripture, as something that can be distilled from the biblical text, and to which the text bears witness. Such a view is highly compatible with a functional-equivalence style of translation, which conveys the essence of the meaning without adhering closely to the wording.

The alignment of different approaches to translating Scripture with different types of Christian believer is complicated by the existence of contradictory ideas about the nature of the Bible within Christianity as a whole. There are certainly those for whom the exact wording is deeply important, and who therefore are suspicious of functional equivalence, even demanding a 'word-for-word' rendering.[27] Such an attitude probably lies behind some of the Catholic hierarchy's preference at present for the English Standard Version, and the slightly greater literalism of the recent Revised New Jerusalem Bible over the New Jerusalem Bible. But probably a majority of Christians see the Bible as having a main set of themes, which are conveyed through the words of the text but are not to be identified with them. In the case of the New Testament this goes with a realization that some of the most important words in that collection, namely the sayings of Jesus, are already a translation from Aramaic into Greek anyway. Insistence on the precise wording of these sayings ignores this fairly obvious fact. The case of the Hebrew Bible/Old Testament is different, since that is not a translation at all, so that the exact words can be pressed more strongly. The same is true, of course, of Paul's letters, which were written in Greek and so are not themselves a translation. But at least where the Gospels are concerned, an awareness that the Greek often renders sayings in Aramaic may make one pause before insisting on a very literal translation, and may encourage a functional-equivalence approach. As James Barr put it, the 'very words' of Jesus are in practice preserved only in a Greek translation.[28]

Another religious dimension of biblical translation has to do with the rendering, in the New Testament, of terminology that may point to (and therefore validate) various forms of Church organization. At the Reformation the rendering of terms such as *ekklesia* (church), *episkopos* (bishop) and *presbyteros* (elder/priest) was highly contentious. Protestant Reformers preferred translations that did not appear to equate what apostolic writers were talking about with the institutions of the Roman Catholic Church. Hence they rendered *ekklesia* as 'assembly' or 'congregation' and *episkopos* as 'overseer'. Thus at Philippians 1:1, *episkopoi kai diakonoi*, traditionally 'bishops and deacons', became in Protestant hands less ecclesiastical – compare today the GNB's 'church leaders and helpers'. The Reformers were increasingly aware that the late-medieval Church differed in significant ways from its ancient counterpart, and urged a return, that the Church should change and assimilate itself more closely to the original model. William Tyndale's preference for the 'non-Catholic' renderings of such terms was one of the reasons why Church authorities objected to his translation, resulting in his execution. When the King James Version was being commissioned, the translators were explicitly instructed that 'the Old Ecclesiastical words [were] to be kept, viz. the Word *Church* not to be translated *Congregation*, &c'.[29]

Modern translations, even when made by Catholic translators, have on the whole followed the same principles as Tyndale, recognizing that the Church's organization has developed since New Testament times. Thus the Jerusalem Bible has 'presiding elders' for *episkopoi* at Phillippians 1:1 (though the more conservative Revised New Jerusalem Bible, published in 2019, has reverted to 'bishops'). There is an awareness that the Church has changed drastically since its beginnings, and that the forms of ministry it now has cannot simply be equated with those in the Churches founded by Paul and other apostles. Those at the time of the Reformation who placed great emphasis on how these 'ecclesiastical' terms were translated were correct to see that they had wide-ranging implications for the polity and life of the Church. If the Church of New Testament times is to be a model for today, the much vaguer categories articulated in modern translations, by Catholics and Protestants alike, are less easily deployed in support of dogmatic adherence to traditional types of ordained ministry.

OBJECTIONS TO FUNCTIONAL EQUIVALENCE

Functional equivalence now seems to many such an obviously correct way of translating the Bible, providing readers with a readily comprehensible version in language attuned to their own needs and style, that it may be surprising to learn that not everyone by any means agrees with it. There are several possible objections, and it is not clear that biblical translators who modernize the Bible are always aware of them.

First, functional equivalence presupposes that the meaning of a text is detachable from its wording.[30] On the level of the gist of a whole book there is something in this, but translations proceed in much smaller chunks than that, and at a granular level it is harder to extract a meaning that can be captured in different words from the original. It implies what may be called an instrumental theory of language: that language is a medium or tool for conveying meaning, but meaning itself is non- or pre-linguistic. Though this view may make sense when it comes to translations of instruction manuals or other purely factual texts, it doesn't when we are dealing with poetry or literary prose, where the wording is inseparably part of the meaning. And much of the Bible surely falls into this category. Instructions in Leviticus on how precisely to offer a sacrifice may be one thing, but the literary texts that make up so much of the narrative books of the Hebrew Bible, or the Gospels, are another. (And Leviticus may have more literary traits in its ancient context than are obvious to most readers today, especially non-Jewish ones.) In these cases literary art and the conveyance of meaning are bound up together, and the skill of the translator lies in doing justice to both. As James Barr wrote, commenting primarily on the procedures of the translation panel that produced the New English Bible Old Testament,

> The underlying theory of translation among some philologists is something like this: translation is a procedure simply and purely linguistic: from his comparative Semitic learning the philologist is able to decide what is the correct meaning, and this is then put into English; questions of literary criticism, exegesis and theological interpretation can then follow after, and will be based securely on the correct meaning as already established; but in essence they are a separate matter. Such a view is a very naïve one, but there is some evidence that it fits with the philological procedures of NEB.[31]

Robert Alter similarly argues that 'philological clarity in literary texts can quickly turn into too much of a good thing. Literature in general, and the narrative prose of the Hebrew Bible in particular, cultivates certain profound and haunting enigmas, delights in leaving its audiences guessing about motives and connections, and, above all, loves to set ambiguities of word choice and image against one another in an endless interplay that resists neat resolution.'[32] This is opposed to the philological tendency to want to find a straightforward, non-ambiguous meaning in texts.

As Barr also notes, this impulse can have a somewhat conservative effect, in that it leads one to read the text as coherent even if it isn't. It implies that 'there can be a poetry separate from philology, and a philology separate from poetry'.[33] It does not ask literary questions, limiting itself to the meanings of words and not attending to wider issues of interpretation. It produces a somewhat positivistic approach to the text, where the meaning exists at a basic factual level and is not to be located in style or register. Thus on this view the meaning can easily be paraphrased without loss, so that functional equivalence is entirely viable.

The idea that words and meaning can be separated is controversial not only when it comes to the translation of the Bible, but in translation studies in general, and among literary critics. Against the instrumental view of language, they point out that it is not as though the meaning of a text exists independently, and is then converted into words: the wording and the meaning form an indivisible whole, and translating well requires attention to both. Literary texts have a certain *Gestalt*, a shape or coherence or form made of words and ideas, wedded together indissolubly. 'There is no "content" to be smelted from the biblical ore; each biblical context exists in its own unitary and indissoluble *Gestalt*, a *Gestalt* at least as indissoluble as that of a true poem.'[34] The idea that the meaning can be simply extracted and reformulated is indeed naïve, in ignoring the fact that 'it is impossible to transmit the content without at the same time transmitting the form. How something is said is not peripheral to what is said.'[35]

All this raises the question: what kind of literature is the Bible? For Nida and for functional-equivalence translators in general it is a *message*, which can be clothed in a variety of garbs without changing its essential nature. For the opponents of functional equivalence, the Bible is something more like a poem or a novel, which cannot be reduced to a basic message but communicates by its form as well as by its overt content. There is an interesting difference between Christian and Jewish readers on this point. Jews, with a Hebrew text that has been more or less fixed for more than 1,000 years, tend to be more committed to the exact biblical wording than do Christians, whose own contribution to the Bible, the New Testament, exists in many manuscripts in divergent forms, and has never been finally standardized. For them it comes more naturally to think that there is a central thrust that can be conveyed in many different linguistic forms. There is also little propensity among many Christians to see the Bible as a work of art or high literature, and so a greater willingness to read it rendered into a colloquial English style. And at least in the case of Paul's letters, we know that he was communicating with a specific (and not specially learned) audience, so that a rendering in everyday English does not seem inappropriate.

A second problem about functional equivalence is its tendency to smooth out the biblical text and eliminate awkward or discordant passages by a fluent translation. Barr notes, and criticizes, over-fluency ('smoothing out') in the NEB.[36] The great opponent of fluent or transparent translation in modern times is Lawrence Venuti, who argues passionately that 'domesticating' translations, in which the foreignness of the original is so far as possible concealed, represent what he calls 'ethnocentric violence', forcing the source text into the language and values of the target language. Many writers on translation use the image of glass, arguing that the translation should be a clear window on to the original: 'I see translation as the attempt to produce a text so transparent that it does not seem to be translated. A good translation is like a pane of glass . . . It should never call attention to itself.'[37] Venuti puts the exactly opposite case. Any translation inevitably acculturates the source text to some degree within the target language's norms, but this is to be resisted as much as possible, not affirmed. The translator's task, he argues, is not to create the text the author would have produced in our culture, but to render the text in all its alien character. Consequently Venuti favours 'foreignizing' translations. Functional equivalence reduces the distance between today's reader and the original text, whereas, as Henri Meschonnic puts it, 'The distance from which a message reaches us is part of the message.'[38]

This view will come as a surprise to many readers in the Anglophone tradition, where transparency in translation tends to be taken for granted as the primary goal. As we shall see in Chapter 3, there is an alternative tradition among some Continental thinkers. Venuti sums up the contrast:

> One approach can be called *instrumental*. On the empiricist assumption that language is direct expression or reference, the instrumental model treats translation as the reproduction or transfer of an invariant which the source text contains or causes, typically described as its form, its meaning, or its effect. The other approach can be called *hermeneutic*. On the materialist assumption that language is creation thickly mediated by linguistic and cultural determinants, the hermeneutic model treats translation as an interpretation of the source text whose form, meaning, and effect are seen as variable, subject to inevitable transformation during the translating process.[39]

The instrumental approach has been the norm in modern biblical translation, and especially under the influence of Nida. As we shall see, the 'hermeneutic' model will result in quite a different type of translation from functional equivalence.

For Venuti, 'transparent' translation is an expression of colonialism, annexing the source text to Anglophone values, and in effect inventing authors who would have been modern Americans or Britons if they could. (He does not much discuss translations into languages other than English.) Anglophone, and particularly functional-equivalence, translators often seem to feel that their work is respectful of those for whom they translate by using idioms native to their language and culture – speaking to them on their terms rather than talking down to them in someone else's. In fact, Venuti argues, to produce a translation that looks as though it was written originally in the target language disrespects not only the original – by falsifying it – but also the readers in the target language, by failing to challenge them with the essential foreignness of the text. By making the translator invisible, fluent and transparent translation thus does an injustice both to the source text and to its recipients.[40] We shall see in Chapter 3 how far a formal-equivalence translation can escape these strictures.

Jorge Luis Borges (1899–1986) once argued that the classics of literature may be even better read in translation than in the original:

> Borges . . . conjectured that one of the possible advantages of a translation over an original is its likelihood to eschew aspects of a work involving historical or linguistic idiosyncrasies that have little to do with why the work is worth reading in the first place. That is why Borges would at times recommend to young writers that they read great works of literature in translation rather than in the original: 'It is better to study the classics in translation to appreciate the substantive and to avoid the accidental.'[41]

The distinction between what is essential in a work and what is accidental sounds close to the contrast between message and medium that is inherent in functional-equivalence translation. Applied to the Bible, it would favour versions that make the text familiar and approachable rather than culturally distant. Venuti would presumably strongly disagree with Borges on this point, or at least would say that the only kind of translation of which Borges's proposal might be true would be a strongly 'foreignizing' one.

Ultimately translations that conceal their translatedness are dishonest, as is argued in an attack on the Canadian Translation Bureau's definition of authenticity in translation: 'Authenticity is the impression conveyed by a translation that it is not, in fact, a translation, that it was composed in the target language from the outset, that it is an original piece of writing.'[42] 'It is, to say the least,' writes Ian Mason, 'an interesting twist to our understanding of the notion of "authenticity" to extend it to a process whereby something which is, in fact, a translation is presented as something which is not!'[43]

Something similar happens in the European Union, where every version of a document officially translated into the languages in which the EU operates is interpreted as being the 'original' text, even though each is manifestly a rendering of a text originally written in just one of them. There are naturally legal reasons why this fiction has to be maintained, to prevent any member state from appealing behind the document in its own language to the actual, but concealed, original.

A third, and much more obvious, danger of functional equivalence is that it may simply falsify the meaning of the original text in its anxiety to make it readable in the target language. To take the figs=bananas equation again, this will create the mistaken impression that Jesus was familiar with bananas. On a more serious level, phraseology that is

accessible in the target language may reflect its own cultural assumptions in a way that falsifies those of the source text. J. B. Phillips's
rendering of 'friend' (Greek *phile*) as 'my dear fellow' at Luke 14:10
situates Jesus in the English upper-middle-class world of the 1950s to an
extent that could be argued to be seriously misleading. Another draw-
back of functional equivalence is a tendency to overexplain and in the
process to falsify. Thus at Romans 2:28–9 Paul says that a Jew is not one
who is one outwardly (that is, circumcised), but one who is one inwardly.
The New International Version translates, 'A person is not a Jew who is
one only outwardly, nor is circumcision merely outward and physical' –
which softens Paul's tone as it tries to explain his meaning.

We can already find such subtle misreadings in the Greek translation of the Hebrew Bible/Old Testament in the last couple of centuries
BCE. There are places where the Greek translators may have deliberately changed the sense of the Hebrew to produce what was from
their point of view a theologically more satisfactory version. This is
clear in the Greek Bible's attitude to life after death. The Hebrew Bible
is noticeably reticent about any kind of afterlife, tending to portray
the world of the dead as shadowy and mysterious and as lacking in
any positive features, very much like Hades in Homer. Sheol, as that
world is known in Hebrew, is a place where the praise of God has
ceased and where people can no longer enjoy fellowship with him. In
the Psalms, particularly, the worshipper prays to be delivered from
Sheol, in the sense not of rising from the dead, but of being rescued
just in time to avoid going there – for now:

> The snares of death encompassed me;
>> the pangs of Sheol laid hold on me;
>> I suffered distress and anguish.
> Then I called on the name of the LORD:
>> 'O LORD, I pray, save my life!'
>
> For you have delivered my soul from death,
>> my eyes from tears,
>> my feet from stumbling.
> I walk before the LORD
>> in the land of the living.
>
>> (Psalm 116:3–4, 8–9)

The Greek version sometimes changes this, understanding prayer to be released from the power of Sheol as a longing for resurrection. Take Psalm 16 (15 in the Greek Bible), where in verses 9–10 the Hebrew speaks of God saving the suppliant from untimely death: 'you do not give me up to Sheol, or let your faithful one see the Pit'. In the Greek we find instead that God will save him from Hades, into which he *has already fallen*, just as is implied in the way the Psalm is read in Acts 2:31 where it is applied to the resurrection of Jesus.

The Greek translation also introduces resurrection language where there is no hint of it in the Hebrew. For example, at Psalm 1:5 we read in the Hebrew that the ungodly 'will not stand in the judgement', which means they will not be able to stand up in court and be judged to be in the right – it is a concern wholly of this world. The ungodly will not be accorded any standing among the righteous, in particular in the town assembly. But the Greek translates 'stand' with the word that usually means 'rise from the dead' (*anastesontai* rather than the more literal *stesontai*): 'The ungodly will not rise to take part in the council of the righteous', understood to mean their assembly in heaven after death. This gives an entirely different flavour to the Psalm – one that Christians, understandably, came to prefer.

Similar slips occur when, for example, 'Gehenna' in the New Testament is translated as 'hell' in English, a term which carries with it all the overtones of eternal punishment it has in Western Christian culture, which it arguably lacked for Jews in the first century CE.[44] To retain 'Gehenna' is undoubtedly to 'foreignize' the text, since the word does not occur in modern English; but to render it 'hell' transposes the New Testament into a post-biblical world-view, and gives a misleading impression. As Bart Ehrman argues, the detailed ideas of heaven and hell that Christianity developed in the centuries after the composition of the New Testament do not rest on nearly as strong a biblical foundation as many assume. Indeed, the New Testament itself records the evolution of interest in an afterlife and the kind of interplay between Scripture, translation and theology that contributed to this evolution, in that its interest partly rests on ideas imported into the Old Testament on its translation into Greek. The thinking of the New Testament writers was at least partly conditioned by the fact that they were more familiar with the Septuagint than with the Hebrew Bible.

A fourth objection to functional equivalence is raised by Robert Alter, whose own translation of the Hebrew Bible we shall examine in Chapter 4. This is that functional equivalence shows what he calls 'a rage to explain' or the 'heresy of explanation'.[45] 'The translators appear to work on the assumption that readers of the Bible are rather dim and thus repeatedly need to have things spelled out for them.'[46] Partly, no doubt, because functional-equivalence versions are often intended for specific, sometimes not very literate, readerships, translators reshape the text to make its logical structure clearer. In particular they tend, as we have already seen, to smooth out awkwardnesses in the text and to replace paratactic structures (sentences where clauses are simply joined with 'and') with subordinate clauses. They substitute 'therefore' and 'thus' and 'hence' for the ubiquitous Hebrew 'and', and break up long Greek sentences in the more convoluted sections of Paul's letters into short and more easily digested ones. In a way this could be seen as an unfair objection, given that some such translations are indeed intended for those who need explanations, but Alter shows that it applies also to the NEB, REB and JB, which are all aimed at literate readers. The effect is to conceal the style of the original and to replace it 'with the style of a middlebrow novel', as Alter puts it.[47]

Fifthly, functional equivalence tries to make the Bible more accessible for modern readers by adjusting both the vocabulary and the style to fit our conventions. But that invites the question, who are 'modern readers' and who are 'we'?[48] The objection often levelled against the NEB was that the readers for whom it worked best were highly educated academics, rather than the 'people in the pew'. The style was complex, and avoided accessible features of the narratives in the Hebrew Bible and the Gospels: the paratactic linking of clauses with 'and' mirrors much ordinary conversation, whereas the more convoluted subordinate clauses that replaced it do not. Any translation of the Bible has to envisage an extremely heterogeneous collection of readers, rendering the task almost impossible. But it is fair to point out that to aim at a 'modern style' is a rather unattainable goal. There are many modern styles of writing, among them 'biblical English' modelled on the KJV. There is a danger that the cultivation of up-to-date English may produce a version that proves to be quite ephemeral, as colloquial style changes quickly, and also that it will be marked for social class as

Phillips's version, and arguably the NEB, were. There is no neutral 'modern English' usable on all occasions.

Also important, sixthly, is the fact of linguistic change in the biblical languages themselves. Parts of the Hebrew Bible, especially some old poems such as Judges 5 and Genesis 49, probably seemed archaic by the last few centuries BCE; and in the New Testament some passages, notably Luke 1–2, are written in an archaizing 'biblical' style. To render them in a uniform modern English arguably distorts the impression they made on readers when the books of the Hebrew Bible were settling into the form we recognize today and the New Testament was being written. We shall look at this issue in detail in Chapter 5, but for now it is worth noting as a problem for functional-equivalence translation, which aims at producing a version readily comprehensible to a reader of today unfamiliar with the Bible in the original languages.

A final point is that much of the Bible, especially the Hebrew Bible, is poetic in character, and to aim at a plain translation that makes no attempt to imitate the poetry is, again, to falsify the impression the text will have made on its original readers. The idea of a core 'message' separable from the language in which it is couched again proves itself to be based on a misunderstanding of how poetic language works. Some translations of the Bible do, as we have seen, aim to do justice to its more poetic language; but in general the effect is to level the English to what is thought to be readily comprehensible to the 'average' reader. The last word on this can be left to Paul Valéry:

> Ordinary spoken language is a practical tool. It is constantly resolving immediate problems. Its task is fulfilled when each sentence has been completely demolished, annulled, and replaced by the meaning. Comprehension is its end. But on the other hand poetic usage is dominated by personal conditions, by a conscious, continuous, and sustained musical feeling.
>
> Here language is no longer a transitive act, an expedient. On the contrary, it has its own value, which must remain intact in spite of the operations of the intellect on the given propositions. Poetic language must preserve itself, through itself, and remain the same, not to be altered by the act of intelligence that finds or gives it a meaning.[49]

3

Taking the Reader to the Bible

DEFENDING LITERALISM

In the second century CE a Jewish translator normally known as Aquila, believing the existing Greek rendering of the Hebrew Bible to be not only too influenced by Christian interpretations but also too loose and paraphrastic, decided to produce a more literal version.[1] In Hebrew there is a special particle, *et*, which can precede the direct object of a verb, and does so in Genesis 1:1, which runs: 'In the beginning created God *et* the heavens and *et* the earth.' There is also a homonym *et* which means 'with': so Aquila rendered the verse 'In the beginning God created with the heavens and with the earth.' It marks one of literalism's pinnacles: even grammatical particles were to be given a translation. And of course the result was less, not more, accurate than a more natural version would have been.[2]

Literalism in that extreme sense is not regarded as an option by any modern translator. As we noted in the previous chapter, it lies at or even off one end of the spectrum just as much as complete paraphrase does off the other. But within viable options for translators there are formal-equivalence possibilities that adhere much more closely to the wording of the source text, and yet are just as clearly faithful translations, as are the moderate forms of functional equivalence we have just been considering. Such translations, in Schleiermacher's terms, move the reader towards the text rather than the text towards the reader.

Schleiermacher thought this preferable,[3] but formal equivalence has traditionally had a rather bad press, especially among Anglophone writers.[4] It is thought to be wooden and stilted, even accused of 'trans-lationese'. The classic theorists, such as Dryden, speak ill of 'literalism' (metaphrase, as he called it):

> 'Tis much like dancing on Ropes with fetter'd Leggs: A man may shun a fall by using Caution, but the gracefulness of Motion is not to be expected: and when we have said the best of it, 'tis but a foolish Task; for no sober man would put himself into a danger for the Applause of scaping without breaking his Neck.[5]

Indeed, it is hard to find many defences of translating word-for-word, as opposed to sense for sense, before the twentieth century. Jerome himself opposed such translations in general, though he made something of an exception for the Bible, 'in which even the order of the words is a mystery' (meaning 'a divine revelation' rather than a puzzle).[6] In this chapter we shall see that some recent approaches to translating the Bible join hands with Jerome, as well as with twentieth-century theorists, in defending formal equivalence against the widespread acceptance of functional equivalence worldwide.

An important study of early translation theory does, however, point to pre-modern theorists who defended something we could identify as formal-equivalence translation. One such was Sir Thomas North (1535–1604), who translated from Jacques Amyot's comments in French as follows: 'The office of a fit translator consisteth not only in the faithful expressing of his author's meaning, but also in a certain resembling and shadowing forth of the form of his style and manner of his speaking.'[7] His basic argument, that translations should imitate the manner as well as the content of the source text, is picked up in a number of modern comments on Bible translation. James Barr criticizes modern translations on just these grounds, pointing out that the New English Bible is 'better at saying in its own way what the biblical writers had *meant* than in conveying what was the *biblical way of saying it*. It did not convey the biblical speech, the biblical style, the grain of the biblical diction.'[8] This 'grain' might include bumpy places where, often because of an underlying clash between two originally independent documents that were subsequently amalgamated to form a single account, the source text does not run smoothly, but the NEB along with other modern renderings chooses to buff away these rough edges. Buber sums up the problem neatly: *how* something is said is not peripheral to *what* is said.[9]

Robert Alter has continued this line of attack, excoriating modern biblical translators for their insistence on turning the Bible into an easy read by suppressing the distinctive features of biblical speech such as repetition, parataxis and the use of a restricted vocabulary that avoids both technical terms and 'elegant variation' (a traditional way of describing the use of many synonyms as a means of improving the style, a practice alien to Hebrew). Here is the New Jerusalem Bible's functional-equivalence rendering of Exodus 1:8–14, followed by Alter's comments on it:

> Then there came to power a new king who never heard of Joseph. 'Look,' he said to his people, 'the Israelites are now more numerous and stronger than we are. We must take precautions to stop them from increasing any further, or if war should break out, they might join the ranks of our enemies. They might take arms against us and then escape from the country.' Accordingly they put taskmasters over the Israelites to wear them down by forced labour. In this way they built the store-cities of Pithom and Rameses for Pharaoh. But the harder their lives were made, the more they increased and spread, until people came to fear the Israelites. So the Egyptians gave them no mercy in their demands, making their lives miserable with hard labor: with digging clay, making bricks, doing various kinds of field-work – all sorts of labor that they imposed upon them without mercy.

Alter writes:

> This modernizing translation is probably the most egregious of all the twentieth-century versions, but the others are not much better . . . The forward movement of the prose is interrupted by the tic of explanatory phrases – 'accordingly', 'in this way', and, most shamefully, an entire clause that has no equivalent whatever in the Hebrew, 'So the Egyptians gave them no mercy in their demands.' The impulse to spell out everything for the reader at the cost of both rhythm and stylistic decorum is especially evident in 'We must take precautions to stop them from increasing any further.' . . . These are words that, both in sound and diction, could easily come from a bureaucratic report or a

pedestrian newspaper article . . . The cadenced grandeur of the Hebrew writer's narrative of the oppression of the people of Israel in Egypt can scarcely be heard.[10]

The contrast with traditional versions such as the KJV and Luther's Bible could hardly be greater: Luther 'gave the Bible some room'.[11] Such versions were not slavishly 'word-for-word', any more than Jerome's Latin had been, but they followed the contours of the Hebrew and Greek more closely than functional-equivalence translations – such as the Jerusalem and New Jerusalem, New English and Revised English Bibles – have done in our own day.

RESPECT FOR THE TEXT

Where formal equivalence is defended, it is often, as we have just seen with Alter, in terms of respect for the original text – a moral, not merely an aesthetic, point. As suggested in the previous chapter, this may not be wholly fair. Functional equivalence also tries to respect the Bible, but holds that this aim is best served by making it more comprehensible to a modern reader. Equally unwise is the argument that formal equivalence makes for a more 'accurate' reading, as we find in the Preface to the Revised New Jerusalem Bible: 'Attention has . . . been given to rendering the language and imagery of the original languages accurately rather than by dynamic equivalence.'[12] 'More literally' is not necessarily the same as 'more accurately'.

There remains a good case to be made for formal equivalence. It represents less of an intrusion by the translator, less of an assumption that he or she knows what the text 'really means'; a greater humility[13] in the face especially of obscure or problematic texts. Goethe (1749–1832) divided translations into three types (not corresponding exactly to Dryden's threefold classification) as 'informative, that brings over the message "in our own sense"; the parodistic remaking of a work according to the cultural norms of the translator; and the "interlinear version", in which the translator penetrates to the essence of the original through close imitation of language use'.[14] 'Interlinear' here does not mean literally a 'crib' proceeding word by word, but a very close following of the style and manner of the source text. Until recent times it was regarded as quite normal in translating the Bible, partly because of the perceived sacredness of the original text. More on this below.

Perhaps in preference to 'formal' equivalence we should speak more stridently, as Venuti does, of 'foreignizing' translations: renderings that display the non-native origin of texts such as the Bible. If, like Alter, we prefer to retain the parataxis that so characterizes both Hebrew narrative and, by imitation of it, much of the narrative in the Gospels (even though they are in Greek), we are deliberately reminding readers that these texts come from a culture different from their own.[15] The author of Exodus is not a contemporary novelist, still less a contemporary bureaucrat, but someone from a time and culture distant and strange to us. The temptation to erase this – because of a desire for the Bible to be relevant to us still – is great, but it is important to hold on to it if we are to 'give the Bible some room'. We might even want to raise the stakes and say, with Vladimir Nabokov, that 'the person who desires to turn a literary masterpiece into another language has only one duty to perform, and this is to reproduce with absolute exactitude the whole text, and nothing but the text. The term "literal translation" is tautological, since anything but that is not truly a translation but an imitation, an adaptation or a parody.'[16] Even to use different words to render the same word in different places in the original text can be argued to transgress this principle – the KJV deliberately does so at times, and for it incurred condemnation by Nicholas Culpeper (1616–54), who for that reason preferred the Geneva Bible.[17] (In the 1880s the panel that produced the now largely forgotten Revised Version tried but failed to correct this 'fault' in the KJV.) But 'absolute exactitude' is a chimera: no translation can be absolutely exact in rendering a text in a different language.

It might be thought that formal-equivalence translations will tend to be archaizing, pale imitations of the KJV at best. 'Foreignizing', however, is not synonymous with archaizing, nor indeed with a high-brow approach, as can be seen from a remarkable recent translation intended for the general reader, *The Old Testament for Everyone* by John Goldingay. This is published as part of *The Bible for Everyone*,[18] which originally appeared book by book but is now available as a complete work. The New Testament part is the work of Tom Wright, and offers a good, moderately functional-equivalence version. But for the Old Testament Goldingay explicitly espouses formal equivalence, even seeking to use the same English word for the same Hebrew word where practicable. The result is a spare translation that mirrors the Hebrew text rather closely while feeling entirely free to use modern words, and even – in this like the Good News Bible – avoiding technical terms. The effect can be quite startling. Here, for example, is the story of Elijah and what the KJV calls the 'still small voice':

> He came to a cave there and stayed the night there. And there, Yah-weh's word came to him. He said to him, 'What is there for you here, Eliyyahu?' He said, 'I've been very passionate for Yahweh, the God of Armies, because the Yisra'elites have abandoned your pact. Your altars they've torn down; your prophets they've killed with the sword. I alone am left, and they've been seeking my life, to take it.' He said, 'Go out and stand on the mountain before Yahweh.' There was Yahweh passing, and a great, strong wind, splitting mountains and breaking up cliffs before Yahweh (Yahweh was not in the wind), after the wind an earthquake (Yahweh was not in the earthquake), after the earthquake a fire (Yahweh was not in the fire) and after the fire a low murmuring sound,
>
> (1 Kings 19:9–12)

The repeated 'there', the names – Yahweh, Eliyyahu and Yisra'elites – no longer in their conventional English forms, 'pact' for covenant, the parenthetical insertions about God's absence from wind, earthquake and fire, and the translation 'of Armies' for Sabaoth (traditionally 'hosts') – all these are a faithful representation of the Hebrew. This is a version that definitely takes the reader to the text rather than bringing the text to the reader. But it is certainly not archaizing, even using modern contractions such as 'I've'.

The 'call' of Isaiah is similarly striking:

> In the year King Uzziyyahu died, I saw the Lord sitting on a throne, high and lofty, with his train filling the palace. Seraphs were standing above him; each had six wings. With two it would cover its face, with two it would cover its feet, with two it would fly. One would call to another, 'Sacred, sacred, sacred, Yahweh of Armies, his splendour is the filling of

the entire earth.' The doorposts on the sills shook at the sound of the one who called, while the house was filling with smoke.

I said, 'Aagh me, because I'm ruined, because I'm a man polluted of lips, and I live among a people polluted of lips, because my eyes have seen the King, Yahweh of Armies.' But one of the seraphs flew to me, in his hand a coal that he had taken with tongs from on the altar. He made it touch my mouth, and he said, 'There, this has touched your lips, and your waywardness will depart, your wrongdoing will be expiated.'

(Isaiah 6:1–7)

Again this captures the flavour of the Hebrew, even down to 'his splendour is the filling of the entire earth' rather than the traditional 'the whole earth is full of his glory', which smooths out some apparently bumpy Hebrew. 'In his hand a coal', with no verb, is how the Hebrew runs. The translation feels rough in some ways, and so does the underlying Hebrew.

Goldingay in his Preface makes explicit that he 'sticks close to the way the Hebrew (and Aramaic) works rather than paraphrasing it, so that the readers can get as close as possible to the details of the original text ... Nowadays translations are more inclined to aim at translating sentence by sentence, which has opposite advantages and disadvantages to translating word by word. My translation moves in that older direction.'[19] This marks it out as clearly a formal-equivalence version. Tom Wright's *New Testament for Everyone* is also said to 'stick closely to the original'[20] but in practice tends far more towards a more functional-equivalence approach to the Greek text, rendering Paul's frequent *gar* ('for') as 'you see' and *christos* not only as 'Messiah', which is indeed what it means ('anointed one', corresponding to the Hebrew *mashiah*, the origin of the English 'Messiah'), but also as 'King', which is arguably a theological interpretation of the text. Wright's New Testament shares the informal language of Goldingay's Old Testament, but reads more like normal modern English – which means it does not 'move the reader towards the text' in the same way. Goldingay's translations are sometimes startling, but this is because they are so close to the original. Thus the 'man of God' (Elisha) becomes 'the supernatural man',[21] and the high priest is to wear 'shorts' under his tunic. Goldingay manages to be both up to date and yet also 'literal'.

Similar things may be said of Sarah Ruden's translation of the Gospels. Ruden is a highly experienced translator of ancient texts, and applies techniques tested in these to the task of rendering the Gospels: they are discussed in her book on translating the Bible, *The Face of Water*.[22] Like Goldingay, she tends to use quite colloquial English, yet also adheres closely to the source text, keeping proper names and technical terms in something near to their original form rather than using the conventional English equivalents, and often imitating what she takes to be allusions and etymologizations in the Greek:

> And he went throughout Galilaia, giving his news in their synagogues, and expelling demons. And there came to him a man with leprosy, who pleaded with him, [falling on his knees and] telling him, 'If you want, you can cleanse me.' And Iēsous was wrenched with pity; he stretched out his hand and touched him, and said to him, 'I do want to. Be cleansed.' And right away the leprosy left him, and he was cleansed. And snorting a warning to him, Iēsous sent him away right then, telling him, 'See that you say nothing to anybody, but get going and show yourself to the priest, and make the offering for your cleansing that Mōüsēs set out in the law, as proof for them.' But once the man went away, he proceeded to publicize his healing persistently, spreading the story all around, so that Iēsous could no longer go openly into a town. Instead, he remained outside in uninhabited places; but then they kept coming to him from everywhere.
>
> (Mark 1:39–45)

> And on the first day of the festival of bread made without yeast, the students approached Iēsous and said to him, 'Where do you want us to prepare for you to eat the *pascha*?' And he said, 'Get moving and go to the city, to such and such a person, and tell him, "The teacher says, 'My time is near; I'm going to observe the *pascha* at your place with my students.'"' And they did as Iēsous directed, then prepared the *pascha*.
>
> (Matthew 26:17–19)

Note here 'giving his news', 'wrenched with pity', 'snorting a warning', 'the festival of bread made without yeast', 'get moving', and 'the *pascha*' – all defamiliarizing translations that imitate the Greek and remind the reader that the text was not originally written in English.

Also defamiliarizing, though to a lesser extent, is David Bentley Hart's version of the New Testament, which sets out to be literal and explicitly disavows functional equivalence, though he prefers not to regard his translation as deriving from any particular 'theory'. Sometimes the literality leads to unusual and arresting translations of technical titles and terms, as here in the 'parable' of the sheep and goats:

> 'Then he will say to those to the left, "Go from me, you execrable ones, into the fire of the Age prepared for the Slanderer and his angels" . . . And these will go to the chastening of that Age.'

> (Matthew 25:41, 46)

Hart believes that the New Testament should not be too much naturalized by assimilating its language to modern usage: 'one should never be willing to exchange the imagery preserved in ancient turns of phrase for expressions proper to our time, especially where this would mean sacrificing the obscure grandeur and mystery of poetic tropes for the drearily prosaic phrases to which modern languages are more naturally prone'.[23] Like Robert Alter, he sees modern translations as all too often 'explanations' rather than true translations. His work, like Ruden's, is focused on the exact wording of the original in a way that is more typical of Jewish translators of the Hebrew Bible, and resists any appeal to a 'gist' or general drift of the kind favoured by functional-equivalence versions.

Anyone reading Goldingay's, Ruden's and Hart's versions will be aware that the Bible is from an ancient culture different from their own: it is not the Bible we would have written ourselves (whoever 'we' are). In the nineteenth century there was a famous debate between Matthew Arnold and Francis Newman, the brother of Cardinal John Henry Newman, over the translation of Homer. Newman had produced what would now be called a formal-equivalence version, of which Arnold disapproved for many of the reasons discussed in the previous chapter, preferring what we would now call functional equivalence. Arnold was a proponent of 'transparent' translation, and, given the general culture of translation in England, he was generally judged to have won the argument. As Venuti has urged, however, Newman made a case that Arnold did not really answer: 'The English translator should desire the reader always to remember that his work is an imitation, and moreover is in a different material; that the original is foreign, and in many respects extremely unlike our native compositions.'[24] The translator's responsibility, on this view, is to indicate the foreignness of the idiom in the source text by imitating it in the target language, producing a deliberately somewhat awkward rendering that points beyond itself to the original. This is part of the proper humility of the translator.

Should distance in time be registered as well as difference in culture? Translators have usually rendered ancient texts into modern versions of the target language. It would be odd to translate *Don Quixote* into English contemporary with Cervantes; and with the Bible there is of course no English from the last few centuries BCE and the first two CE into which it could even theoretically be translated. But sometimes translators have felt it reasonable to add a patina of age. It is said that the KJV often uses expressions of Tudor origin that were already slightly outdated by the 1610s, just as the Book of Common Prayer of 1662 perpetuates older types of diction, such as 'Our Father, *which* art in heaven'. But with the Bible there can be no consistent archaizing. Attempts to use older English words would simply produce a kind of pseudo-medieval Bible à la Walter Scott or William Morris.

There has perhaps been a swing away from functional-equivalence translation in recent years. One sees it too in liturgy, where the (greatly contested) recent changes in the English text of the Mass have presented Catholics with prayers closer in form to the Latin originals, less approachable and up to date in 'feel'. I don't propose to enter into the controversy over these changes, except to point out that they should not be discussed in terms of 'accuracy'. As we have seen, functional equivalence can be as accurate as formal equivalence. That is not the issue. The issue is a matter of comprehensibility on the one hand and continuity with the past on the other; also perhaps solemnity versus approachability – a large theological issue which we will revisit in Chapter 6.

IMITATIVE TRANSLATION

In Dryden's terminology, 'imitation' is at the furthest stretch from literalism, a kind of translation that is little more than loosely based on the source text – a poem or speech 'in the manner of' a classical author, for example. At the risk of confusing matters and in defiance of his usage, I want to use the term 'imitative translation' for a phenomenon at exactly the opposite end of the spectrum: a translation in which formal equivalence is taken to such an extreme that the Hebrew or Greek becomes really clear beneath the surface, and the target language bends and creaks under the weight of what it is having to accommodate. The KJV with all its parataxis, and Goldingay's version with 'the fullness of the earth is his glory', are already moving a little beyond what normal English prose will stand. One has to imagine an imitation of the source language so much closer even than this that its foreignness is immediately apparent, to the point that it is difficult to read. One might ask why someone would want to produce a barely readable translation, but at all events the twentieth century saw a number of moves in that direction, taking readers so close to the Bible that they could only understand it with difficulty but were certainly treated to a clear exhibition of its foreignness. The most important of these translations is the work of Martin Buber (1878–1965) and Franz Rosenzweig (1886–1929). There is a concise exposition of their work by Everett Fox in *Scripture and Translation*,[25] which I shall follow here.

In 1936 Buber published a collection of his and Rosenzweig's essays on biblical translation called *Die Schrift und ihre Verdeutschung* (*Scripture and Its Translation into German*).[26] Among essays on the nature of Scripture and its (allegedly) originally oral character, much space is devoted to how it should be translated into German so as to preserve its unique features: 'how a translation designed to lead the attentive listener-reader back to the syntactic and stylistic workings of the Hebrew text may serve that end.'[27] The two friends had begun working on translations of biblical books in 1925, and Buber continued it after Rosenzweig's premature death. Psalms and Proverbs were the first to appear, then the Pentateuch, of which there was a revised edition in 1930. Buber continued to work on the translation into the post-war years, producing revisions in the 1950s and 1960s.

The two scholars shared the belief that the exact wording of the Hebrew Bible was crucial to the message it was intended to convey, so that no attempt to produce an 'idiomatic' rendering could ever do it justice. Only a certain kind of literalism – formal equivalence, and that of a very exact and tight kind – was acceptable, if the 'voice' behind the text was to be fully heard in German (or any other target language). So they pioneered an attempt to mimic the Hebrew, often creating new German words to convey what they took to be the essential meaning of Hebrew ones, frequently on the basis of their etymology. For example, 'whole burnt offering' (Hebrew *'olah*) becomes *Darhöhung*, something like 'high-bringing', 'uplifting' or 'raising up', on the basis that the noun comes from the verb *'alah*, 'go up', which in the causative form means to 'raise up'. An altar, *mizbeach*, becomes a 'slaughter-site' (*Schlachtstätte*), deriving as it does from the verb *zabach*, 'to slaughter'.

Also characteristic is the insistence on using the same German word for the same Hebrew one, not just out of stylistic preference or a quest for accuracy but also because they believed that the Bible was characterized by a number of 'leading words' (*Leitwörter*) that functioned rather as leitmotivs do in some music to signal a reference to a larger theme – on this see Chapter 8. A given *Leitwort* would summon up a whole network of what would now be called intertextual allusions, helping to unify the Bible as a single work.

The result makes for strange German, not easily captured in English, but best illustrated by presenting a loose formal-equivalence English translation of two significant passages from the Buber-Rosenzweig rendering:

> *Im Anfang schuf Gott den Himmel und die Erde.*

> *Die Erde aber war Irrsal und Wirrsal.*
> *Finsternis über Urwirbels Antlitz.*
> *Braus Gottes schwingend über dem Antlitz der Wasser.*

> *Gott sprach: Licht werde! Licht ward.*
> *Gott sah das Licht: daß es gut ist.*
> *Gott schied zwischen dem Licht und der Finsternis.*

Gott rief dem Licht: Tag! Und der Finsternis rief er: Nacht!
Abend ward und Morgen ward: Ein Tag.

In the beginning God created the heaven and the earth.

The earth though was confusion and muddle.
Darkness over maelstrom's countenance.
Tumult of God hovering over the face of the waters.

God spoke: Light be! Light was.
God saw the light, that it is good.
God divided between the light and the darkness.
God called to the light: Day! And to the darkness he called: Night!
Evening came and morning came: One day.

(Genesis 1:1–5)

Irrsal und Wirrsal captures the alliterative Hebrew *tohu wa-bohu*, and
I have been unable to imitate this in English. 'God called to the light:
Day!' reads oddly, but reflects the fact that to call someone or something X is in Hebrew formulated as 'to call *to* someone X'. The verb
'call' has the same double usage in Hebrew as in English, meaning
both 'to cry out' and 'to name/designate', but in the second case has to
be followed by 'to' in Hebrew as it does not in English. The translation
here is over-literal, therefore, rather like Aquila's insistence on translating the particle *et*. 'One day' mirrors the Hebrew, which does not say
'the first day' but 'day one' – and that would perhaps have been an
even more faithful formal-equivalent translation of the phrase.

Mosche sprach zu Gott:
Da komme ich denn zu den Söhnen Jißraels,
ich spreche zu ihnen: Der Gott eurer Väter schickt mich zu euch.
sie werden zu mir sprechen: Was ists um seinen Namen? –
was spreche ich dann zu ihnen?
Gott sprach zu Mosche:
Ich werde dasein, als der ich dasein werde.
Und er sprach:
So sollst du zu den Söhnen Jißraels sprechen:
Ich bin da schickt mich zu euch.

Und weiter sprach Gott zu Mosche:
So sollst du zu den Söhnen Jißraels sprechen:
ER,
der Gott eurer Väter,
der Gott Abrahams, der Gott Jizchaks, der Gott Jaakobs,
schickt mich zu euch.

Moshe spoke to God:
So I come to the sons of Yisrael, I speak to them: The God of your
fathers is sending me to you,
they will speak to me: How is it about his name?
What do I then speak to them?
God spoke to Moshe:
I will be there as the one who will be there.
And he spoke:
So shall you speak to the sons of Yisrael:
I AM THERE is sending me to you.
And God spoke further to Moshe:
So shall you speak to the sons of Yisrael:
HE,
The God of your fathers,
The God of Abraham, the God of Yitshaq, the God of Yaakob,
is sending me to you.

(Exodus 3:13–15)

The unusual spellings of the names (*Mosche, Jißrael*, etc.) are closer to
the Hebrew than the normal equivalents in either German or English.
'I will be there as the one who will be there' is Buber-Rosenzweig's
version of the well-known 'I am who I am', and represents one possible interpretation of it. God then becomes HE, HIM and so on rather
than 'Yahweh' or 'LORD' – one way of dealing with the unutterable
holy name of God. This name appears in Hebrew, throughout the
Bible, as four consonants, YHWH, which are understood to be related
to the verb 'to be' (*hyh*), and hence connected with God's self-
description here in Exodus 3:14, which may mean 'I am who I am'.
Whether there really is an etymological connection between YHWH
and *hyh* is a matter of dispute. For a fuller account see Chapter 8.

Buber-Rosenzweig has a French imitator in André Chouraqui, born in Algeria in 1917, who was deputy mayor of Jerusalem under Teddy Kollek, and a great sponsor of interfaith work. His Bible appeared in 1974–9. His translations of the New Testament and the Qur'an were well received, and his work was favoured by André Malraux and by Hans Urs von Balthasar. Even more than Buber-Rosenzweig, his translation of the Hebrew Bible is a kind of imitation of the Hebrew, and he coins even more new words. Thus to be angry is *nariner*, from nostril ('nostrilize'), a priest is a *desservant*, anger is *brûlème*, burningness, descent (*zera'*, literally 'seed') is *semence*, and *toledot*, 'generations', are *enfantements*, 'childings'. Infinitive absolute constructions – the way emphasis is indicated in Hebrew, by adding the infinitive of the verb to the normal tense-form – are rendered by repeating the verb, so 'you shall die, you shall die' (KJV: 'you shall surely die'). 'Let there be light' becomes, very oddly, '*Elohims dit: Une lumière sera, et c'est une lumière*' ('God said: A light will be, and there's a light'). Genesis is called 'Entête', for *bereshith*, its Hebrew name, because the noun is derived from *rosh*, 'head'. The *'olah* is rendered, much as by Buber-Rosenzweig, with *montée*, 'rising up'. The divine name is printed as YHVH with 'Adonai' ('Lord') superimposed on it, while Elohim ('God'), morphologically plural though it takes singular verbs when it refers to the God of Israel, is transliterated, but an 's' is added to the end, making a kind of double plural like older English 'cherubims'.[28]

Another imitative translation in French is by the poet Henri Meschonnic (b. 1932), who, again, emphasizes the need to stick closely to the Hebrew, commenting shrewdly (and with hostility) on Nida's functional-equivalence approach that 'to adapt is to evangelize'.[29] His translations are nearer to normal French than Chouraqui's and rest on very close knowledge of the Hebrew. Here is the beginning of his translation of Lamentations:

> Comme est restée seule la ville plénière de peuple a été comme une veuve
> Plénière entre les nations première entre les provinces a été insolvable
>
> Pleurera pleurera dans la nuit et sa larme sur sa joue nul ne la console
> de tous ceux qui aiment
> tous ses amis ont été infidèles ont été pour elle des ennemis

How has remained alone the city full of people has been like a widow
Full among the nations first among the provinces has been insolvent

Shall weep shall weep in the night and her tear on her cheek no one
consoles her among all who love her
All her friends have been unfaithful have been for her enemies[30]

In English, the main representative of this school is Everett Fox. His translation of the Pentateuch is conceived as a homage to Buber and Rosenzweig, though it is not so extreme in its renderings and sometimes closer to normal English than theirs is to normal German.[31] Here, for example, is his translation of the institution of the Passover:

YHWH said to Moshe and to Aharon in the land of Egypt, saying,
Let this New-Moon be for you the beginning of New-Moons,
the beginning-one let it be for you of the New-Moons of the year.
Speak to the entire community of Israel, saying:
On the tenth day after this New-Moon
they are to take them, each-man, a lamb, according to their
            Fathers' House, a lamb per household . . .

A wholly-sound male, year-old lamb shall be yours, from the
            sheep and from the goats you are to take it.
It shall be for you in safekeeping, until the fourteenth day after
            this New-Moon,
and they are to slay it – the entire assembly of the community of
            Israel – between the setting-times.
They are to take some of the blood and put it onto the two posts
            and onto the lintel,
onto the houses in which they eat it.
They are to eat the flesh on that night, roasted in fire,
and *matzot*,
with bitter herbs they are to eat it . . .

And thus you are to eat it:
your hips girded, your sandals on your feet, your sticks in your
            hand;

you are to eat it in trepidation –
it is a Passover-Meal to YHWH.

(Exodus 12:1–3, 5–8, 11)

The divine name is transliterated rather than rendered with HE as in Buber-Rosenzweig; there are some slightly odd hyphenations to indicate that the original is a single word in Hebrew ('New-Moon', 'each-man', 'Passover-Meal'); and the sentence structure mimics the Hebrew to some extent. As Fox says, 'In practice ... the translator who wishes to bring the language spoken by his audience into consonance with the style of the Hebrew text runs the risk of doing violence to that language, forced as he or she is into "hebraizing" the language. There will of necessity be a certain strangeness and some awkward moments in such a translation.'[32]

Fox makes it clear that he wants to present the Bible 'in English dress but with a Hebrew voice'. Like Buber-Rosenzweig, he often renders what are allegedly the 'root meanings' of verbs, and he repeats words when the Hebrew repeats them: thus in Genesis 32:20–21 he follows B-R in rendering:

He [Jacob] said to himself:
I will wipe the anger from his [Esau's] face
With the gift that goes ahead of my face
Afterward, when I see his face
Perhaps he will lift up my face!
The gift crossed over ahead of his face ... [33]

whereas in modern translations, 'the translators are apparently concerned with presenting the text in clear, modern, idiomatic English. For example, they [the NEB] render the Hebrew *yissa phanai* ["lift up my face"] as "receive me kindly". The NEB translates the *idea* of the text; and at the same time it translates *out* the sound by not picking up on the repetition of *panim* [face] words.' Fox deals with the emphatic infinitive absolute construction by repeating a word and adding 'yes': 'I will make your seed many, yes, many', which again imitates the Hebrew but at the expense of normal English, where traditionally translators add 'indeed', or as in KJV expressions such as 'in blessing I will bless you', which is also an imitative rendering. This makes Fox's a classic formal-equivalence version. Again there is the attention to *Leitwörter* that we find in Buber-Rosenzweig, and the same sense of the Bible as a single whole with wordplay from book to book, which we shall examine in more detail in Chapter 8.[34]

With the exception of Chouraqui (and to some extent Ruden), imitative translators have not worked on the New Testament but only on the Hebrew Bible – the same is true of Robert Alter, whom we will discuss in Chapter 4. The translators we have examined are mostly Jewish (Goldingay is an exception), and their interest in formal equivalence correlates with Jewish attitudes towards Scripture more than with Christian ones. Naomi Seidman quotes Edward Greenstein: 'audience-oriented translation conforms to the evangelical thrust of Christianity as opposed to the covenant-centeredness of Judaism'.[35] In other words, functional equivalence is used in an attempt to convert people to Christianity, formal equivalence to reaffirm the Hebrew text for Jewish readers and ideally to send them back to that text.

This may be an oversimplification, but there is clearly a good deal of truth in it. It reflects real, divergent underlying attitudes to the Bible. As we have already seen, the impulse behind modern functional-equivalence versions has indeed tended to be evangelistic (not always evangelical – Catholic versions such as the Jerusalem Bible have followed the same approach), aimed at presenting the gospel message through the medium of a biblical translation so that the reader is invited to accept it, rather than leading the reader to want to study the exact wording of the original text. (Greenstein uses 'evangelical' of Christian approaches in the quotation in the previous paragraph, but probably means 'evangelistic' – focused on conversion.) In Judaism the text itself is more important, even down to details that could be regarded as sub-semantic such as letter-shapes and spelling, whereas Christians have seldom been interested in, or even noticed, such things in either Testament. We note again that for Christians the Bible in Hebrew has not usually functioned as the scriptural canon, but instead the Old Testament has been read in Greek, Latin or some other language. The translatability of the Bible has been a normal perception for Christians almost from the beginning, where for Jews it has been more problematic. Consequently Jewish scholars have been inclined to prefer translations that point more clearly to the underlying Hebrew.

The contrast should not be exaggerated. Christian translations before modern times, though not so formal-equivalent in character as the work of Buber-Rosenzweig or Fox, were traditionally far from the kind of functional equivalence that would one day turn figs into bananas. The KJV often imitates the underlying Hebrew of the Old Testament and the Greek of the New, resulting in what is recognizable now as 'biblical English'. Luther, similarly, retains Hebrew idioms and constructions, including parataxis and the rendering of the infinitive absolute with repetition of the verb. From a typical piece of narrative in the KJV it is normally possible to reconstruct the underlying Hebrew, even if not so readily as from Buber-Rosenzweig, whereas one could hardly do so from the Good News Bible, or any of the Jerusalem Bible family, or from the New English or Revised English Bibles. In English the tradition of quite 'literal' translation of the Hebrew Bible goes back certainly to Tyndale, and behind him to Jerome's Latin, and indeed the Greek of the Septuagint. It is to this tradition that we owe such expressions as 'stiff-necked' and 'hard-hearted', though not (as might have happened) 'long-nosed' for merciful.

Nowadays there are evangelicals who do not at all share Nida's preference for functional equivalence, and who argue that a strict literalism is the only way of doing justice to the Bible – in this standing closer to what we have just identified as a more characteristically Jewish approach. There is an excellent survey and analysis of this tendency by Dave Brunn,[36] who as a linguist argues that there cannot strictly speaking be such a thing as an absolutely literal version of any text, and succeeds in showing that translations that are purportedly literal are sometimes in practice less so than more mainstream versions. Some of the translations he discusses are hardly known outside the evangelical constituency, but within it are, in some cases, influential. This is especially true of the New International Version, widely regarded as the soundest Bible for evangelicals to use.

This is mainly because the translators are all known to be evangelicals themselves, and so are trusted by Christians of the same persuasion to be reliable (see Chapter 1). But it is also partly because of the way they render certain crucial passages. An example is Isaiah 7:14 (also mentioned in Chapter 1). This is the verse quoted in the New Testament (Matthew 1:23) as 'the virgin shall conceive and bear a son'. There is almost unanimity among Old Testament scholars that the relevant Hebrew word (*almah*) means 'young woman' and does not imply virginity. This does not (against what is commonly argued by both sceptics and some theologians) mean that Jesus' virginal conception or 'virgin birth' must be a myth derived from the text in Isaiah – for if no one thought the word meant 'virgin' in Hebrew, then the doctrine cannot derive from the verse, but must have been read into it. This happened with help from the Septuagint, which does have 'virgin' (*parthenos* in Greek). But for some evangelicals (and some traditional Catholics) it is important that the sentences in Matthew and Isaiah should correspond exactly, and that both should bear witness to Mary's virginity. So the NIV duly translates 'virgin' in Isaiah 7. Apart from this and similar examples, the translation is not (as remarked already) particularly partisan. It is in no meaningful sense literal: it is about as formal-equivalent in style as the KJV or RSV. The Introduction to the NIV in fact expresses what amounts to a mild functional-equivalence philosophy of translation: 'accurate translation will not always reflect the exact structure of the original language. To be sure, there is debate over the degree to which translators should try to preserve the "form" of the original text in English. From the beginning, the NIV has taken a mediating position on this issue.'[37]

IMPACT ON THE TARGET LANGUAGE

Lawrence Venuti quotes a significant passage from Rudolf Pannwitz (1881–1969):

> The fundamental error of the translator is that he stabilizes the state in which his own language happens to find itself instead of allowing his language to be powerfully jolted by the foreign language.[38]

The 'jolt' referred to has been crucial to many proponents of formal-equivalence translation, who argue that the smooth, transparent appearance of other kinds of rendering canonizes the norms and underlying culture of the target language. By aiming to produce the text that the author would have written, had he or she been a native speaker of the target language, a translator refuses to allow the source text to challenge those norms. At the end of that road stands Pope's Homer 'in a powdered wig declaiming in a baroque theatre', giving us no clue of just how radically different from our world was that of ancient Greece. Surely a translation should reveal this difference, not paper over it? And in the process it should challenge us to learn from the ancient text, and even to learn its language.[39] Fox, as we saw, is aware that there may be a need to distort the target language in a challenging but useful way.

This is the essence of what Venuti calls the hermeneutic approach, alien to the Anglophone tradition but present in many Continental theories of translation. This has been so at least since Schleiermacher's proposal that the translator's task can be to move the reader towards the text, not just to bring the text to the reader, even though he admits elements of both. It is this understanding that lies behind the celebrated but controversial (and no doubt rhetorically exaggerated) suggestion by Walter Benjamin that the translator has no business to be concerned with the reader *at all*:

> When seeking insight into a work of art or an art form, it never proves useful to take the audience into account . . . No poem is meant for the reader, no picture for the beholder, no symphony for the audience.
>
> If translation were intended for the reader, then the original would also have to be intended for the reader. If the original is not created for the reader's sake, how then can this relationship allow us to understand translation?[40]

Benjamin saw translation as important because it showed that the work was translatable and thus of major significance: its translatable quality was part of what we should now call its reception history, its resonance down the years. He also suggested that there was an optimum time for the translation of certain works, often long after their creation, and through such translation their aura might be enhanced. Making a foreign text easily accessible to someone who happens not to know the language was, as it were, a collateral effect of a good translation, almost too trivial to mention.[41]

For Benjamin, furthermore, translation showed the affinity of all languages, and thus pointed to a kind of underlying universal language in which all texts met.[42] This rather mystical idea is hard to 'cash' – what is its practical result for either translators or readers? Benjamin, characteristically, did not think in terms of practical benefits, at least at this level. Art for him was a transcendent reality far removed from such questions.[43] But he did strongly defend 'literal' translation, as being more just to the source text:

> True translation is transparent: it does not obscure the original, does not stand in its light, but rather allows pure language, as if strengthened by its own medium, to shine even more fully on the original. This is made possible primarily by conveying the syntax word-for-word, and this demonstrates that the word, not the sentence, is translation's original element.[44]

One result of jolting the target language and its culture is to improve them. Where Anglophone translators are interested in making the source text sound like a native one, those working in the hermeneutic tradition have been concerned to elevate their own language by assimilating features of it more closely to the source language of the text being translated. Buber and Rosenzweig tried to reinvent German so that it was capable of conveying the patterns, structures and vocabulary of the Hebrew text, 'to make the German alien by means of the Hebrew'.[45] As Jürgen Habermas was to argue,[46] 'Translation expands our original language so that we can express what is expressed in the language we are translating.'

These ideas have their roots in the German soil of the seventeenth and eighteenth centuries, amid a sense that German literature had in its grasp the possibility of attaining a comparable status to French, but could do so only by 'expanding' the capacities of the German language. The English language's time of self-awareness and self-assertion had come earlier, in the late Middle Ages with writers such as Chaucer, and in modern times English has never lost its sense of being a world-language: hence a certain arrogance leading to the 'ethnocentric violence' of translations into English of which Venuti complains so vehemently. Pannwitz, again, argued that translators should not 'germanize' Hindi, Greek or English but should 'hinduize, graecize, and anglicize' German.[47] Introducing idioms from other languages would improve German, but this could only be accomplished if translations from those languages were rather literal. This need not be a problem, for, as Borges remarks, 'it might be said that literal translations make not only, as Matthew Arnold pointed out, for uncouthness and oddity, but also for strangeness and beauty'.[48] Francis Newman would have had a much warmer welcome in German circles than he had in England. Schleiermacher had already seen that a major translation alters the target language. Serious translators realign their own language just as much as they are shaped by it. In translation proper, as opposed to mere 'interpreting', there is a twofold relationship to language:

> Every human being is, on the one hand, in the power of the language he speaks; he and all his thoughts are its products. He cannot think with complete certainty anything that lies outside its boundaries; the form of his ideas, the manner in which he combines them, and the limits of these combinations are all preordained by the language in which he was born and raised: both his intellect and his imagination are bound by it. On the other hand, every free-thinking, intellectually independent individual shapes the language in his turn. For how else if not by these influences could it have gained and grown from its raw beginnings to its present, more perfect state of development in the sciences and arts?[49]

There is here an earnestness about the relation of translation to language that can be lacking in the Anglophone tradition, which often sees translation primarily as simply a transfer of information from one tongue to another without serious loss. The hermeneutical tradition is much more attuned to the effect that translation has on the target culture by augmenting its linguistic character.

'Strangeness and beauty' can certainly be found in Luther's translation of the Bible, made before much of this theorizing began. But they can also be found in the tradition of English Bible translation, where approximating the English to the Hebrew (and Greek) goes back at least to Tyndale. As we have seen, like Jerome he preserved Hebrew idioms such as 'stiff-necked' and 'long-suffering', and also retained the syntactic structures of Hebrew rather than turning them into 'elegant' English – thus bequeathing to modern readers a certain simplicity and directness of style not always to be found in the functional-equivalence versions of our own day. The translation of a work as massive and as culturally significant as the Bible throws the target language off balance. Those in the hermeneutic tradition of translation do not try to resist this, but embrace it as a way of changing the target language, perhaps for ever.

In Luther's case, his rendering pulled together the many varieties of German – which still exist at the oral level, far more pronounced than regional variations in English – into a written vernacular used by all.[50] Spoken German in rural areas around Hamburg in the north and Munich in the south can sound as almost two different languages, and mutual comprehension can occasionally be difficult. But thanks to Luther, written German, the so-called *Hochsprache*, is more or less standardized everywhere. He achieved this, however, by attending to everyday speech, steering his Bible between dialects to forge a language that could be understood by all in German-speaking lands. As he put it in his *Open Letter on Translation* of 1530:

> You don't ask Latin literature how to speak German, you ask the mother at home, the children in the street, the common man in the market – look at how they speak, and translate accordingly. Then they will understand it, and they will see you are speaking German to them.[51]

The need to render the Bible intelligible to speakers of the many variants of German thus administered more than just a 'jolt' to the written language. To a great extent, it remade it.

The English Bible had a comparable, albeit less dramatic, effect in Britain – though this in fact preceded the publication of the KJV in 1611, which in itself did not stimulate much change. Tyndale and his successors had already worked their magic by then.[52] And English was already more cohesive than German, so that translations of the Bible did not need to unify the language as Luther had to. Undeniably, however, the various versions culminating in the KJV ensured that biblical turns of phrase and modes of thought would become central to Anglophone culture. As we shall see, the classic tradition of English Bibles, of which the KJV is in practice the only one that is still widely read today, makes all retranslations problematic, just as Luther's version has done for German-speaking readers. Many biblical expressions are now no longer perceived as Hebraic, but as English: the language has changed to accommodate them.

OBJECTIONS TO FORMAL EQUIVALENCE

Just as functional equivalence, for all its attractions, is still open to criticism, so too is formal equivalence, even when it does not take the easily caricatured form of 'literal' translation, in the sense of a mere interlinear gloss or crib. In the work of Nida, as we have seen, it is shunned because it makes the gospel message harder to understand. But there are other reasons, grounded in translation theory rather than religious principles, why not everyone is convinced even by the ethical reasoning of Venuti and others in support of a mode of translation supposedly less prone to 'ethnocentric violence'. Here are three.

First, formal-equivalence translations do appear on the face of it to have a degree of accuracy and objectivity not found in functional equivalence, where the translator has much more latitude to match the words to the audience; and therefore (it could be argued) it shows more humility in face of the source text – greater faithfulness, less arbitrariness. Functional-equivalence renderings, it is felt, impose the translator's own interpretations on the text, whereas formal-equivalence ones simply transfer the essential or literal meaning into the target language. We saw that the Revised New Jerusalem Bible presents itself in just that light, and the same is true of recent revisions of the Catholic liturgy in a more conservative, literal direction. But is that really the case?

It is easy to think of instances where literal translation conveys a different sense from the original, but functional equivalence the same sense. We saw this in Chapter 2 with the case of American versus French headlines. It applies also to road signs: the French *signalisation horizontale effacée* does not 'mean' 'effaced horizontal signalization' but 'no white lines' or 'no road markings'. The more 'literal' version is also less accurate, not only in its semantic meaning ('signalization' has no obvious meaning in English) but also in its force ('look out, be careful!'). In the Bible there are similarly phrases which do not work well in a literal translation, such as Paul's optative *me genoito*, literally 'may it not be' but traditionally, and surely correctly, rendered 'God forbid', even though this damages concordances by introducing a reference to God that is not 'really in' the source text.[53] 'May it not be' falls much more flat, and does not convey nearly so absolute a wish to avoid the feared outcome.

The apparent neutrality of formal-equivalence language is sometimes an illusion, because all words tend to have a personal resonance for particular readers, and this is as true when the rendering is more literal as when it is freer. All words used in the Bible, in any kind of translation, can ring bells because of events and usages that have arisen since the particular rendering was produced. For instance, the KJV translation of Greek *monai* (dwelling places) as 'mansions' in John 14:2 ('in my Father's house are many mansions') may conjure up the wrong picture for a modern reader because the word now refers to a large and expensive house, so that one could argue that the KJV has changed in meaning over time: 'mansion' no longer has its Latin implication in English as simply a place to stay (from *maneo*, 'to remain').[54] It was a formal-equivalence translation in the seventeenth century but nowadays is simply misleading.

Secondly, formal equivalence can be used, as we have seen, in order to 'foreignize' – to alert the reader to the fact that the translation *is* a translation and not an original text. This argument may take the moral high ground, as in Venuti, insisting that functional-equivalence translations assimilate the source text to the target culture and thus evacuate it of its context in its own setting, whereas formal equivalence draws attention to that context. Emphasis on the original culture also has a context, however, as David Damrosch points out:

> Of course, one may or may not share this preference for 'minoritizing' or 'foreignizing' translations. Their popularity today clearly accords with the rise of multiculturalism and our new attention to ethnic difference; just as the melting pot has lost favor as a model for immigrant experience, so too assimilative translation is increasingly disfavored. 'Foreignizing' efforts are the translational correlate of the contemporary championing of ethnic identity. A proponent of a more universalist view of world literature could well object that foreignness can be overdone, not only in producing potentially unreadable texts but also by

creating a separatist mode of translation that undermines the reader's sense of connection to a common human experience.

He goes on to concede that

... even a reader with universalist principles should also object to a translation that simply assimilates the foreign work entirely to contemporary American values, a process that gets us to no common ground beyond our own local cultural position.[55]

This begins to suggest that translation needs to combine features of both functional and formal equivalence, a possibility we shall take up in the next chapter. But Damrosch clearly sees problems in leaning too far towards the source text, which may produce an unintelligible version of a work that was not originally unintelligible, a rendering which certainly signals the foreignness of its source but gives little help in actually understanding it. In which case, why bother with translation at all? Just insist that the reader learn the original language. (Yet even that would not solve the problem, for the foreigner virtually never attains native-speaker competence in another language.) Insisting too hard on formal equivalence and foreignizing can lead to a *reductio ad absurdum* of the whole project of translation.

Unless one is an absolute cultural relativist, one is likely to see similarities between even mutually remote cultures, and in bringing texts across the divide the translator will want to show not only difference but also likeness. This is particularly likely to be so when the text being translated is a classic such as the Bible. Translators of Greek tragedy try to bring out the human universals in the text as well as the obvious cultural gap between ourselves and ancient Greeks. The Bible seems to call for the same treatment. It is certainly in many ways an alien book, as popular reactions to its bloodier passages make clear, and the translator has no business to gloss over that. Yet it also continues to speak, and translations that deliberately make that harder to understand seem rather perverse.

The discussion about the right kind of biblical translation thus leads, inevitably, into wider questions about the nature and status of the Bible. We saw how John Goldingay's *Old Testament for Everyone* follows a somewhat foreignizing approach (with 'Yahweh', names

spelt according to Hebrew conventions, odd repetitions and parataxis), while Tom Wright's *New Testament for Everyone*, though by
no means extreme in observing functional equivalence, nevertheless
makes Paul, for example, into something more like a modern lecturer,
as Wright himself indicates: 'Paul's letters, though capable of poetic
brilliance, often seem to reflect the kind of animated discussion you
might have after a lecture in a crowded room.'[56] One and the same
volume thus raises a central issue about which course to follow. It is
hard not to feel that Goldingay's approach sometimes distances the
Bible rather more than is comfortable for most modern readers.
Whether that is a salutary challenge or a bridge too far is up for discussion, and we should be clear that it is not a question confined to
the world of translation, but concerns our whole understanding of the
Bible, and indeed of texts in general, both ancient and modern. As
George Steiner argues, all understanding is a form of translation –
even within a shared language, since each of us personalizes our own
vocabulary stock, grammar and syntax. Formal equivalence, especially in the service of foreignizing, may make it seem that the source
text is somehow unusual in this respect, when in fact in all understanding, even of speech in our own tongue, we necessarily have to
recognize the words as coming from an alien source.

Imitative translations such as Buber-Rosenzweig thus do more
than remind the reader how different the underlying text is from anything we would write now. They also take up a position on the wider
hermeneutical debate about how texts convey meaning, and they
stress – some would say exaggerate – the differences between cultures. They do drive us back to the original texts, but at the expense
of making them seem even more strange than perhaps they are. Once
one gets inside another language, it stops seeming strange. For
example, putting the verb at the end of subordinate clauses is counter-
intuitive for English-speakers, but one does not have to get far into
learning German for it to start seeming entirely natural. Producing
an English version of a German text that deliberately replicates this
feature then comes to seem rather perverse, almost a refusal to credit
the speakers of another language with common sense. In the same
way it is not long before the learner of Hebrew starts to be unable to
read it from left to right and automatically begins each line at the

right without thinking about it. To signal the foreignness of a Hebrew text by writing all the words of the translation backwards would
certainly foreignize it, but would surely not be sensible. Sometimes
Buber-Rosenzweig strikes me as almost doing that, torturing the German language to give a sense – and even then, of course, only a vague
sense – of the original Hebrew. Asserting the importance of a language by translating it into a much-distorted version of another thus
has its drawbacks.

Thirdly, the distance of the modern translator from ancient texts such
as the Bible is of course temporal as well as cultural. Even in reading a
nineteenth-century novel in one's own language it is impossible not to be
aware of changes in the meaning of words over time: how much more
with a document from up to 3,000 years ago in imperfectly understood
tongues. But to mark this difference by archaizing diction, refusing to
modernize it at all, is arguably just as much a betrayal of the original as
it is to over-modernize it. Steiner quotes Stephen MacKenna: 'Plato
was modern to Plato.'[57] To give a reader the impression Plato made on
his contemporaries, some kind of functional-equivalence translation
seems to be called for, in which we gain a sense of the freshness of his
writing, not just of its distance from us. Plato was writing what for him
was modern Greek, as we see by the presence of quotations from Homer,
in much older Greek, within his work – he was manifestly aware himself
that the language had changed.[58] We cannot readily signal this unless we
translate Plato's own words into normal modern English.[59] (The question of archaizing will be revisited in Chapter 5.)

Where the Bible is concerned, stressing the temporal distance can
be a way of removing the sense that it is still relevant. We know it is
an old book: there is no need to emphasize that in the way it is translated. Isaiah was modern to Isaiah. Formal equivalence can easily
make him seem dated.

We seem to have reached an impasse. The next chapter will explore
the possibility of a way forward.

4

Translation in Equilibrium

Rabbi Judah said: One who translates a text literally is a liar; one who adds anything to it is a blasphemer. (Babylonian Talmud, Kiddushin 49a)

COMPROMISE

Writing about various translations of a number of ancient Egyptian poems, David Damrosch comments that 'they achieve their full force as world literature when we translate them in such a way as to preserve both their immediacy and their distance from us, both their universality and their temporal and cultural specificity'.[1] In Schleiermacher's terms, texts need to be moved towards readers at the same time as readers need to be moved towards texts. But is that possible?

Our discussion so far suggests that it isn't. The NRSV's Preface 'To the Reader' claims that the translators have been 'as literal as possible, as free as necessary', which sounds an admirable aim. But in reality there is a strong clash of opinions between those who favour Schleiermacher's first option – achievable, in the case of the Bible, only by some kind of functional equivalence – and adherents of the second, which requires fidelity to the original at the level at least of the sentence and perhaps, if Benjamin was right, even at the level of the individual words. Both, surely, cannot be correct. We could soften the dilemma a bit by suggesting that different approaches are required for different purposes, and I shall return to this idea in the Conclusion. A Bible in missionary use, it can be claimed, needs to prioritize functional equivalence, even if that means turning 'white as snow' into 'white as a cockatoo's feathers'. One for liturgical reading in a Western church should be fairly literal but allow for places where the biblical idiom is strange, adjusting it to the congregation's needs. A study Bible, thirdly, should follow the original so closely that every word should somehow be represented in the translation, with notes to elucidate difficulties. Beyond the spectrum these three positions cover, there might even be a place for interlinear cribs at one end and, at the other, free paraphrase – as we have seen, there are some good paraphrases available for many biblical texts. All these might qualify as translations of the Bible, and on the principle of 'horses for courses' we might affirm them all, and leave the matter there. Michel Foucault suggests this amicable division of labour for translations in general:

> It is quite necessary to admit that the two kinds of translation exist; they do not have the same function or the same nature. In one, something (meaning, aesthetic value) must remain identical, and it is given passage into another language; these translations are good when they go 'from like to same' ... And then there are translations that hurl one language against another ... taking the original text for a projectile and treating the translating language like a target. Their task is not to lead a meaning back to itself or anywhere else, but to use the translated language to derail the translating language.[2]

To some extent this may be a contrast between literary translation on the one hand and purely informative translation on the other.[3] But in the case of the Bible, at least, the two major options, functional and formal equivalence, are not usually defended as merely acceptable options among others, or as suitable in different circumstances, but are each presented as the only correct approach to translating Scripture. Formal equivalence is touted as more 'accurate' and also as avoiding ethnocentrism, two *ethical* arguments that would seem to rule out mere preferences. Functional equivalence is presented as the only way of making the Bible comprehensible, other approaches being fit only for 'translators with time on their hands' and who care little for the work of evangelism. One approach emphasizes the text's distance from us, the other its universal applicability. Can there possibly be any common ground?

George Steiner, in his ground-breaking book *After Babel*, points towards a way of recasting the discussion. Steiner proposes starting not with the binary contrast that has preoccupied us so far – because it has preoccupied the modern treatment of translation – but instead with a fourfold scheme of his own design for what he calls 'the hermeneutic motion'. It offers the possibility of more meeting of minds and a wider consensus on what a good Bible translation needs to be like.

FOUR STAGES IN TRANSLATION

All translation, according to Steiner, proceeds in the same way, whatever school it may be aligned with. Its first stage precedes any actual translation, and consists in the trust that the text is worth translating. Where the Bible is concerned this is probably a given for most of those who have ever translated it, but with other texts it may be an open question. To translate any text is to affirm its status and importance, however, so that the decision to do so is not taken lightly. The would-be translator may find that the text is much emptier than it looked, that, in Dorothy Parker's words, 'there is less here than meets the eye'. The biblical translator will hope not to have that experience, since, whether or not one believes in the message or contents of the Bible, it would generally be regarded as a non-trivial text. Still it is important to note that the translator begins from a position of trust. Benjamin, as Steiner notes, commented that there can be texts whose time to be translated has not yet come: the receiving culture is not yet ready for them.[4] But that, again, is hardly true of the Bible.

The second stage Steiner identifies as aggression. This may seem an odd word to use, but it corresponds to the sense many translators share that the text they are working on is yielding to an attack: Jerome spoke of what the translator gets from the text as a kind of plunder. The meaning is brought home captive. 'Every schoolchild,' says Steiner, 'but also the eminent translator, will note the shift in substantive presence which follows on a protracted or difficult exercise in translation: the text in the other language has become almost materially thinner, the light seems to pass unhindered through its loosened fibres. For a spell the density of hostile or seductive "otherness" is dissipated.'[5] At this moment, to develop Jerome's metaphor, there is a feeling of having invaded the text, and then having brought its contents home with you. This is part of moving the text towards the reader, in Schleiermacher's terms.

The same is true of the third stage, which Steiner calls incorporation. The translator, having grasped the meaning of the text, expresses it in his or her own language. This may involve a good deal of functional equivalence, as one strives to find terms and turns of phrase that capture the source text's ideas in one's own language, though it may also require some literalness in the rendering – at this stage the process is unstable, and the text oscillates between source language and target language. For good or ill, the translated text may complement, improve or damage existing texts in the target culture.

Thus a new Bible translation can destabilize the whole existing religious culture, much as the changes to Catholic liturgy derived from the Second Vatican Council in the 1960s rocked traditions of many kinds in the Catholic Church. (Indeed, these included major effects on translation, both of the Bible and of liturgical texts, with a swing towards functional equivalence as part of the desire to make official texts more user-friendly.) But it can also be transformative, opening people's eyes to what is in the Bible, as it can be argued that Luther's rendering did for the incipient Protestant movement. The Bible became a possession for ordinary Christians to an extent it had not been before. The translated text also takes its place among other literary monuments, changing them in the process in the ways T. S. Eliot described in his essay 'Tradition and the Individual Talent'.[6] At the same time the newly translated text, if it is a significant one such as the Bible, becomes part of the literary canon in the target language, and that sets up all sorts of interrelationships with the existing canonical texts, which influence how the new text is read. Steiner argues that German translations of Shakespeare changed the German language, much as all agree that Luther's Bible did.[7]

But for Steiner there is an all-important fourth stage, a stage that the usual binary or three-way analyses of translation we have outlined do not have properly in their sights, and which he calls compensation or restitution. This is the attempt to make the new text speak with its own voice even after it has been translated. In practical terms, it may involve moving it back towards the original setting and perhaps re-literalizing some parts of it to avoid its being too cosily incorporated into the new setting. It is hard not to feel that the New English Bible could have done with someone attending to this stage, to cut out crassly modernizing features. 'The failings of the translator . . . localize, they project as on to a screen, the resistant vitalities, the opaque centres of specific genius in the original.'[8] These failings may consist either in having embroidered or 'improved' the source text, or in having cut it down to size or trivialized it, and so reduced it.

A reduction can be seen in some renderings of the poetic books of the Hebrew Bible. Take, for example, the Jerusalem Bible version of Psalm 73:6–16:

> So pride is their chain of honour,
> violence the garment that covers them;
> their spite oozes like fat,
> their hearts drip with slyness.
>
> Cynical advocates of evil,
> lofty advocates of force,
> they think their mouth is heaven
> and their tongue can dictate on earth.
>
> This is why my people turn to them
> and lap up all they say,
> asking, 'How will God find out?
> Does the Most High know everything?
> Look at them: these are the wicked,
> well-off and getting still richer!'
>
> After all, why should I keep my own heart pure,
> and wash my hands in innocence,
> if you plague me all day long
> and discipline me every morning?
>
> Had I said, 'That talk appeals to me',
> I should have betrayed your children's race.
> Instead, I tried to analyse the problem,
> hard though I found it.

This conveys the general sense of the Psalm, but it loses its poetic character with prosaic elements such as 'well-off', 'after all', 'appeals to me' and 'tried to analyse the problem'. It is conversational rather than psalm-like in English. Of course, someone might want to argue that this particular Psalm is an argument rather than a hymn, but it still seems to fall badly flat in this version. The translator has reduced it.

Improving the source text is also a failing: as Dr Johnson, his sights set on Dryden, put it, 'A translator is to be like his author; it is not his business to excel him.'[9] Steiner suggests that, as well as translations, musical settings can often do this. For example, Wilhelm Müller's poems have been seen by some as having been quite feeble until Schubert set them as *Die Winterreise,* and notoriously the libretti of many operas would stand no chance as plays, being elevated only by the music.[10] 'Betrayal by augment' is Steiner's description of this process. Does it happen at all with the Bible? Some would argue that the Bible is so sublime that no translation could possibly improve it, but a case can be made that some translations do precisely this. The Pauline letters are not in origin great literature, nor were they designed to be so. They are occasional pieces, of course carefully considered and constructed since they were meant to be read and reread, but never intended as *literary* monuments. The same is almost certainly true of the Gospel according to Mark, written in rather rough-hewn Greek. But in both cases translators in many languages have raised them to a high literary level. Take, for example, the King James Version at 2 Corinthians 6:1–10:

> We then, *as* workers together *with him*, beseech *you* also that ye receive not the grace of God in vain. (For he saith, I have heard thee in a time accepted, and in the day of salvation have I succoured thee: behold, now *is* the accepted time; behold, now *is* the day of salvation.) Giving no offence in any thing, that the ministry be not blamed: but in all *things* approving ourselves as the ministers of God, in much patience, in afflictions, in necessities, in distresses, in stripes, in imprisonments, in tumults, in labours, in watchings, in fastings; by pureness, by knowledge, by longsuffering, by kindness, by the Holy Ghost, by love unfeigned, by the word of truth, by the power of God, by the armour of righteousness on the right hand and on the left, by honour and

dishonour, by evil report and good report: as deceivers, and *yet* true; as unknown, and *yet* well known; as dying, and, behold, we live; as chastened, and not killed; as sorrowful, yet alway rejoicing; as poor, yet making many rich; as having nothing, and *yet* possessing all things.

In Paul this is a rhetorically constructed list, but it does not have nearly as dramatic an effect as KJV gives it, largely through its command of rhythm, especially with the climax in the last phrase. Certainly the translation does not fall short of the source text, and I would argue enhances it. This transgresses the Johnsonian precept, but is hard to regret. Compare Tom Wright's moderately functional-equivalence version:

So, as we work together with God, we appeal to you in particular: when you accept God's grace, don't let it go to waste! This is what he says:

I listened to you when the time was right,
I came to your aid on the day of salvation.

Look! The right time is now! Look! The day of salvation is here!

Wright's version of the passage ends (vv. 11–13):

We have been wide open in our speaking to you, my dear Corinthians! Our heart has been opened wide! There are no restrictions at our end; the only restrictions are in your affection! I'm speaking as though to children: you should open your hearts wide as well in return. That's fair enough, isn't it?

This captures well a sense of the passage as coming from a personal letter, but, in contrast to KJV, reduces it somewhat by making it too colloquial: Paul was after all aiming at a certain degree of solemnity, and expecting his letter to be pondered on, not discarded. It does, however, help us to see that KJV may be exaggerating the degree of formality.

The proper task of the translator, according to Steiner, is to *balance* the relationship between target and source, a task that hardly ever succeeds but should be always in mind. Fidelity or faithfulness in translation is not a matter of 'accuracy' in a literalistic sense, nor of exact correspondence in a functional-equivalence sense, but of the relation of source to target such that nothing is lost that can be conveyed in either way. 'The translator, the exegetist, the reader is *faithful to* his text, makes his response responsible, only when he endeavours to restore the balance of forces, of integral presence, which his appropriative comprehension has disrupted.'[11] There then arises a kind of exchange between source and target that leads the reader to feel that what is offered is the real text. It retains the marks of its original setting in the source language and that language's era, culture and idiom, yet also seems to belong in the target culture without causing disruption. And at the same time it avoids not just translationese, but even the kind of unidiomatic English (or other target language) which, while not being exactly wrong, strikes the native speaker as not quite the natural way of putting something.[12]

Such translations of course hardly ever occur: they are works of genius. Steiner cites one, from a surprising source: G. K. Chesterton (1874–1936), rendering a sonnet by Joachim du Bellay (1522–60):

> *Heureux qui, comme Ulysse, a fait un beau voyage,*
> *Ou comme cestuy là qui conquit la toison,*
> *Et puis est retourné, plein d'usage et raison,*
> *Vivre entre ses parents le reste de son aage!*
> *Quand revoiray-je, hélas, de mon petit village*
> *Fumer la cheminée, & en quelle saison*
> *Revoiray-je le clos de ma pauvre maison,*
> *Qui m'est une province, & beaucoup d'avantage?*
> *Plus me plaist le sejour qu'on basty mes ayeux,*
> *Que des palais Romains le front audacieux:*
> *Plus que le marbre dur me plaist l'ardoise fine,*
> *Plus mon Loyre Gaulois que le Tybre Latin,*
> *Plus mon petit Lyré que le mont Palatin,*
> *Et plus que l'air marin la douceur Angevine.*

Happy, who like Ulysses or that lord
     Who raped the fleece, returning full and sage,
With usage and the world's wide reason stored,
     With his own kin can wait the end of age.
When shall I see, when shall I see, God knows!
     My little village smoke; or pass the door,

The old dear door of that unhappy house
    That is to me a kingdom and much more?
Mightier to me the house my fathers made
    Than your audacious heads, O Halls of Rome!
More than immortal marbles undecayed,
    The thin sad slates that cover up my home;
More than your Tiber is my Loire to me,
    Than Palatine my little Lyré there;
And more than all the winds of all the sea
    The quiet kindness of the Angevin air.[13]

Chesterton hits the tone of the sonnet, exactly as a functional-equivalence version would do, yet he renders every word of it as much as any formal-equivalence translator. Some words are expanded, but it cannot be said that the wonderful 'the quiet kindness of the Angevin air' travesties '*la douceur Angevine*'. At the same time as the sonnet is incorporated into the stock of English homesickness poems and poems about being content with one's home, it is also plainly still French, and not only for its overt references to the Loire and Anjou. It is also, incidentally, Chestertonian: 'all the winds of all the sea' stretches '*l'air marin*' in a characteristic way. It translates Du Bellay's sixteenth-century French into modern English, though an English that suggests antiquity – 'rape' in the sense of theft was already outdated when Chesterton was writing, but readers will have been aware of Pope's satirical *Rape of the Lock*, about the theft of a lock of hair. For our present purposes its importance is that it cannot easily be assigned to either of the ideal types we have been working with, but represents a genuine fusion: it is hard not to feel that Nida and Venuti might both approve of it. It truly holds the source and the target text in equilibrium.

The same can be said of some of the translations of medieval Latin poems by Helen Waddell (1889–1965). These too tend in a functional-equivalence rather than a literal direction, choosing verse forms that do not always correspond to the original and introducing many changes, yet still rendering the whole sense of the source text without remainder. Here, for example, is one of Peter Abelard's Good Friday hymns:

Solus ad victimam procedis, Domine,
morti te offerens quam venis tollere:
quid nos miserrimi possumus dicere
qui quae commisimus scimus te luere?

Nostra sunt, Domine, nostra sunt crimina:
quid tua criminum facis supplicia?
quibus sic compati fac nostra pectora,
ut vel compassio digna sit venia.

Nox ista flebilis praesensque triduum
quod demorabitur fletus sit vesperum,
donec laetitiae mane gratissimum
surgente Domino sit maestis redditum.

Tu tibi compati sic fac nos, Domine,
tuae participes ut simus gloriae;
sic praesens triduum in luctu ducere,
ut risum tribuas paschalis gratiae.

Alone to sacrifice thou goest, Lord,
    Giving thyself to death whom thou hast slain.
For us thy wretched folk is any word,
    Who know that for our sins this is thy pain?

For they are ours, O Lord, our deeds, our deeds,
    Why must thou suffer torture for our sin?
Let our hearts suffer for thy passion, Lord,
    That sheer compassion may thy mercy win.

This is that night of tears, the three days' space,
    Sorrow abiding of the eventide,
Until the day break with the risen Christ,
    And hearts that sorrowed shall be satisfied.

So may our hearts have pity on thee, Lord,
    That they may sharers of thy glory be:
Heavy with weeping may the three days pass,
    To win the laughter of thine Easter Day.[14]

Very little in the source text here escapes attention, from the repeated '*nostra*' rendered as 'our deeds, our deeds', to the play on '*compati*' and '*compassio*'. 'Whom thou hast slain' is not quite right for '*quam venis tollere*', but the sense is not falsified. The elegiac tone captures Abelard's text exactly, despite the huge gap in culture and in chronology. This is not what Abelard would have written if he had been a modern Englishman: it remains a foreign text. Yet it seems transparent to the original, enabling us to hear it in English. As with so many of Helen Waddell's translations, the balance between source and target seems near-perfect. She was a remarkable translator, famous in her day, through her deep penetration of her sources combined with an English style that is perhaps occasionally slightly precious for a modern reader, yet surely still speaks as it did in the early twentieth century. She deserves to be better known.

REBALANCING BIBLICAL TRANSLATION

Are there any biblical translations that achieve this same feat? There are passages in the King James Version that surely approach it. In the New Testament, parts of Luke's nativity stories capture both the simplicity and the 'biblical' flavour of the original, which is written in Greek imitative of the Septuagint, with much parataxis:

> And there were in the same country shepherds abiding in the field, keeping watch over their flock by night. And, lo, the angel of the Lord came upon them, and the glory of the Lord shone round about them: and they were sore afraid. And the angel said unto them, Fear not: for, behold, I bring you good tidings of great joy, which shall be to all people. For unto you is born this day in the city of David a Saviour, which is Christ the Lord. And this *shall be* a sign unto you; Ye shall find the babe wrapped in swaddling clothes, lying in a manger.
>
> (Luke 2:8–12)

This is a formal-equivalence, almost word-for-word version, but it captures the rhythm and clarity of the original in real English. (As always, it adds in italics the words needed to understand the text that are not explicit in the Greek.) It is not only closer to the Greek than Eugene Peterson's version, which we looked at in Chapter 2, but also in highly comprehensible English of its period. The continuing popularity of the KJV at carol services in England confirms that people still have no difficulty in understanding it.

A modern example is the Jerusalem Bible's rendering of Nahum 2, on the fall of Nineveh, the Assyrian capital, to the Babylonians in the late seventh century BCE:

> A destroyer advances against you.
> Mount guard on the rampart,
> watch the road, tuck up your cloaks;
> muster all your forces.
> The shields of his fighting men show red,
> his warriors are dressed in scarlet;
> all the steel of the chariots flashes
> as they are thrown into battle;
> the horsemen are impatient for action;
> the chariots storm through the streets,
> they hurtle across the squares;
> they look like blazing flames,
> like lightning they dash to and fro.
> The picked troops are called out;
> the columns clash,
> they hurl themselves against the rampart,
> the mantelet is already in place.
> The gates that give on the river are opened,
> in the palace all is panic.
> The Lady is carried off, taken into exile,
> her handmaids raise the dirge, with sighs
> like the moaning of doves,
> and beat their breasts.
> Nineveh is like a pool
> whose waters are draining away.
> 'Stop! Stop!'
> But no one turns back.

'Plunder the silver! Plunder the gold!'
There are endless treasures,
tons of valuables.
Raid and ravage and ruin!
Heart fails and knees give way,
fear is in the loins of all
and every face grows pale.

(Nahum 2:2–11)

This translation, which has survived with only minor changes in the Revised New Jerusalem Bible, captures the breathless panic of the original, and in 'raid and ravage and ruin' even renders the alliteration in the Hebrew (*buqah umebuqah umebullaqah*). ('The Lady' may be the queen or queen mother, or conceivably an Assyrian goddess.) The language is modern but not obtrusive – only 'tons' perhaps seems modernizing and rather colloquial. The translation does not over-elevate the passage poetically, but it gives a very fair impression of the tone of the original without archaizing. There is something like the balance between source and target that Steiner desires.

In the Hebrew Bible, Seidman suggests that Buber-Rosenzweig also brings the target to the source and the source to the target in equal measure, but I am more sceptical about this. As we have seen, their version seems much better at taking the reader to the text than at bringing the text to the reader, because the German is so manifestly unusual and signals the underlying Hebrew much more than presenting a viable translation for a modern readership. Yet there are places where it does seem to achieve a kind of equilibrium. For example,

Sie hörten SEINEN Schall, Gottes, der sich beim Tageswind im Garten erging.

Es versteckte sich der Mensch und sein Weib vor SEINEM, Gottes, Antlitz mitten unter den Bäumen des Gartens.

ER, Gott, rief den Menschen an und sprach zu ihm:

Wo bist du?

Er sprach:

Deinen Schall habe ich im Garten gehört und fürchtete mich, weil ich nackt bin, und ich versteckte mich.

Er sprach:

Wer hat dir gemeldet, daß du nackt bist?

Hast du vom Baum, von dem nicht zu essen ich dir gebot, gegessen?

Der Mensch sprach:

Das Weib das du mir beigegeben hast, sie gab mir von dem Baum,
und ich aß.

Er, Gott, sprach zum Weib:

Was hast du da getan?

Das Weib sprach:

Die Schlange verlockte mich, und ich aß.

They heard the sound of HIM, God, who was walking in the garden at the day's breeze.

The human and his woman hid themselves before HIS countenance, God's, among the trees of the garden.

HE, God, called to the human and spoke to him:

Where are you?

He spoke:

Your sound I heard in the garden and was afraid, because I am naked, And hid myself.

HE spoke:

Who told you that you are naked?

Have you eaten from the tree from which I commanded you not to eat?

The human spoke:

The woman whom you gave me to be with me, she gave me from the tree, and I ate.

HE, God, spoke to the woman:

What have you done here?

The woman spoke:

The snake seduced me, and I ate.

(Genesis 3:8–13)

Apart from the treatment of the divine name as *Er*, HE, this is not far removed from the King James Version in its essentials. It has few idiosyncrasies of style, and is simply an almost word-for-word rendering of the Hebrew. Yet it achieves perfectly good communication with a modern reader.

There are also mainly functional-equivalence translations of the Bible that manage to create an equilibrium between source and target. I have said harsh things of the New English Bible, but at times it succeeds strikingly in being both modern and true to the original. Here is the beginning of the third chapter of Lamentations, the quintessential lament in the Hebrew Bible:

> I am the man who has known affliction,
>> I have felt the rod of his wrath.
> It was I whom he led away and left to walk
>> in darkness, where no light is.
> Against me alone he has turned his hand,
>> and so it is all day long.
> He has wasted away my flesh and my skin
>> and broken all my bones;
> he has built up walls around me,
>> behind and before,
> and has cast me into a place of darkness
>> like a man long dead.
> He has walled me in so that I cannot escape,
>> and weighed me down with fetters;
> even when I cry out and call for help,
>> he rejects my prayer.
>
> (Lamentations 3:1–8)

The translation captures the prosody of the original, in which the indented lines generally have two beats or stressed syllables in Hebrew against the three in the others – the so-called *qinah* or lament metre, which 'limps'. NEB has caught this by using four beats to three, which is more feasible in English but produces a similar effect. At the same time it has achieved a piece of unfussy and spare English.

Thus the true contrast may be not between functional and formal equivalence, but between those translations that successfully marry source and target so that both are respected, and those that are unbalanced between them.

The most successful modern translation of the Hebrew Bible in this respect is Robert Alter's in three magnificent volumes. His solo endeavour tends more in the formal- than in the functional-equivalence direction, but without being doctrinaire about this – despite his invective against 'the heresy of explanation', which argues for formal equivalence. The quality of the translation is evident as early as Genesis 1:2, where the NRSV renders 'the earth was *tohu wa-bohu*' as 'the earth was a formless void', but Alter captures the rhyme and has the alliterative 'welter and waste'. (Luther experimented with '*Irrsal und Wirrsal*', picked up by Buber-Rosenzweig, as we saw.[15])

Here are two excerpts from Alter's translation, one prose, the other verse. First, the intervention of a wise woman from Tekoa when King David is mourning for the banishment of his son, Absalom, who has taken the life of another of David's sons, Amnon, in revenge for his rape of Absalom's sister. The woman constructs a clever parallel, purportedly from the doings of her own two sons, one of whom has killed the other and is supposedly being sought for execution, thus depriving the woman of both sons. She then applies the story to David:

> And the woman said, 'Let your servant, pray, speak a word to my lord the king.' And he said, 'Speak.' And the woman said, 'Why did you devise in this fashion against God's people? And in speaking this thing, the king is as though guilty for the king's not having brought back his own banished one. For we surely will die, like water spilled to the ground, which cannot be gathered again. And God will not bear off the life of him who devises that no one of his be banished. And so now, the reason I have come to speak this thing to the king my lord is that people have made me afraid, and your servant thought, "Let me but speak to the king. Perhaps the king will do what his servant asks. For the king would pay heed to save his servant from the hand of the person bent on destroying me and my son together from God's heritage."' ... And the women said, 'Let my lord the king speak, pray.' And the king said to the woman, 'Pray, do not conceal from me the thing that I ask you.' And the king said, 'Is the hand of Joab with you in all this?' And the woman answered and said, 'By your life, my lord the king, there is no turning right or left from all that my lord the king has spoken! For your servant Joab, he it was who charged me, and he it was who put in your servant's mouth all these words. In order to turn the thing round your servant Joab has done this thing. And my

lord is wise, as with the wisdom of a messenger of God, to know every-thing in the land.' And the king said to Joab, 'Look, pray, I have done this thing. Go and bring back the lad Absalom.'

(2 Samuel 14:12–16, 18–21)

Simple parataxis, as in KJV, moves the narrative and the dialogue along. Where the Hebrew is rather halting and involved, the transla-tion mirrors that: 'the king is as though guilty for the king's not having brought back his own banished one', and 'God will not bear off the life of him who devises that no one of his be banished'. These long clauses perhaps reflect the woman's hesitancy, as Alter suggests in his commentary on the passage. 'My lord the king' or 'the king my lord' preserve the Hebrew idiom (rather than 'Your Majesty' as in other modern translations) and convey the right degree of our distance from the organization of the ancient Judaean monarchy, while remain-ing fully comprehensible. This is largely a formal-equivalence rendering, but adjusted to meet the modern reader. The 'angel of God' has become 'a messenger of God', which is the natural sense of Heb-rew *mal'akh*, though it fairly certainly refers to a non-human figure. The passage has a lot of hidden irony, for in successfully convincing David to bring back Absalom, the woman unwittingly causes the rebellion which will nearly cost David his throne and does cost Absa-lom his life. Alter's rendering runs in exactly the right idiom and style, and thus achieves the elusive balance between source and target.

The same skill is on display in a verse passage. This is taken from an oracle about Moab, a Transjordanian kingdom, ascribed to the prophet Isaiah though probably in origin anonymous, and difficult to give a date to.

> Yes, in the night was Ar sacked,
> Moab was undone.
> Yes, in the night it was sacked,
> Qir Moab was undone.
> They went up to the temple of Dibon,
> to the high places, to weep.
> For Nebo and for Medbah
> Moab wails . . .

Heshbon and Elealeh cry out,
　　as far as Jahaz their voice is heard.
Therefore Moab's picked warriors cry,
　　their life-breath broken up.
My heart for Moab cries out,
　　those who flee her as far as Zoar
　　　　and Eglath Shelishiyah.
For by the Ascent of Luhith,
　　in weeping they go up.
For on the road to Horanaim
　　they rouse disaster's cry.
For the Nimrim waters
　　have become a desolation . . .

For screaming encircles
　　the region of Moab.
As far as Eglaim her wail,
　　to Beer Eilim her wail.
For Dimon's waters are full of blood,
　　yes, I will add still more against Dimon:
for Moab's survivors, a lion,
　　for the remnant of the land.
　　　　　　　(Isaiah 15:1–2, 4–6, 8–9)

Part of the magic is attributable to the exotic and onomatopoeic place names, but – as with the NEB version of Lamentations 3, considered above – the lament is rendered poignantly and simply, without either archaism or anything that grates as unhappily modern. Compare and contrast the NEB 'On the night when Ar is sacked, Moab meets her doom' – surely a more banal rendering. (The Jerusalem Bible translates 'The night when Ar was ravaged Moab collapsed'.) Alter has precisely the measure of this formal yet highly emotional lament.

Alter thus follows Steiner's precept of compensation/restitution to an almost unique extent among modern translators into English. His stated aim is on the whole more in line with formal equivalence, and he disapproves, as we have seen, of 'the heresy of explanation', where the translator makes explicit (for a supposedly stupid reader, as Alter sees it) connections that are latent in the text, and explains (away) awkward pieces of wording by making all smooth. At the same time, he does sometimes modernize the text to prevent the reader from being trapped in an impenetrable past. In Numbers 22–4 'Balaam took up his oracle' (KJV) is consistently rendered 'took up his theme' (compare Jerusalem Bible, 'declaimed his poem'), while 'YHWH Zebaoth' becomes 'Master, LORD of Armies', rather than 'of hosts'. As a translation of the Hebrew Bible it is a triumph, and if someone could produce something similar for the New Testament and, indeed, the Apocrypha, the world would be richer for it.

TRANSLATING UP AND DOWN

How are we to explain the fact that 'literary' translators of the Bible today tend to veer in a formal-equivalence direction, while more popular versions tend towards functional equivalence? As we have seen, the difference partly correlates with the tendency of Jewish translators of the Hebrew Bible to emphasize the exact wording of the text, while Christians may be more concerned with the gist, especially in the case of the New Testament. But this correlation is not complete – in particular, some Christian translations, notably the KJV, have been quite literalistic in both Testaments, as in our own day is David Bentley Hart. The explanation lies elsewhere.

David Bellos has introduced a useful distinction between translating UP and translating DOWN. Translation UP means translating into a more prestigious language than the source, DOWN into a less prestigious one. At the moment, English is the most prestigious language in the world, so that in general all English versions of texts originally written in other languages represent translation UP. The practical effect of this is a tendency towards functional equivalence, with foreign elements in the original text suppressed to produce an English text that is as nearly as possible a text that a native English-speaker might have written. In past centuries, when French was the prestige language in Europe, translations from French into English would have retained many characteristically French expressions and terms, since they were then translating DOWN. Nowadays, on the other hand, French expressions are avoided when French texts are rendered into English, and when English is being translated into French it is English features that are left in (no doubt to the annoyance of the Académie Française). A little foreignizing is acceptable even in translation UP. Thus the ranks of detectives in foreign novels ('Scandi noir', for example) are often not rendered as 'chief superintendent' or 'sergeant' as in British law enforcement, but instead there is some approximation to the equivalent in their own system. But in general the culture and language are made as English as possible. English is treated as the norm or default language, and other languages have to dance to its tune. Hence the accusation of 'ethnocentric violence'.

Traditionally the languages of the Bible were high-status languages, and when translating into English scholars were translating DOWN, and so would leave Hebrew and Greek idioms very much intact: in other words, they would lean towards formal equivalence. The high status of the Bible as a cornerstone of culture and the Scripture of two world religions still predisposes many translators towards formal equivalence, and leads to the sense that a more literal is a more faithful version. But there is a twist. Translations into minority languages are frequently carried out, not from the Hebrew and Greek originals, but from a basic English or Spanish version, since often the translator will not possess any personal knowledge of biblical languages. In that context, the translator is translating UP from what is in effect a low-status 'crib' or guide to the text towards a higher-status target language, so the polarity is reversed. Respect for the target language means that functional equivalence is preferred, just as Nida argued it should be, so as to acclimatize the Bible in the culture of the language in question.

Thus with the Bible it is generally more literary translators, working with the original languages, who practise formal equivalence. Those who do so tend, like Alter, to argue that no other approach is acceptable: in terms of Bellos's model, they regard themselves as translating DOWN, and see anything other than close adherence to the original as a kind of insult to the text. This contrasts with what Nida encouraged: 'Nida's job was to help produce texts that were functionally equivalent to the Bible considered not as sacred script, but as the repository of a sacred story.'[16] But literary translators reject the idea that there is a gist, a basic meaning or story that can be rendered func-tionally, and see something approaching word-for-word translation as the only way of doing justice to the biblical text in which, as we recall that Jerome remarked, 'even the word order is a mystery'. In fact it is virtually impossible to preserve biblical word order in English and still produce a comprehensible text, but it is felt that such should at least be the ideal. Thus we get translations in the tradition of Buber-Rosenzweig, such as Fox and, to some extent, Alter. It was for the same reason that the King James translators, and the versions they drew on, preserved so much Hebrew idiom and syntax. Much of it might, they thought, be an essential feature of the text, which should not be lightly jettisoned in the interests of mere intelligibility in English. The higher a doctrine of the inspiration and authority of the literal text the trans-lator embraces, the more likely the result is to be verbally close to the original, even if this produces a text that is hard to understand. Does authority attach to the text, in its very words, or to the story the text tells? That is often the issue that translators of the Bible, unlike other texts, have to confront. It is a fault line that runs through all discussion of the authority and inspiration of the Bible.

5

Style and Register

RETRANSLATION

Some translations of the Bible are revisions of an existing version: the King James Version begat the Revised Standard Version, which begat the New Revised Standard Version. The intention of the most recent of these, the NRSV, was much the same as that of the KJV in its own day: not to make 'a new Translation, nor yet to make of a bad one a good one . . . but to make a good one better, or out of many good ones, one principall good one, not justly to be excepted against'. The KJV had used Tyndale and Coverdale as well as translations into other languages, such as Luther's German – not to mention the ancient versions, Greek and Latin and Syriac, for the translators were formidable linguists. The modernizing involved, of vocabulary and syntactical choices in the English, may be done well (as with the KJV) or indifferently (as, to my taste, in the NRSV), but it does not raise any issues of principle. An existing translation is being revised.

Not so with modern translations created from scratch. Here the translators are trying to reconceive the task of biblical translation as if it were being done for the first time. The result may be strikingly different from the KJV tradition or from Luther, and we have looked at many versions that strike out in new directions. Some, like Fox, Goldingay or Hart, the New International Version or the Revised New Jerusalem Bible, tend in a formal-equivalence direction; others, such as the Jerusalem Bible (and New Jerusalem Bible), Tom Wright and many translations into languages of the developing world, use functional equivalence. In this chapter, however, that particular distinction will loom less large than before. For what unites all these translations is that they do not take their bearings from an existing version. In English, it means in particular that the KJV renderings are scrupulously ignored.

Nothing produced so much confusion when the New English Bible was first published as the failure to realize this. Those for whom the KJV was simply 'The Bible', hardly thought of as a translation at all but seen primarily as a classic of English literature,[1] talked endlessly in reviews about how the translators had 'changed' the Bible, or showed that a given NEB rendering was inferior stylistically to the KJV one. Elijah's 'still small voice' (1 Kings 19:12) had been replaced with 'a low murmuring sound',[2] destroying (it was said) all the poetry. The correct response to this was emphatically not that 'a low murmuring sound' is as resonant as 'a still small voice' – clearly it is not – but rather that the former is what the Hebrew means. ('Voice', *qol*, is regularly used in the Hebrew Bible to mean 'sound', as when Adam and Eve heard the *sound*, not the voice, of God walking in the garden of Eden in Genesis 3:8.) In fact, the NRSV's 'a sound of sheer silence' is probably more accurate, and actually more evocative, with its oxymoron. But the present point is simply that translators must follow the linguistic evidence rather than the 'magic' of an existing version.

Although such critics misconstrued what it means to translate the Bible from scratch, they had a point. They correctly perceived that an English Bible already exists and has a canonical and authoritative place within the corpus of English literature, and indeed culture. In that corpus many of its renderings, even if inaccurate, are established in tradition and usage. The well-loved hymn 'Dear Lord and Father of mankind, forgive our foolish ways' speaks of the 'still small voice of calm' that quietens our desires, and it would be considerably less effective in this if it were 'a low murmuring sound'. The phrase is part of English idiom. Not to take any notice of this is a definite choice, and saying that one was simply following the Hebrew doesn't change this. This is not to imply that the NEB translators should have retained the still small voice, but that their rebuttal of their critics was itself rather disingenuous, or at least naïve. There was no meeting of minds.

Once there has been a truly canonical translation of any classic work, any new rendering, however accurate, is in effect a retranslation, and will inevitably be judged by comparison with the version that has become standard. To choose 'low murmuring sound' if the corresponding Hebrew phrase turned up, say, in the Dead Sea Scrolls, would be a simple semantic decision; but to choose it in 1 Kings 19 is to reject 'still small voice', which hovers in the background whispering 'choose me'. Other phrases, such as 'the Lord is my shepherd' or 'the spirit is willing, but the flesh is weak' similarly resist 'retranslation', as most people would perceive it.

This is true of very simply literal translations, and equally true of highly functional-equivalence ones: in both cases the translator is not following the KJV, or Luther, or whatever might be the established translation. And that translation rings in the ears of many readers, so that providing an objectively more accurate rendering is not a straightforward decision to use this or that wording, but a decision *not* to use the established one. When Buber-Rosenzweig render 'Light be! Light was' (*'Licht werde! Licht ward'*), they are sticking very closely to the Hebrew, but the reader cannot avoid recalling the traditional '"Let there be light": and there was light' ('*"Es werde Licht!" Und es ward Licht'*), and perhaps also the stupendous crash from the orchestra on the second '*Licht*' in Haydn's *Creation*. In the same way the KJV lurks in the mind of many Anglophone readers when they encounter any modern Bible, and it gets in the way of hearing the new version.

This is not a problem peculiar to the Bible. Rosenzweig himself observed that 'every great work of one language can in a certain sense be translated into another language only once'.[3] As he goes on, 'Voss remains the German Homer, and Luther the German Bible ... A new Homer translation can of course be much better than Voss, but it is not and cannot become a world-historical event.'[4] As Steiner puts it, 'the translator translates after and against his predecessors almost as much as he translates his source'.[5] There are aspects of the first and decisive version that may help in this process of establishing it as definitive. One can be some measure of archaism, which we shall see characterizes the KJV. This suggests that the version is older than it really is, and therefore already a classic: 'it creates an illusion of remembrance which helps to embody the foreign work into the national repertoire'.[6] Steiner says that Chateaubriand's translation of Milton 'suggests that it has behind it an equivalent to an Authorized Version [of the Bible]. As is often pointed out, no such equivalent exists. But its imaginary felt presence is unmistakable when French masters translate those works of English poetry and prose in which the Bible is a shaping precedent.'[7]

It can be argued that the classic status of the KJV and its lighter revisions makes a new translation almost an impossibility. There are many excellent modern translations of the Psalms in particular, but Anglican clergy of my generation have behind them years of reciting, in their daily prayers, not actually the KJV but one of its sources, the even older version of Miles Coverdale, used in the Book of Common Prayer. For all its many defects, this rendering of the Psalms, which was not even made directly from the Hebrew (a language Coverdale did not know), to me simply *is* the Psalms. Even where they are clearly inaccurate, I know them by heart, and they slip unbidden into my mind. New versions, however good, cannot compete with this. The best that can be done is for a translator to be aware of the competition, and not to pretend that the traditional renderings can simply be set aside and forgotten. Buber argued that a new version was needed in German because Luther's Bible had become, as he put it, a 'palimpsest', overlaid with familiar ideas, and that it needed to be defamiliarized.[8] But this is a very difficult task, for the established translation, being part of the individual's memory as well as that of the denominational community memory, obtrudes whenever a new version is attempted. All of us who have grown up with the Bible have personal connections with given turns of phrase in the version we know, which in Anglophone culture is still often the KJV. (This has no doubt changed for many, and it is important to remember that for most modern Catholics in Britain the version that is settling in their minds is the Jerusalem Bible, the version normally used at Mass – though, as we shall see in Chapter 6, this may be changing.) As Steiner puts it, 'interpretation [of a text], except in the first momentary instance, is always reinterpretation'.[9]

COLLOQUIAL AND FORMAL LANGUAGE

Twentieth- and twenty-first-century translations of the Bible into English normally aim to produce a version in readily comprehensible modern parlance. But most translators would agree that this is by no means simple, both because modern English is not a uniform language, and because the style of the Bible varies from book to book, and even from passage to passage. In the Hebrew Bible in particular, some books seem to be an amalgam of several underlying documents that have been woven together to make a slightly uneven whole, and we can detect this precisely because of divergent styles (see Chapter 9 for examples). Most versions recognize the problem, at least in theory. Thus the Jerusalem Bible has in its Introduction:

> The translator of the Bible into a vernacular may surely consider himself free to remove the purely linguistic archaisms of that vernacular, but here his freedom ends. He may not, for example, substitute his own modern images for the old ones: the theologian and the preacher may be encouraged to do this, but not the translator. Nor must he impose his own style on the originals: this would be to suppress the individuality of the several writers who responded, each in his own way, to the movement of the Spirit. Still less must it be supposed that there should be throughout a kind of hieratic language, a uniform 'biblical' English, dictated by a tradition however venerable. There is no doubt that in forfeiting this we lose something very precious, but one hopes that the gain outweighs the loss.[10]

The JB certainly did avoid mimicking the language of the KJV ('a uniform "biblical" English'), though in its turn it established a new JB style that can easily be discerned throughout the translation. This is characterized by an avoidance of parataxis in narrative and its replacement by varying conjunctions such as 'then', 'but', however', and so on, and a more typically modern inserted 'he said' after the first few words of a speech, where the Hebrew has 'and he answered and said' always before any words are quoted. In verse there is often a slightly disjointed style, which does capture the jerkiness, to an Anglophone reader, of Hebrew poetry. The JB also presents well, in the case of Paul's letters, the sense of a sustained argument. Here are some examples:

> After the death of Saul, David returned from his rout of the Amalekites and spent two days in Ziklag. On the third day a man came from the camp where Saul had been, his garments torn and earth on his head. When he came to David, he fell to the ground and did homage. 'Where

do you come from?' David asked him. 'I have escaped from the Israelite camp,' he said. David said to him, 'What happened? Tell me.' He replied, 'The people have fled from the battlefield and many of them have fallen. Saul and his son Jonathan are dead too.'

(2 Samuel 1:1–4)

Draw yourself up against Babylon, surround her,
all you who bend the bow.
Shoot! Do not spare your arrows.
Raise the war cry against her from all sides.
She surrenders! Her bastions fall!
Her walls collapse!
This is the vengeance of Yahweh. Take revenge on her.
Treat her as she has treated others.
Deprive Babylon of the man who sows,
of the man who wields the sickle at harvest.
Escape from the destroying sword,
let everyone return to his own people,
let everyone escape to his own country!

(Jeremiah 50:14–16)

If a person's faith is not strong enough, welcome him all the same without starting an argument. People range from those who believe they may eat any sort of meat to those whose faith is so weak they dare not eat anything except vegetables. Meat-eaters must not despise the scrupulous. On the other hand, the scrupulous must not condemn those who feel free to eat anything they choose, since God has welcomed them. It is not for you to condemn someone else's servant: whether he stands or falls it is his own master's business; he will stand, you may be sure, because the Lord has power to make him stand.

(Romans 14:1–4)

Especially in the case of Paul, the English of the Jerusalem Bible, as of the New English Bible and many other modern versions, is somewhat colloquial. In narrative, the conventions being followed are those of the modern novel. In verse, there is an attempt to imitate the Hebrew, but in the process the translation becomes rather exclamatory. All three types assimilate the biblical text to modern norms (that is, technically speaking all are functional-equivalence versions, moving the text towards the reader and asking, how would someone today say that?). But all seem to me to do so in a positive and useful way. There are, however, some issues of principle involved.

First, how far were the various books of the Bible written, in Hebrew or Greek, in the rather colloquial style into which the Jerusalem Bible and other modern versions render them? In the case of Paul, for example, too much can be made of the fact that he wrote in koine Greek, the vernacular that had established itself in the Mediterranean world by the first century CE. Sometimes his use of it is cited as showing that he wrote in a colloquial style, but that seems predicated on the idea that he might have written in classical, Attic Greek but chose a more democratic option instead. This is unlikely to be the case. Paul wrote the kind of Greek that was current in his day. This justifies a translation into modern English, but not therefore also into a colloquial register.

The New Testament may, it is true, be described as informal or unofficial writings. The early Christians were a sect, not part of an establishment that produced a national literature, and the books they did write were mostly not meant for wide circulation. By the first century CE most of the Hebrew Bible, by contrast, was already recognized by Jews everywhere as authoritative. Some parts of it seem to have become 'holy Scripture' much earlier than this: many scholars think that the book of Deuteronomy, for example, was already an official document by the sixth century BCE. So it would not be surprising if New Testament books had been written in a less formal style. This reasonable expectation, however, is not wholly borne out by the evidence of the text we have. In the ancient world, writing a document as long and complex as a Gospel, or one of Paul's letters, was not a casual undertaking even within a small in-group such as the early Christians. It required expensive materials and a trained scribe, and would have been undertaken only if the resulting text was expected to be kept for a considerable time, read and reread, probably when the Church assembled for worship. This solemn setting should make us pause before thinking of the books of the New Testament as informal enough to justify rendering them in a colloquial form of any target language.

Thus Paul's letters are not chatty, but have a certain formality and gravitas. They were written to be returned to time and again and pondered deeply. The approach of a translator such as J. B. Phillips, making Paul into someone having an informal conversation with his readers, surely misses the mark here, and so does the Jerusalem Bible. Even the NRSV is mistaken when it implies in its Introduction that Paul's Greek is informal or conversational:

> Another aspect of style will be detected by readers who compare the more stately English rendering of the Old Testament with the less formal rendering adopted for the New Testament. For example, the traditional distinction between *shall* and *will* in English has been retained in the Old Testament as appropriate in rendering a document that embodies what may be called the classic form of Hebrew, while in the New Testament the abandonment of such distinctions in the usage of the future tense in English reflects the more colloquial nature of the koine Greek used by most New Testament authors except when they are quoting the Old Testament.[11]

The distinction between *shall* and *will* is a good deal more complicated than this suggests. There is little agreement among writers of English about it, and few readers will really notice the difference between the Testaments on this front. (The great Fowler brothers, in *The King's English*, commented that 'It is unfortunate that the idiomatic use, while it comes by nature to southern Englishmen ... is so complicated that those who are not to the manner born can hardly acquire it' – a counsel of despair.[12] Though I am a southern Englishman, I'm not nearly so assured as my Edwardian forebears on *shall* and *will*.) But even though Paul's letters are occasional pieces of writing, usually dealing with some particular concern in the Christian group they are addressed to, they are not casual or informal. They are solemn and serious, and the Jerusalem Bible and other modern translations can diminish this sense.

The Greek of the Gospels contains many Semitisms, which implies that the evangelists (perhaps with the exception of Luke) were probably first-language Aramaic-speakers who had koine Greek as their second language, or else spoke a Greek that was heavily Semitized.

But again this should not be equated with the idea that their Greek was colloquial, or that their writings were meant to be ephemeral or casual. In the case of John, his Greek is some of the most simple and pared down in the New Testament, yet he uses it to an often dramatic effect in a way that belongs to very serious literature. The characters in the story certainly do not chat.

The Hebrew Bible, as just noted, seems in any case to consist largely of 'official' literature, which clearly justifies a formal register for a translation. Goldingay's *The Old Testament for Everyone* is, as we have seen, relatively literal (formal-equivalent) in character, but the English register he deems appropriate for the equivalence may sometimes be too low. It conveys the sense very accurately, but often implies a light tone inappropriate to such formal writing. The translation does not 'balance' with the original in the way described in the previous chapter. For example, the death notices of the kings of Israel and Judah in the books of Kings regularly include the note 'As for the rest of the deeds of King X, are they not written in the book of the chronicles of the kings of Y?' This formulation conveys, in a formal tone, that there is a document where other details can be found: the force of 'are they not written?' is something like 'they are certainly to be found', this kind of (rhetorical) question being a trick of formal Hebrew style. Goldingay, however, renders it 'written on the document about things of the time, aren't they?', implying both that the reader should know this already – which this kind of formulation almost certainly does not imply – and also that the tone is conversational, which it isn't.

Perhaps the Revised Standard Version conveys best the level of formality of Hebrew Bible narrative, capturing the rather laconic style and the slightly elevated register. A high register is difficult to sustain in modern English, in which formality almost demands a measure of archaism: it is hard to be solemn without lapsing into 'biblical' English, and perhaps there is no point resisting it. Here is the RSV rendering of 2 Samuel 6:16–17, 20–23:

> As the ark of the LORD came into the city of David, Michal the daughter of Saul looked out of the window, and saw King David leaping and dancing before the LORD; and she despised him in her heart. And they brought in the ark of the LORD, and set it in its place, inside the tent

which David had pitched for it; and David offered burnt offerings and peace offerings before the LORD.

And David returned to bless his household. But Michal the daughter of Saul came out to meet David, and said, 'How the king of Israel honoured himself today, uncovering himself today before the eyes of his servants' maids, as one of the vulgar fellows shamelessly uncovers himself!' And David said to Michal, 'It was before the LORD, who chose me above your father, and above all his house, to appoint me as prince over Israel, the people of the LORD – and I will make merry before the LORD. I will make myself yet more contemptible than this, and I will be abased in your eyes; but by the maids of whom you have spoken, by them I shall be held in honour.' And Michal the daughter of Saul had no child to the day of her death.

We might guess that this is not exactly what Michal and David said to each other, but rather a stately, sanitized version of it. It is the way people are supposed to speak about improper things at a royal court – with profanities omitted. Much is left to the reader's imagination. The style might well remind us of a scene from the *Arabian Nights* in its familiar translations. The New English Bible flattens this impression, rendering 'when he exposed his person in the sight of his servants' slave-girls like any empty-headed fool', which manages to be wordy and yet unidiomatic at the same time. It ends, 'Michal . . . had no child to her dying day', taking refuge in a familiar English idiom ('dying day') rather than keeping the rhythm and high register of 'the day of her death'. Of course the information imparted is the same, but the tone in the NEB is subtly off because the translators have hit the wrong register. To put it in terms we have already used, it needed a bit more foreignizing.

HEBREW VOCABULARY AND GENRE

One issue specific to the Hebrew Bible is its comparatively small vocabulary – just 2,000 root words across its books. Particularly in prose texts, the same word is often repeated where in English an attempt would be made to vary the language. To revert to the story of Balaam's ass in Numbers 22: every time the animal is mentioned it is called 'the ass'. Never is there any elegant variation ('the animal', 'the creature', 'Balaam's mount'), as might be the preference of a writer in English. There was clearly no dislike of repetition in writing Hebrew prose. This may be either the cause or the effect of the limited stock of words used in the narrative texts of the Hebrew Bible. Robert Alter has argued that Hebrew vocabulary used in speech in the period covered by the Hebrew Bible (perhaps tenth to second centuries BCE) may have been much larger than the Bible would lead us to think, and that this is probably confirmed by Mishnaic Hebrew – the Hebrew of the first few centuries CE – which preserves many quite different words for the same objects or concepts.[13] Perhaps, he speculates, in writing formal prose only certain words were conventionally acceptable. The nearest analogy would be French classical drama – Racine, Corneille, Molière – which has a tiny vocabulary not at all in keeping with normal spoken French of the seventeenth century. Only specific words and turns of phrase were deemed suitable for the stage. This is the very opposite of Shakespeare's huge word stock of more than 20,000 words, including perhaps 1,500 that are his own coinages.[14]

If Alter is correct, then this poses a conundrum for the translator. To be true to the original, translators would need to maintain a restricted vocabulary in the target language, too. His persuasive theory is that a rather stripped-down English would be appropriate for prose narratives, especially if the aim is an 'imitative' rendering. It would be ridiculous to try to establish an artificially restricted English vocabulary to correspond to the Hebrew, but considerable restraint seems to be required in using elegant variation there, and perhaps the avoidance of both technical terms and colloquialisms. Alter illustrates this in relation to the vocabulary choices in the story of Noah's ark in Genesis 7:17–18. Here is the King James Version:

> And the flood was forty days upon the earth; and the waters increased, and bare up the ark, and it was lift up above the earth. And the waters prevailed, and were increased greatly upon the earth; and the ark went upon the face of the waters.

Alter cites the Revised English Bible, Jerusalem Bible and the Jewish Publication Society Tanakh, all of which use a wider range of vocabulary: 'earth' and 'ground', and 'the ark floated on the surface of the swollen waters' in the REB; 'the ark drifted away over the waters' in the JB; and 'the Flood ... raised the ark so that it rose above the earth' in the JPS.[15] Both parataxis and repetition are avoided, making the story more modern in tone by varying the expression and in particular eliminating 'went' in favour of more nautical terminology. In all these more functional-equivalence versions there is a gain in variety but a loss in the simplicity and almost fairy-tale quality that the KJV preserves from the Hebrew. The modern versions seem more factual, almost like a news report by comparison. This is a distortion, for the original Hebrew, with its spare language captured well by the KJV, does not read like a news bulletin at all, but like the description of something more legendary or mythic.

This raises an important point. What is the genre of stories like the Flood narrative? Should we translate it so as to give the impression of a modern eyewitness report or a section from a novel? A piece of historical writing or a story from a collection of legends? To say that we need to render it in 'normal modern English' begs the question, because modern English allows all four registers but marks them differently. To translate the passage so that it sounds like a novel or a report or a piece of historiography is surely a genre-mistake. The modern versions Alter examines tend to muddle up the possibilities, so that we gain no clear impression of what kind of material we are dealing with. The KJV with its restricted vocabulary and bald style may come closest to indicating the impression the Hebrew gives, that this is a piece of folklore. If we wanted to demonstrate the different possibilities, we might produce the following:

> The flood lasted forty days, and the water took the ark up with it. The ark stood no chance in the water. It was growing all the time and it was carrying the ark with it.
>
> (eyewitness)

> The water took forty days to cover the earth, and lifted the ark up until it was well above the surface of the flooded ground. Then the ark travelled across the water.
>
> (novel)

The great flood must have lasted for about a month and a half. The ark evidently floated on the surface of the water, which completely covered the earth and practically obliterated it.

(historical narrative)

Forty days the flood continued, and the waters increased and lifted up the ark high above the earth. And the waters prevailed over the earth and covered it entirely; and the ark floated away on the surface of the waters.

(legend)

All convey the same information, but they are generically incompatible with each other in style. Translators have to decide which genre the passage in question is assigned to before they consider style and register. My judgement is that the last, a legendary style, does best justice to the original – in which case one might as well settle for either the KJV or a modernized version of it such as the Revised Standard Version. But some might prefer to think of Genesis as essentially factual, something like an eyewitness report (by God, presumably), in which case the first version would be preferable. Which is correct depends on how we approach the Bible, and indeed what is our notion of Scripture; but my point is that the question cannot be avoided, and that too few modern translators ask it.

Goethe opposed varying the style of translation for the Bible's different genres, at least in versions intended for general consumption:

> Luther took a work written in a highly varied style, took all its diverse lyrical, historical, hortatory, and didactic tones, and presented them to us in our native language as if all had been cast in the same mold. In so doing he furthered the cause of religion far better than if he had striven to reproduce the various peculiarities of the original. In vain have later translators labored to make Job, or the Psalms, or the other biblical poems available for our pleasure in their particular poetic form. For the great mass of people that one is aiming at, a plain translation is always best; critical translators attempting to rival the original serve only the private delectation of the learned.[16]

This raises two questions: who, nowadays, are the 'learned', and what can properly be described as a 'plain' translation. Without wishing to disagree with Goethe, I feel sure that modern translators should at least get these issues in their sights.

This has taken us away from the question of vocabulary, but it does have a bearing on it. Even the question of whether to translate 'water' (prosaically) or 'waters' (poetically) depends on genre, as does the use of 'prevailed', which would be unsuitable in an eyewitness account but is wholly appropriate in a legend. Similarly, historical narrative is likely to contain some markers of opinion or probability, as indicated above, but these would be out of place in a novel, at least in one with an omniscient narrator. Parts of the books of Samuel may be regarded as novel-like, and here one might at least consider a style more approaching a modern novel, as the New English Bible does.

Hebrew verse presents a different challenge, because there (as in poetry in many languages) there is a much larger vocabulary, including many words that do not occur in prose at all. This invites the translator to use similarly 'poetic' terms in the target language. Alter does this when he renders an unusual Hebrew word for windows at Genesis 7:11 as 'casements', following Keats's usage.[17] Because many poetic words occur nowhere else in the Hebrew Bible or in other bodies of Hebrew, translators are sometimes at a loss to know how they should be rendered. Here similar words in other Semitic languages may sometimes be helpful, since it can be suggested that the corresponding word in Hebrew has the same meaning. There is, however, a general consensus that, in the Old Testament of the New English Bible, speculations based on other languages ran riot: one purpose of the Revised English Bible was to tame them. Cognate words in related languages do not always have the same meaning: *actuel* in French and *aktuell* in German do not mean 'actual' in English, but 'current' or 'topical', even though etymologically they are 'the same word'. The same is bound to be true of many words in Hebrew and in the other Semitic languages, such as Akkadian and Arabic, that have supplied scholars with possible equivalences for previously unknown Hebrew words.

A notorious NEB example, though from prose rather than verse, is Judges 1:13–14:

Othniel, son of Caleb's younger brother Kenaz, captured it [Kiriath-sepher], and Caleb gave him his daughter Achsah. When she came to him, he incited her to ask her father for a piece of land. As she sat on the ass, she broke wind, and Caleb said, 'What did you mean by that?'

Compare the NRSV:

And Othniel son of Kenaz, Caleb's younger brother, took it: and he gave him his daughter Achsah as wife. When she came to him, she urged him to ask her father for a field. As she dismounted from her donkey, Caleb said to her, 'What do you want?'

The extraordinary and startling rendering 'broke wind' rests on the hypothesis that alongside the Hebrew word normally translated 'dismounted' there was a homonym with this other, flatulent meaning; that in turn rests on the fact that similar verbs with that meaning can be found in other Semitic languages related to Hebrew. But really the translation is a flight of fantasy.[18]

THE HISTORY OF
THE BIBLICAL LANGUAGES

Though the New Testament writers all have individual styles, they all write relatively correct koine Greek (exceptions are Mark and Revelation, on which more below). This differs from the classical Greek of Plato or Thucydides by having simplified some features: there is no longer a really functioning optative mood alongside the subjunctive, and the use of prepositions is less subtle. In the Gospels, as already noted, there are Semitisms, Aramaic turns of phrase and construction. A few books, notably the Letter to the Hebrews, are in a slightly more sophisticated style than others, sufficiently for most scholars to be convinced, for example, that Hebrews cannot be by Paul. Origen, in the third century, had already noticed this. Most think also that the Pastoral Letters, 1 and 2 Timothy and Titus, are similarly not Pauline, mainly because of differences of style. Very few of the differences can really be captured in translation, however: Hebrews could be made smoother and the genuine Pauline letters slightly more angular, but virtually no reader would notice.

One exception to this is the beginning of the Gospel according to Luke. The main narrative in Luke begins in chapter 3, with the proclamation of John the Baptist. The proclamation is dated in detail in Luke 3:1–2, and the presence of this dating material has suggested to some that the Gospel originally began here, without the stories of Jesus' birth and childhood with which Luke now starts. (Mark, after all, which was one of the sources Luke drew on, also begins with John the Baptist.) This is the hypothesis known as 'proto-Luke', now generally out of favour among New Testament scholars, despite its plausibility. Chapters 1–2 of Luke are taken up with a kind of prequel, the account of the birth of John and Jesus, and are the primary source for most of the traditional Christmas story. Here the Greek style is palpably different, clearly modelled on the narratives in the Greek translation of the Hebrew Bible, the Septuagint. It also contains three hymns or psalms, which are still used in Christian worship as the Magnificat (Luke 1:46–53), the Benedictus (Luke 1:68–79), and the Nunc Dimittis (Luke 2:29–32). There is clearly a case here for marking the distinct styles in a translation. The simplest way would be to begin with an older version such as the King James Version in chapters 1–2, followed by a more modern rendering for the rest of the Gospel. We might preserve 'lo, the angel of the Lord came upon them', and 'they were sore afraid' (Luke 2:9), rather than, for example, the NRSV 'Then an angel of the Lord stood before them', and 'they were terrified'.

Interlacing translations in such a way would capture the dissonant styles of the original, but it would have at least one significant religious or theological implication: it would make these chapters sound more like folklore or legend. So long as the whole Gospel is translated into the same register of English, whether modern or archaic, the reader treats it as one kind of work. But as soon as Luke 1–2 is marked off as a different type of material, best captured in an English that is obviously older than that used for the rest of the Gospel, then the implication that these stories are generically different becomes unavoidable. Thus once again the type of translation chosen raises the question of genre. If the shepherds were 'sore afraid' when other people, elsewhere in the Gospel, are 'frightened' or 'terrified', then the story of the shepherds reads more like a legend. Modernizing translations of Luke 1–2 have the effect of cancelling out that perception.[19] Of course, that may be right: perhaps these stories are genuine historical memory. But translators need, once again, to ask the question, and to recognize the theological weight of their choices. The small shift in style would signal, and trigger in the reader, reflection on the status and authority of the Gospels as a genuine historical record.

If koine Greek is a single language, give or take local variations, the same is not true of Biblical Hebrew. The New Testament was produced over less than a century; the Hebrew Bible includes texts that probably span the better part of a millennium, perhaps from the tenth to the second century BCE. It would be remarkable if Hebrew had not changed over this period. Experts on Biblical Hebrew (BH) identify at least three phases: Archaic BH, Classical BH and Late BH. The Archaic version is found mainly in a few old poems: Exodus 15, Judges 5 and Habakkuk 3 are among these. Classical BH is the form that modern students learn, and it predominates in the Hebrew Bible: particularly characteristic are the narratives in the books of Samuel and Kings. After the exile of the sixth century BCE, when many Judaeans were forcibly removed by the Babylonians to what is now Iraq, Hebrew altered in significant ways, as can be seen from texts such as Ecclesiastes (probably third century BCE), on the path to developing into the Hebrew found in early Jewish texts such as the Mishnah (early third century CE). The main differences can be found in vocabulary – ABH in particular includes many words not found later, even in verse – and in the verb system. There are also changes in spelling between Classical and Late BH, which can already be seen in Chronicles (perhaps from the fourth century BCE).

Should any of these changes be marked in translation? The aim of most modern translators is to render the text in contemporary English (or whatever the target language may be), conveying the impression the text will have made on its original readers or hearers, in accordance with MacKenna's principle that 'Plato was modern to Plato'. Thus we should translate Exodus 15 into modern English because it was modern to those who heard it in (maybe) the tenth century BCE, and Ecclesiastes similarly because it was modern to people in the second century BCE. And we should bear in mind that what Goethe called a 'plain' translation is better for those who are not 'learned' – people who do not, in Nida's phrase, 'have time on their hands'.

Yet to the author of Ecclesiastes, Exodus 15 will have sounded archaic, much as Homer did to Plato, and 2 Samuel will have sounded old-fashioned. It might be desirable to mark that in some way, just as it makes sense to indicate that Luke 1–2 harks back to an earlier 'biblical' style. If we are to vary our style of translation to mirror different genres, it is a small step to allow it also to indicate Hebrew's different phases. Imagine, for example, a Bible that rendered ABH in King James English,[20] CBH in Revised Standard Version English and LBH in New English Bible English, all of them comprehensible to a modern reader but quite distinct in tone and style. If how 2 Samuel sounded to its first readers is important, so too is how it sounded to the writers of Chronicles and Ecclesiastes. There needs, in fact, to be a certain reception-historical element in biblical translation, paying attention to how earlier texts were received and appreciated by the authors of later ones.

The sense that some biblical texts sounded archaic even within later 'biblical times' was to some extent captured by the King James Version, which (as we saw) used a mildly outdated form of English, so that the Bible was slightly 'pre-aged'. The KJV translators did not do what I am suggesting and distinguish different texts as older or later by the way they translated them, but they did make sure that the Old Testament in particular had what Steiner aptly calls a 'patina'. They used obsolescent verb forms ('shaked' rather than 'shook', for example), and words that were already passing out of use. The result was a version that in 1611 sounded as though it was a weathered monument of English – not just of Hebraic – culture, and which did not strive to be up to date in language, though of course it did seek to be comprehensible.[21] My own suggestion is that adding a patina of age to at least some parts of the Hebrew Bible in translation would be appropriate, in order to indicate how it sounded in the ears of the later readers who also wrote the books that came at the end of the biblical period. As with a good historical novel, the period flavour should not be laid on too thick: no one wants the Bible to contain 'gadzooks' or 'forsooth'. But enough distance from modern English to signal the antiquity of the text might represent an acceptable 'foreignizing' element. This, of course, flies in the face of the commitment of modern translations to contemporary language, and shows again how many more dimensions there are than the single formal/functional equivalence axis.

TRANSLATING SPEECH

Both Testaments contain a great deal of direct speech, and every translator must confront the question of how colloquial to make it. In general, throughout the Bible, whoever is speaking does so in a style very like that of whoever is writing. There is no attempt in the Gospels, for example, to signal the Galilean speech of Jesus and the disciples, even though occasionally a word or two is quoted in Aramaic, as is also the case in Paul: *talitha cum* (Mark 5:41: 'little girl, get up'), *ephphatha* (Mark 7:34: 'be opened'), *abba* (Galatians 4:6: 'Father'), *maranatha* (1 Corinthians 16:22: 'our Lord, come'). Even in the account of Peter's denial, when he is recognized as a Galilean by his speech (Matthew 26:69–75), no adjustment is made to the Greek to imitate this, which would indeed be a hard thing to do and would be unlikely to have occurred to the writers of the Gospels.

In the Hebrew Bible there is one notorious place where we seem to have an imitation of really informal speech: Genesis 25:30, in the story of Esau selling his birthright to his younger brother for what the King James Version calls 'a mess of pottage' (probably a lentil stew). The hungry Esau says to Jacob, according to the NRSV, 'Let me eat some of that red stuff, for I am famished!' But the Hebrew is more incoherent, capturing Esau's desperation by repeating 'red' with no noun: 'Let me gulp from that red red, because I am famished.' Robert Alter renders it 'Let me gulp down some of this red red stuff, for I am famished'; Goldingay, even more colloquially, 'Please let me wolf down some of the red stuff, this red stuff, because I'm faint.' In my own west London vernacular Esau would have said, "Ere, gis [= give us] a nosh of that red wossname [= what's its name], 'cos I'm perishin' 'ungry', though no translator is likely to want to imply that Esau grew up on a London housing estate. In general translators do not attempt to render vernacular speech, partly because of this very difficulty – which variety of English, which regional or social[22] type of speech to imitate? Here is Bellos on the subject:

> The movement of translation towards the standard form of the receiving language can be highlighted by the fate of regional and social dialects. Bournisien, one of the minor characters of Flaubert's *Madame Bovary*, speaks with turns of phrase and vocabulary items that are comically typical of the region where the action is set – rural Normandy in the 1830s. English obviously does not have a conventional way of representing the speech of nineteenth-century countryfolk from Normandy. In principle, a translator could make Bournisien speak in English like a Wessex farmer out of Thomas Hardy or a Scottish preacher invented by Walter Scott. But representing one regional dialect of the source by some regional dialect of the target is rarely attempted in translation. Most people currently think it is just silly to make a Bavarian dairy farmer use Texas cowboy slang, or to have a woman on the St Petersburg tram express herself in Mancunian in order to suggest her geographic and linguistic distance both from the capital and the standard language. The culture of translation as it presently exists in English as well as in French and many other languages eradicates regional variation in the source. It drives written representations of dialectal speech towards the centre.[23]

All that said, a recent British television adaptation of *Les Misérables* gave the peasants broad Yorkshire accents, which shows that the task can be carried out if one insists, though perhaps at the risk of offending people in the areas chosen to provide the dialect of the downtrodden. Esau's speech is very difficult to render satisfactorily, though at least we should avoid 'for', which no English-speaker today uses in colloquial speech in place of 'because'.

There is another place, not noted by Alter, where non-standard Hebrew occurs. It is in Jezebel's words to King Ahab after Naboth has refused to sell him his vineyard, in 1 Kings 21:7. This is supposed to have happened in the ninth century BCE, and is used by the author of Kings as an indication of the injustices in Israelite society in the age dominated by the prophet Elijah. Ahab, in asking to buy Naboth's vineyard, is offending against the principle that family property is

inalienable – even when it is the king who wants to acquire it. Jezebel, deeply unimpressed by her husband's subsequent sulk, asks him
(according to the NRSV) 'Do you now govern Israel? Get up, eat
some food, and be cheerful; I will give you the vineyard of Naboth
the Jezreelite.' But in Hebrew her words begin, 'You now do kingship
over Israel?', which is quite unidiomatic. H. G. M. Williamson[24] has
suggested that this is an imitation of the non-Israelite, Baal-
worshipping Jezebel's foreign speech: not only is she an idolater and
a crook, but she can't even speak proper Hebrew! A translator could
experiment with various ways of imitating this, given that written
English has established methods for signalling that a foreigner is
speaking.

A high style is easier to imitate: supplicants addressing the king in
the books of Samuel and Kings can be made to say 'Your Majesty' (as
in the New English Bible) without that sounding odd, though the
more literal 'my lord the king' is perfectly acceptable in English and
raises no issues, as well as adding an attractive slight foreignization.
In general the tendency of translations is to elevate the style of speech
somewhat, though in any case we can assume that (Esau apart) characters in biblical narrative are made to speak more formally than they
would really have done. The biblical narrators are not aiming to preserve the whole speech of their characters, but to summarize what
they said: this is particularly evident with Paul's speeches in Acts,
which cannot possibly have been as short as in the form the author
gives them. In the Hebrew Bible, too, speeches are in general very
terse, and consequently attempts to render them in a conversational
style mostly fail, because this highlights their implausibility as complete utterances. This is a besetting problem in most modern-language
translations, which ignore the formulaic and abbreviated character of
much biblical speech. It is seldom modelled on the utterances of real
speakers, but instead expresses the basic content of their message in a
summary form. The nearest comparison with readily available texts
in English is with Icelandic sagas as translated in the Penguin Classics
series, where events and speeches alike are presented as tersely as
possible – very differently from the expansive style of a novel. Dialogue in the Bible is seldom realistic; rather it is stripped to the bare
bones.

TRANSLATING NONSENSE

There is one passage in the Hebrew Bible which intentionally contains nonsense: Isaiah 28:9–13. The prophet is here telling his audience that because of their sins God will bring about an invasion by the Assyrians, and he reports a mocking question asked him by that audience, but the meaning of the question is unclear in traditional English translations. Here, for example, is the NRSV:

> 'Whom will he teach knowledge,
>> and to whom will he explain the message?
> Those who are weaned from milk,
>> those taken from the breast?
> For it is precept upon precept, precept upon precept,
>> line upon line, line upon line,
>> here a little, there a little.'
>
> Truly, with stammering lip
>> and with alien tongue
> he will speak to this people . . .
>
> Therefore the word of the LORD will be to them,
>> 'Precept upon precept, precept upon precept,
>> line upon line, line upon line,
>> here a little, there a little';
> in order that they may go, and fall backwards,
>> and be broken, and snared, and taken.

'Meaning of this verse uncertain', NRSV adds, as well it might. What seems clear is that Isaiah is telling his listeners that they will be invaded by a people whose speech they cannot understand ('alien tongue'), presumably the Akkadian-speaking Assyrians. The sinners' complaint is that Isaiah's message is fit only for babies; very well then, the prophet retorts, you will be subject to those whose speech you will understand no better than a baby can Hebrew. But what is meant by 'precept upon precept', and so on?

The simplest explanation is that the words have no real meaning at all, even though they *can* be translated as above (to make a largely meaningless sentence), but are meant to imitate the babbling of a baby. Accordingly, the Revised New Jerusalem Bible (following the earlier Jerusalem Bible) simply transliterates the Hebrew:

> To whom should he give his teaching,
> to whom explain his message?
> Babies just weaned?
> Babies just taken from the breast?
> For it is *Sav lasav, sav lasav,*
> *kav lakav, kav lakav,*
> *zeer sham, zeer sham*!
> For he will talk to this nation
> with stammering lips and a foreign tongue ...
>
> So the word of the LORD to them is,
> *Sav lasav, sav lasav,*
> *kav lakav, kav lakav,*
> *zeer sham, zeer sham.*
> So that when they walk they will fall over backwards,
> broken, trapped and taken captive.

This may be a sensible solution to the problem – the Luther Bible adopts it too – though it would puzzle anyone hearing the translation read aloud without explanation. The Revised English Bible produced a more functional-equivalence rendering, or rather an explanation, of the text:

> Who is there that can be taught?
> Who makes sense of what he hears?
> They are babes newly weaned,
> just taken from the breast.
> A babble of meaningless noises,
> mere sounds on every side![25]
> So through barbarous speech and a strange tongue
> the Lord will address this people ...
>
> Now to them the word of the LORD will be
> a babble of meaningless noises,
> mere sounds on every side.

> And so, as they walk, they will fall backwards,
> they will be injured, trapped, and caught.

This makes sense of the passage by abandoning any attempt to imitate it in English. It would fall under Robert Alter's condemnation of the 'heresy of explanation', but it is a serviceable solution to a real problem. His own translation reads 'filth-pilth' and 'vomit-momit', in a clever imitative rendering of the Hebrew words. This is the kind of passage that stretches the ingenuity of translators.

BAD GREEK AND ECCENTRIC HEBREW

One particular problem in translating the New Testament is the presence of substandard Greek. In Mark, and still more in Revelation, there are examples of Greek that is wrong not just by classical but also by koine standards. Revelation, for example, has a preposition followed by a noun in the nominative case – a slip which causes classicists to gasp.[26] As with non-standard forms of the source language belonging to particular locations or social classes, there is a convention that translators also do not register grammatical errors.[27] Producing deliberately ungrammatical English to convey ungrammatical Greek might suggest a fault in the translator rather than in the source. It could be argued that at least the translator should obey the Johnsonian precept (see Chapter 3) and not actually *improve* the source text, as arguably the King James Version does with Revelation. Betty Radice, for many years editor of Penguin Classics and herself a prolific translator of Latin texts for the series, once said, in defending her version of Terence against a critic who thought it 'relentlessly nice', 'my prose is "relentlessly nice" because I see this as a flaw in the poet ... I confess I was often tempted to improve on my original.'[28] It is doubtful, though, whether she would have sought to reproduce actual grammatical howlers in the original text if there had been any.

We have no way of knowing whether there is any bad Hebrew in the Bible, apart from the speech of Esau and Jezebel already discussed, since our knowledge of its rules and norms is insufficient for us to judge. Long as the Bible may seem, it represents a small corpus from which to reconstruct the Hebrew language, and ancient inscriptions and graffiti offer no more than a tiny supplement to its evidence. Many variants may have existed of which we know nothing, and the language may have been artificially standardized by scribes at any stage in its development. There are, however, books where the Hebrew seems strange when measured against what we do know of its history, in particular Job and Hosea. In the latter case, it has been suggested that this prophet from the Kingdom of Israel may have used a northern dialect of Hebrew rather than the version standard in the Kingdom of Judah to the south – the version that became Classical Biblical Hebrew – and that Kings and some Psalms also preserve 'Israelian' Hebrew.[29] This can only be a surmise, but it would discourage scholars from emending the text of Hosea, Psalms or Kings to make the Hebrew more 'correct'. Though it could of course be done, it's hard to imagine that any translator of the Bible into English would take to rendering Hosea in Scots, or a Cumbrian dialect, to indicate that his Hebrew is distinctively northern. Hugh Pyper has translated Ecclesiastes into Scots, without any implication that the book is northern in origin, and there exists a translation of parts of the New Testament into lowland Scots, in which the devil in the temptation narratives speaks Received Pronunciation English, marking him out as an Englishman.[30] But that is all about relations between the English and the Scots in the second millennium CE, not a serious comment on the New Testament and its language in the first.

Translating non-standard language is always a problem. I would not want to suggest that there is a great deal of such language in the Bible, but where it does occur the translator is faced with some difficult choices – ones that believers too may be obliged to confront. The fact that the Bible is not written throughout in the best varieties of its languages, but can even contain bad Hebrew or Greek, is hard to square with claims that it is inerrant or perfect. Revealing these imperfections in the way the Bible is rendered into a modern language may to some more conservative Christians seem scandalous. Yet these linguistic flaws are just one of many challenges to a belief in the Bible's perfection that are contained within it: inconsistencies, conflicting versions of the same events, textual variants and passages that strike most readers today as morally repugnant. None of these should be exaggerated, but equally they should not be ignored; the higher the claim to a privileged status is made for the Bible, the more of a problem its flaws become. A translation can force these problems on our attention or suppress them.

6

Worship and Inclusive Language

SOLEMNITY OR INFORMALITY

Many translations of the Bible are designed to be read in churches, and this can raise contradictory expectations, depending on the style of worship in the given church. One is that the translation will have a certain formality and sonority, as does the KJV, and will throughout make for a dignified and elevated liturgy. The other is that it will reflect an informal style of worship and so will be easily comprehensible and colloquial in style. Clearly there is no way of combining these two expectations, and worshippers tend to fall into two camps, supporting one or the other. After the Second Vatican Council, Catholics in the United Kingdom and Ireland, who previously had no great tradition of hearing or studying the Bible in English, quickly developed a liking for the comparative informality of the Jerusalem Bible, which obtained the franchise for public liturgical use. The style was in many ways similar to that of new translations of the liturgy; and when Pope Benedict XVI decided to revise the liturgy in a more formal-equivalence direction by going back to a more 'accurate' translation of the Latin (which had remained the norm against which all translations of the Mass were assessed), this resulted in widespread disaffection. At the same time the Jerusalem Bible, by now in its second edition (the New Jerusalem Bible) was also being retranslated, again (as mentioned in Chapter 2) in a more 'accurate' direction – that is to say, to make it more nearly formally equivalent to the text in the original languages. It remains to be seen how this Revised New Jerusalem Bible will be received in the Catholic Church, if it replaces the original Jerusalem Bible in the readings at Mass – though at the time of writing the still more conservative English Standard Version seems likely to be chosen anyway.

The question of solemnity versus informality runs through many reactions to biblical as well as to liturgical translation. It is a far from trivial topic, which can be symbolized by the move in the Eucharist in Catholic and Anglican churches from the traditional arrangement in which the celebrant faces the altar to the modern one, where the celebrant (now often 'president') faces the congregation. Oversimplifying, the change can be said to be from a belief in a God 'out there' to a God 'in our midst'. Worshippers necessarily believe that God combines both characteristics, being, in the technical jargon, both transcendent and immanent. But different kinds of Christian stress either one or the other, and are drawn to correspondingly different styles of worship. With these preferences goes an attachment to formal or informal biblical translations, an alternative we may in shorthand describe as KJV versus JB. Compare, for example, the two versions' renderings of Colossians 3:5–11:

> That is why you must kill everything in you that belongs only to earthly life: fornication, impurity, guilty passion, evil desires and especially greed, which is the same thing as worshipping a false god; all this is the sort of behaviour that makes God angry. And it is the way in which you used to live when you were surrounded by people doing the same thing, but now you, of all people, must give all these things up: getting angry, being bad-tempered, spitefulness, abusive language and dirty talk; and never tell each other lies. You have stripped off your old behaviour with your old self, and you have put on a new self which will progress towards true knowledge the more it is renewed in the image of its creator; and in that image there is no room for distinction between Greek and Jew, between the circumcised or the uncircumcised, or between barbarian and Scythian, slave and free man. There is only Christ: he is everything and he is in everything.
>
> (Jerusalem Bible)

> Mortify therefore your members which are upon the earth; fornication, uncleanness, inordinate affection, evil concupiscence, and covetousness, which is idolatry: for which things' sake the wrath of God cometh on the

children of disobedience: in the which ye also walked some time, when ye lived in them. But now ye also put off all these; anger, wrath, malice, blasphemy, filthy communication out of your mouth. Lie not one to another, seeing that ye have put off the old man with his deeds; and have put on the new *man*, which is renewed in knowledge after the image of him that created him: where there is neither Greek nor Jew, circumcision nor uncircumcision, Barbarian, Scythian, bond *nor* free: but Christ *is* all, and in all.

(King James Version)

The 'cash value' of the two passages is much the same, once one allows for some archaism in the KJV. But the atmosphere is surely different. In the JB there is an air of someone reasoning with his audience and trying to persuade them – 'kill everything in you that belongs only to earthly life', 'you, of all people', 'your old self', 'which is the same thing as worshipping a false god'. In creeps what Alter calls the heresy of explanation. The KJV is closer to a set of directives from on high, issued without entreaty or explanation, with sonorous and absolute diction.

A consistent preference for one of these styles over the other generally correlates with a theological difference. Defenders of the KJV tend to believe in a God of majesty and power; proponents of the JB and similar versions veer towards a more relatable 'God in our midst'. Of course, both ideas of God occur in the Bible itself, so that one cannot argue that one is more faithful to the biblical presentation than the other. To object to KJV English on the grounds that 'no one talks like that now' is to miss the point that it is used precisely because it is not current, and its elevated style points to a transcendent and majestic God. No one spoke quite like that even when the KJV was being produced. Equally, to object to JB English on the grounds that it brings God down to our level is also inappropriate, since that's the whole point of it: to make the Christian message relevant to a current generation. Solemn High Mass and prayer meetings both have their place, and different types of translation fit better with one or the other. Similarly the Good News Bible might be appropriate for worship with children, for example. Context is all, and we recall again that although some translations can be wrong, none can be uniquely right.

It still makes sense to ask about the original level of the biblical text. We saw in the previous chapter that some at least of the Old Testament narrative material was probably written as semi-official literature, so it invites (though it does not force) us to translate it in a relatively formal style. How formal our rendering of Paul should be, however, is a moot point. As we have seen, Paul's writings are, on the one hand, genuine letters, so that the declamatory style of the KJV may set the register rather too high. On the other hand, a letter in the ancient world – and especially one to an entire community – was not at all like a postcard, but a serious document intended to be kept and read again and again. That points towards a reasonably formal style, and suggests that J. B. Phillips ('a hearty handshake all round'), and even the Jerusalem Bible or the New International Version, may be setting the register a little too low. If we want, during an act of worship aimed at all comers, to read Paul and hear him as he was originally heard, some midpoint such as the RSV or REB (the first more formal-equivalence in style, the second more functional-equivalence, but both rather sober) may hit the mark best:

> No, in all these things we are more than conquerors through him who loved us. For I am sure that neither death, nor life, nor angels, nor principalities, nor things present, nor things to come, nor powers, nor height, nor depth, nor anything else in all creation, will be able to separate us from the love of God in Christ Jesus our Lord.
>
> (Romans 8:37–9, RSV)

> ... and yet, throughout it all, overwhelming victory is ours through him who loved us. For I am convinced that there is nothing in death or life, in the realm of spirits or superhuman powers, in the world as it is or the world as it shall be, in the forces of the universe, in heights or depths – nothing in all creation that can separate us from the love of God in Christ Jesus our Lord.
>
> (Romans 8:37–9, REB)

The REB is more explanatory than the more formal-equivalent RSV, but both give a fair impression of the passage with its reference to non-human powers.

THE PSALMS

The Psalms, and hymns based on them, are a special case because they are not simply read as lections during worship but in many traditions are actually sung, and thereby rather obviously affirmed by the congregation, to a greater extent than most of the Bible. It is this that makes the imprecatory passages in the Psalms so troubling: it is one thing to hear of harm inflicted by Israelites on their enemies in Hebrew Bible narratives, but another actually to pray for our enemies to be annihilated. The most notorious example of this is Psalm 137:8–9:

> O daughter Babylon, you devastator!
>> Happy shall they be who pay you back
>> what you have done to us!
> Happy shall they be who take your little ones
>> and dash them against the rock!
>
> (NRSV)

In most churches such passages are nowadays officially censored, and not sung. If they are, as still in some monastic communities, then they tend to be allegorized, with the 'little ones' interpreted as human sins or failings, as in this from C. S. Lewis:

> I can even use the horrible passage in 137 about dashing the Babylonian babies against the stones. I know things in the inner world which are like babies; the infantile beginnings of small indulgences, small resentments, which may one day become dipsomania or settled hatred, but which woo us and wheedle us with special pleadings and seem so tiny, so helpless that in resisting them we feel we are being cruel to animals . . . Against all such pretty infants . . . the advice of the Psalms is the best. Knock the little bastards' brains out.[1]

But Psalm 137 is only an extreme example of a problem that recurs in singing many of the Psalms, with their bellicose approach towards often unspecified enemies. Translators preparing Psalters for use in worship tend to seek ways of avoiding the more vindictive passages, usually by marking them for removal or even not presenting them at all. Anglican Psalters since the proposed Prayer Book of 1928 have bracketed the unacceptable verses, but in Catholic liturgical books they are simply omitted.

An alternative is to provide notes, introductions and the like. On Psalm 137, the RNJB rather guardedly writes in its Introduction 'To the modern mind the poignant pathos of the first six verses is somewhat spoilt by the stark vengefulness of the last three, a limitation of the contemporary moral vision ... It is however a call for justice.' 'Somewhat' is, perhaps, an understatement.

Translating the Psalms so that they can function as hymnody for modern worshippers is in any case a challenge. The Book of Common Prayer incorporated the Psalms from Coverdale's Bible, which are therefore much earlier than the KJV and are not translated directly from the Hebrew but, as we have seen, from the Greek and Latin Bibles. Set to Anglican Chant they have become the staple of cathedral worship in the Church of England and in many parish churches. They contain many inaccuracies and even almost meaningless verses. Take, for example, Psalm 68:30 in this version: 'when the company of the spearmen and multitude of the mighty are scattered abroad among the beasts of the people, so that they humbly bring pieces of silver' – perhaps best prayed allegorically as a prayer for biblical translators. But the eye for rhythm is unfailing, making these Psalms peculiarly memorable:

> For man walketh in a vain shadow, and disquieteth himself in vain; he heapeth up riches, and cannot tell who shall gather them. And now, Lord, what is my hope? Truly my hope is even in thee. Deliver me from all mine offences, and make me not a rebuke unto the foolish. I became dumb, and opened not my mouth, for it was thy doing. Take thy plague away from me; I am even consumed by the means of thy heavy hand. When thou with rebukes dost chasten man for sin, thou makest his beauty to consume away, like as it were a moth fretting a garment; every man therefore is but vanity.
>
> (Psalm 39:7–12, Coverdale)

Few modern translations can match this, but perhaps with one exception: the Grail version. The Grail Psalter was in its day innovative in the way it both simplified the text and also mirrored the Hebrew better than more traditional versions. It was a translation into English of the Psalms in the original *Bible de Jérusalem* (the French version), and preceded the translation of the rest of that Bible as the Jerusalem Bible. It was published in 1963, and soon established itself as a version preferred by many in the new vernacular liturgies of the Catholic Church. A revised version from 2010 has been incorporated into the Revised New Jerusalem Bible. What is particularly striking is the way that it uses a 'sprung' rhythm, indebted to the poetry of Gerard Manley Hopkins, to imitate the rhythms of the Hebrew text. A line of Hebrew verse requires a fixed number not of syllables, but of stresses, and the Grail Psalter constructs its translation on the same principle – just as Hopkins did. Typically there are three stresses per line, but sometimes two, and in laments a three-stress line is usually followed by a two-stress one, producing the so-called 'limping' pattern discussed in Ch. 4. The importance of stress can be seen in these examples from the Grail:

> The Lórd is my shépherd;
> there is nóthing I shall wánt.
> Fresh and gréen are the pástures
> where he gíves me repóse.
> Near restful wáters he léads me;
> he revíves my sóul.
>
> (Psalm 23:1–3)

> He shall endúre like the sún and the móon
> through áll generátions.
> He shall descénd like ráin on the méadow,
> like shówers that wáter the éarth,
> In his dáys shall jústice flóurish,
> and great péace till the móon is no more.
>
> (Psalm 72:5–7)

The Revised Grail version is a remarkable marriage of ancient and modern, which manages to give an impression of reading the original Hebrew, while being in contemporary English – something approaching the state of equilibrium that we saw in Chapter 4 to be so desirable, but also so elusive.

THE CASE FOR INCLUSIVE LANGUAGE

The topic of 'inclusive language' has already arisen, but it is in the use of the Bible in public worship – that is, in contexts where it is read aloud – that it becomes most prominent. The use of gender-neutral terms to avoid giving an impression that the Bible is addressed only or primarily to men can sometimes be justified even on formal-equivalence grounds, since it is clear that, for example, when Paul addresses his 'brothers' he usually means both male and female members of his congregations, the Greek *adelphoi* ('brothers') being intended as a generic term (like 'siblings' in English) that covered women too. But much more often in the Bible the text really speaks directly and exclusively to men, and the decision to add women is justifiable on neither formal- nor really even on functional-equivalence grounds, but is instead about making the Bible relevant to the modern reader. The issue arises particularly, again, with the Psalms, whose use in public worship means that all-male language grates on many modern ears, much as the imprecatory language does. The recent Church of England Psalter, used in the *Common Worship* series of liturgical books, inclusivizes the original wherever possible. I was involved a little in this myself, and know how difficult it is to produce a text that does not appear to prioritize men but also does not read as though it has been deliberately doctored to avoid that. Often it can be done by using plurals: 'Happy is the man who . . .' becomes 'Happy are those who . . .', with no obvious loss of meaning and a gain in applicability. Texts such as these, which are actually sung by worshippers, expose the gap between the sensibilities and culture of some of the authors behind the Bible and our own, and the need for inclusive language translation to reconcile or navigate this especially acute problem. All-male references, just like the curses, are even more apparent when sung by the congregation than when read, since the singers appear to be actively assenting to them.

Indeed, it can be urged that translators have an obligation to aspire to gender-neutral language, that this is a moral imperative if the Bible is not to serve as an agent of the oppression of women. The German *Bibel in gerechter Sprache* (Bible in Inclusive Language),[2] following the lead of the earlier *Bibel im heutigen Deutsch* (Bible in Today's German), introduces many references to women even when they are not clearly implicit in the original text, on just these grounds.[3] As we shall see, this can produce forms such as 'apostolesses', whose historical foundation is shaky, but which are meant to jolt the reader into considering just how inclusive Paul's Churches may have been.

There is an alternative feminist viewpoint, which argues that where the Bible is scandalously androcentric the translator has an obligation to make sure that that is conveyed in the translation. Otherwise it is a fudge, pretending that the Bible is better disposed to women than it truly is, and thus sanitizing the text. There are feminists who make much of the women who do appear as strong and resourceful in the Hebrew Bible – Deborah, Jael, Abigail, Michal, Esther – but there are others who stress just how exceptional they are, and how male the overall atmosphere of the Bible is; and, accordingly, argue that inclusive language lets the Bible off the hook too lightly. Translators have to navigate this issue as best they can. Their dilemma is well summed up by Paul Ellingworth:

> Translators ... aim to transfer to the receptor or target language, not only the meaning of individual words, but the meaning of the text as a whole ...
>
> On the one hand, if they apply [this principle] without modification, readers of the translation will sometimes receive a different impression from readers of the original. For example, the subordination of women, or the use of male-oriented language, may be part of the stock of assumptions which the original readers took for granted, and in which the specific message of the text is set; whereas for readers of the translation, the subordination of women may be so alien, may create so much 'noise', as to 'interfere' with communication of the main point of the text.
>
> On the other hand, if translators modify [this principle] in order to reduce the 'noise' or 'interference', they may be open to the charge of transculturation, 'watering down' the text, or even adulterating the

Word of God ... they are liable to be accused of concealing the cultural, and perhaps the revelational, 'otherness' of the text, and thus to some extent being unfaithful to it.[4]

Which in a nutshell is the old problem of formal versus functional equivalence, as it bears upon this particular issue.

PROBLEMS WITH
INCLUSIVE LANGUAGE

Introducing inclusive language in biblical translation is not plain sailing, clearly. Translators, such as the editors of the Revised New Jerusalem Bible, sometimes blame the English language for the problems in producing a gender-neutral rendering. It is true that English lacks two features that help in inclusivization. One is a non-gendered third person singular pronoun, which would avoid having to use 'he or she' or 's/he', both of which seem inelegant. This is a problem shared by Indo-European languages in general: the only major language in Europe that possesses a genderless third-person singular pronoun is Finnish, which is not Indo-European. The other lack is that English has no single noun meaning 'human person' as opposed to 'male human'. English has only 'man', just as French has only *homme*, where German and Dutch have the useful gender-neutral terms *Mensch/mens* alongside *Mann/man*. Greek likewise has *anthropos* as well as *aner*, and Hebrew *adam* alongside *ish*. (In Psalm 1, 'happy is the man ...' actually uses *ish*, the term for a male person, not the more generic *adam*, though this has not stopped translators from inclusivizing it, usually by putting it in the plural.) In the past it was generally considered reasonable in English to use 'man' as the default form even when encompassing women, as with 'mankind', and it is disingenuous to claim that all those who did so really had a secret male bias. But English has changed, and 'man' now clearly implies a male person. The change is a recent one: in the *Liturgical Psalter*, produced by David Frost to accompany the Church of England's *Alternative Service Book* in 1980, 'man' was still freely used generically. But this soon became a reason to dislike this otherwise excellent translation. It would now be deliberately reactionary to create a version that used 'man', and it would be equally disingenuous to maintain that to do so was simply to follow older precedent, and that women were really meant to be included too.

The NRSV translators in their address 'To the Reader' sum up the difficulties well:

> The mandates from the Division specified that, in references to men and women, masculine-oriented language should be eliminated as far as this can be done without altering passages that reflect the historical situation of ancient patriarchal culture. As can be appreciated, more than once the Committee found that the several mandates stood in tension and even in conflict. The various concerns had to be balanced case by case in order to provide a faithful and acceptable rendering without using contrived English.

The limitations of the English language do certainly pose a problem for the translator. It is not difficult in an official document to adopt 'he or she' (or 'she or he'), but in biblical prose to be read aloud, still more in psalms intended to be sung, the usage is inescapably clunky. In the *Common Worship* Psalter devices such as 'the human race' and 'humankind' were used at times.[5] 'Man' was retained only in the phrase 'man and beast' in Psalm 36:6. English presents difficulties, but they are rarely insuperable; neither are they the translator's fault.[6]

A more substantial dilemma arises when the often androcentric culture of the Bible rears its head, and a particular idea resists equalization. A typically difficult case can be seen in Psalms 127 and 128. These are respectively about the blessings of many sons, and the advantage for a man of having a wife who bears many children:

> Sons are indeed a heritage from the LORD,
>   the fruit of the womb a reward.
> Like arrows in the hand of a warrior
>   are the sons of one's youth.
> Happy is the man who has
>   his quiver full of them.
> He shall not be put to shame
>   when he speaks with his enemies in the gate.
>   (Psalm 127:3–5, NRSV)

Your wife will be like a fruitful vine
within your house;
your children will be like olive shoots
around your table.
Thus shall the man be blessed
who fears the LORD.
(Psalm 128:3–4, NRSV)

It is hard to see how these passages can be inclusivized, and I know of
no translation that attempts it. In the opposite direction, the praises of
the 'woman of worth' in Proverbs 31 can hardly be treated as if they
were about a 'man of worth':

A capable wife who can find?
She is far more precious than jewels.
The heart of her husband trusts in her,
and he will have no lack of gain.
She does him good, and not harm,
all the days of her life.
(Proverbs 31:10–12, NRSV)

– but no one is asking for that anyway.

But such instances are only the tip of an iceberg. In the book of
Proverbs, sayings are often addressed to 'my son' (see for example
Proverbs 1:8, 2:1, 3:1, 3:11, 5:1), and it is generally supposed that
these were originally meant for instruction in some kind of school,
the students of which would almost certainly have been exclusively
male. The choice for the translator is either to inclusivize, as in NRSV
('my child'), thereby falsifying the original reference, or to retain the
original androcentric intention on the grounds of faithfulness to the
original and risk excluding half of the audience. It may be felt, in
the interests of equality of the sexes, that the former is better; but it
results in a kind of soft focus for the text, which no longer has its
original sharpness of reference. How far should the Bible be brought
into line with modern concerns, and how far left in its original state?
If we translate 'my son' in Proverbs as 'my child', we are implying

that the book is addressed to women as well as to men. This is true, in the sense that the Bible is a book for liturgical reading in the church or the synagogue, now; but it is probably not true as a description of the original purpose of the book of Proverbs, taken as a text with a specific historical context. For the latter, only the translation 'my son' does justice to the original. Which Bible is the translator meant to be translating, the ancient Hebrew Bible, or a modern Christian or Jewish one? The words are the same, yet the meaning may be different.

Inclusive language is thus not simply something that can be endorsed or rejected on feminist grounds alone. It obliges us to ask what kind of translation we are making. Are we translating the text the ancient author might have written, had he been writing now, or are we trying to give an impression of how the text will have appeared to its original readers? In other words, we are back with the dispute between functional-equivalence and 'foreignizing', formal-equivalence translation. Some of the opposition felt towards inclusive language is undoubtedly misogynistic or arises from objections to 'political correctness'; but some genuinely derives from a commitment to rendering the text against its historical background, with formal equivalence. Proponents of inclusive language do not always see this, or do not believe it is a genuine motivation for opposition to gender-neutral phraseology. It is in fact entirely possible to be a committed feminist and still oppose inclusive language, perhaps arguing, as suggested above, that we should confront just how sexist much of the Bible really is. From that perspective inclusive language is whitewashing, scouring Scripture for the modern reader and eliminating problems that ought to be shown in their true colours. David Bentley Hart resists inclusive language in his rendering of the New Testament because, he says, 'I would dislike the pretense that the text does not use the sort of language that it does, and I think readers can be trusted to know that these are first-century writings.'[7]

True modernization of the biblical text would presumably also need to change references to exterminating non-Israelites, eliminate all suggestions that Yahweh, the God of ancient Israel, has physical characteristics, remove positive references to slavery in both Testaments, and so on. The *Bibel in gerechter Sprache* makes a start on this agenda, though it does not go very far. It does seem misleading to apply the method to only one feature now perceived as offensive, the androcentric slant of the text; yet to carry it through with complete consistency would leave very little of the Bible unchanged. To make a few texts less androcentric than they really are is to pick at a small loose thread, only to find that the whole garment starts to unravel.

To return to the Psalms, however: perhaps there is a special case to be made in the case of a biblical text that is regularly sung in worship, not just read through. Have the Psalms become a Christian and Jewish hymn book, which communities from both religions are free to adapt for their own uses? The Psalms are, after all, scarcely ever used to prove points of doctrine or of religious practice in either Judaism or Christianity. Maybe we can treat them as somewhat malleable?

A good illustration of this is Psalm 100, much used in Christian worship in many traditions. Older translations, such as the KJV and Coverdale (as used in the Book of Common Prayer) render verse 3, 'it is he who hath made us, and not we ourselves', whereas modern versions unanimously translate it 'it is he who made us and we are his'. Which of these translations is correct, and which should be (or may be) used in worship? To investigate this a digression is needed into the Hebrew language and the history of the Bible. Large theological questions hang on apparently tiny features of the biblical text.

Biblical Hebrew has a pair of homophones, spelt respectively *lo'* and *lo*, both pronounced 'lo'. (The apostrophe in *lo'* represents the Hebrew letter aleph, originally signalling a light glottal stop but silent at the end of a word in the classical language, so the two words are pronounced in exactly the same way.) In a number of places there is doubt as to which ought to appear in the text, since, as can easily be imagined, a scribe taking dictation might well write the wrong one. The Hebrew Bible in its present form, the form reproduced in modern editions, has a system of marginal notes (the Masorah), which comment on textual difficulties and call attention to problems of this kind. It was produced by scribes known as the Masoretes, who curated the biblical text towards the end of the first millennium CE. Often one reading is found in what is written/printed in the main text (the *ketib*, 'that which is written'), while another is recorded in the margin as what is actually read aloud (the *qere* or *qeri*, 'that which is read'). There is much dispute about the purpose of the system, but it can be argued that the marginal *qere* records what the Masoretes thought was really the correct reading, but instructs the scribe nevertheless to leave alone what was traditionally written. The *qere*, that is, tells the reader that the text should be read as if it were different, but this does not give the scribe licence actually to change or correct it when copying out the text, since the written form was regarded as sacrosanct. There are places where the *ketib* has *lo'* ('not') and the *qere* has *lo* ('to him'), or vice versa, and the modern scholar has to decide which is likelier to represent the original sense of the text.

In the case of these two words there is often in practice little difficulty, since they have extremely different meanings, and usually only one makes sense in context. Nevertheless, in one important instance there is genuine uncertainty, and both possible readings have important things to say about the relation between God and humanity. Psalm 100:3 is a verse whose *ketib* version has had a great afterlife. It says that God made us *ve-lo' anachnu*, 'and not we'. 'It is he that hath made us, and not we ourselves' is familiar to anyone who uses the Church of England's Book of Common Prayer Psalter, but exactly the same reading is implied in the 'Old Hundredth' metrical version, 'All people that on earth do dwell' (by W. Kethe, d.1594): 'without our aid he did us make'. The Greek Old Testament, the Septuagint, also has this reading. On this basis it is possible to discourse on the independence of God from any kind of human co-operation in creation, a theme which fits well with classical Christian (and Jewish) theism: God does not need us, or indeed anything but himself, and we have no part in our own making.

But the *qere* of Psalm 100:3 records the reading *ve-lo anachnu*: he made us, 'and to him we', in other words, in Hebrew idiom, 'we belong to him', 'we are his'. This reading has become normal in modern translations of the Bible. At the purely textual level it is impossible to decide which is correct; but our understanding of the thought-world of ancient Israel suggests that the *qere* is right. Did people then really ever entertain the thought that they might have made themselves – even to rule it out? It is an idea that seems to belong to a later, more philosophical theology. Whereas to say that human beings belong to God because he made them fits naturally into the religious conceptuality of ancient Israel. So, at least, it could be argued.

(How then did the form *lo'*, 'not', come to appear in the text at all? We cannot know, though one intriguing possibility – one less reliant on human error – is that there was a time when this was simply an alternative way of writing *lo*, so that the two words were homographs as well as homophones!)

This raises an important point. Generations of Christians, whether using the Prayer Book (Coverdale) Psalm 100 or the identical KJV, or the metrical version, have through singing this Psalm affirmed humanity's total dependence on God for its very existence, and (in a rather Pauline way) disclaimed its ability to form itself – rather than simply saying that people belong to God, as the Psalmist probably originally intended. Could it not be argued that this *ketib*-based translation of the Psalm, though not strictly speaking accurate, nevertheless represents a valuable reworking of the text, especially as the reading in question is actually attested within the Hebrew tradition? Is there not a case for continuing to sing it? This may be especially acceptable given that it in no way contradicts what is probably the superior reading.

But this is perhaps a dangerous slippery slope, encouraging the translator to accept other, less plausible changes to the text until the point is reached where it is no longer the Bible at all. Peterson's *The Message* veers dangerously close to this, sometimes producing what the Bible ought to have said rather than what it does say. But in moderation minor refashionings of the biblical text in the process of translation can be justified, especially where they have a long pedigree, and are to be sung in worship rather than used to determine doctrine or practice.

We have strayed some distance from inclusive language, but the point is the same. Psalm 1 really is talking about the *man* who is righteous, not the person (of either sex). But for use in worship the pluralization that avoids the more 'sexist' implication seemingly does little harm to the text, and is important for its effect on the worshipper, who cannot nowadays generalize things said of men to cover both sexes, as was common in the past, because the English language has changed. Many remain intolerant of this change, and find the fuss about gender-specific terms such as 'man' and 'he' deeply irritating, but if their concern is the integrity of the original, it can be noted that the change to the meaning of the text entailed is nearly always very slight in practice.

For the Psalms, this represents a functional-equivalence tinkering with texts otherwise mostly rendered in a formal-equivalence mode, and I have already argued that compromises between the two approaches are often justified, for particular uses of texts. Use in worship is just such a special case, and may require adjustments to the text, just as it may also require omissions.

Most widely discussed examples of inclusive language affect only the avoidance of exclusively male terms where a gender-neutral alternative is available. 'Inclusive' can be taken to have a wider reference, however, including race and the ordering of society as well as sex or gender. Such a larger agenda is pursued in the German *Bibel in gerechter Sprache*, 'Bible in Inclusive Language', already mentioned. It is the work of a panel of established scholars, though each has translated a different book or books, so that it is not a committee product in the same way as the New English Bible, or the Jerusalem Bible family. Its Introduction makes it clear that it is intended as an instrument of human liberation, and so wants to avoid not only gender-stereotyping but also common assumptions about power-relations of all kinds. In the Gospel parables, for example, the 'kingdom of God' is replaced by 'God's world': thus 'God's world can be compared to a grain of mustard seed ...' (Matthew 13:31), avoiding the use of royal language for God. (This is not, however, pursued in the 'royal' Psalms (93, 97, 99), where God is still described as king.) Thomas's exclamation on seeing Christ risen, 'My Lord and my God!', becomes 'I worship you and wish to obey you, you are the living one, my God!', presumably to avoid the language of 'lordship', which sounds both male and feudal – that anyway is my guess.

The version of the Ten Commandments in Exodus 20 translates what English-speakers know as 'do not commit adultery' with the common German idiom *Geh nicht fremd*, 'do not go strange', but in Deuteronomy 5, where the Commandments are also listed, we have 'Do not injure your life-partnership', implying, at least potentially, a rather different ordering of society from the patriarchal one that the Hebrew Bible seems to envisage. Exodus is here being translated in a formal-equivalence, Deuteronomy in a functional-equivalence manner. In both, the prohibition of coveting the neighbour's wife or property is extended to both sexes – 'do not covet your fellow human being's male or female partner' (Exodus 20:17), 'do not covet other people's male or female partner' (Deuteronomy 5:21). The problem about Proverbs is resolved by using 'My son, my daughter', at least on some occasions.

There is no doubt that the resulting translation can feel clumsy. For example, the king of the Ammonites (2 Samuel 10:1) becomes 'the king of the Ammonitesses and Ammonites' (*der König der Ammoniterinnen und Ammoniter*)'. In 1 Corinthians 12:28 the inclusivizing implies a decision about Paul's ideas on Church order: 'God has set up various gifts in the community: first apostolesses and apostles, secondly prophetesses and prophets, thirdly female and male teachers . . .'. (In double references such as these it is usual in German to put the feminine form first, as in *Studentinnen und Studenten*.) 'Brothers', *adelphoi*, is translated *Geschwister*, 'siblings'. Many will dislike all this, but the project mostly avoids absurdity and presents a challenge to the reader. It is hard to rule out some distortion of the society from which the biblical text comes if one allows gender-neutral language, and this is perhaps a logical inevitability, once a functional-equivalence approach is adopted and the criterion of accuracy is how the text would have been written today. There are of course texts that resist inclusivization, and the *Bibel in gerechter Sprache* is not doctrinaire about this. Even 1 Corinthians 14:34–5, which enjoins women to keep silent in church, is rendered faithfully – though with an endnote mentioning the (widespread) view that it is a conservative interpolation in the text, rather than actually from Paul's own hand.

There are other non-negotiable examples of androcentrism, such as 1 Timothy 2:8–15:

> I desire, then, that in every place the men should pray, lifting up holy hands without anger or argument; also that the women should dress themselves modestly and decently in suitable clothing, not with their hair braided, or with gold, pearls, or expensive clothes, but with good works, as is proper for women who profess reverence for God. Let a woman learn in silence with full submission. I permit no woman to teach or to have authority over a man; she is to keep silent. For Adam

was formed first, then Eve; and Adam was not deceived, but the woman was deceived and became a transgressor. Yet she will be saved through childbearing, provided they continue in love and faith and holiness, with modesty.

(NRSV)

There are many Christian Churches around the world where this counsel is taken quite literally, but for many today it seems hopelessly outdated. There is, however, not much a translator can do about it, and the *Bibel in gerechter Sprache* translates it exactly, without trying to inclusivize it, which would be a lost cause.

A further issue is the presence of arguably antisemitic language in the New Testament. A particular case of this is the frequent adverse reference to 'the Jews' in the Gospel according to John, where the other Gospels tend to speak only of the Pharisees as Jesus' opponents. John is here obviously rather misleading, since Jesus and his disciples were themselves Jews. A contentious case is John 20:19, where the disciples are meeting, after Jesus' death, in a locked room 'for fear of the Jews'. Modern translations tend to say 'the Jewish authorities', though this, like many inclusive reworkings, is really a bowdlerization of a text felt to be offensive rather than a translation of it, unless we fall back on a functional-equivalence argument and say that this is what John would have written had he been constructing his Gospel today. Tom Wright's *Bible for Everyone* deals with the problem by deploying 'the Judaeans', justifiable on purely historical grounds but unlikely to catch on. The Contemporary English Version opts for 'the Jewish leaders'. The whole issue of supersessionism, the idea that Christianity has replaced Judaism, which is arguably propounded in the Letter to the Hebrews, is at stake – a heavy burden to place on the shoulders of the translator.

INCLUSIVE LANGUAGE ABOUT GOD

The focus so far has been on the men and women of the Bible, but what to do with language about God? God in Hebrew and in Greek alike is treated as male, in keeping with the masculine grammatical gender of the words for 'god' in the two languages – respectively *elohim* and *theos*. But it can be argued that since God in truth has no gender, some alternative should be found.

Here again the question is complex. Some would argue that the overwhelmingly male treatment of God in the Bible should be retained even though, or even precisely because, it is scandalous to modern eyes; others that God's essential maleness is a revealed truth. Both camps, though positioned at opposite ends of the spectrum, meet in preferring gendered language to be used in translations. Those who think that the Bible is hospitable to the idea that God is neither male nor female, on the other hand, treat the application of gendered language to God as a constraint of the Hebrew and Greek languages, and urge that gender-neutral language should be used in translations into modern vernaculars. When the new Dutch Bible was being produced in the early 2000s, it was decided after much public wrangling to translate YHWH as 'LORD' (HEER) in the traditional way, only for four female members of the translation panel to resign in protest at this male and hierarchical image of God.[8]

In some languages, such as German and French, the word 'divinity' (*Gottheit, déité*) is feminine, and can sometimes be used instead of the masculine word for God (*Gott, dieu*). Perhaps an expression like 'the Godhead' in English could be treated as feminine too. Sometimes the 'spirit' of God, or God's 'wisdom', is used by biblical translators instead of 'God', since both words are feminine in Hebrew (though 'spirit' is neuter in Greek – Hebrew has no neuter gender). But the grammatical gender of a noun in languages that are far more gendered than English does not necessarily imply physical genderedness or sex – French *personne*, for example, is feminine and requires feminine agreements, but can perfectly well be used of a male person. The very small amount of grammatical gendering in English can mislead the Anglophone reader to treat the gender of foreign nouns as more significant than it is. When Hebrew uses 'spirit' or 'wisdom', both feminine nouns, to refer to what are almost beings alongside God, nothing compels us to translate pronouns referring to them as meaning 'she' rather than 'it'. There are places in the Hebrew Bible where wisdom is certainly portrayed as a woman, for example in Proverbs 8, but elsewhere 'wisdom' is often simply an attribute of God. And 'spirit' never seems to be treated as female, even though the word, *ruach*, is grammatically feminine. One equally cannot argue from the fact that the Greek word for spirit, *pneuma*, is neuter that the New Testament sees it simply as a 'thing' – that is to misunderstand how grammatical gender works. Thus in German the word for girl, *Mädchen*, is neuter, but that does not mean that German-speakers regard girls as inanimate objects. It is simply constrained by the fact that the word is a diminutive form: all German diminutives are neuter in grammatical gender.

It seems to me that the Bible really does treat God as male, though lacking most of the physical and sexual characteristics that constitute maleness in human beings, and that this should be indicated in translation. I would add that the Bible is mistaken in this, since God, as any theologian can tell you, has no gender. Whether or not it is a scandal to speak as though God has, the fact that the Bible does so should be indicated in the translation, not airbrushed out.

TRANSLATING THE DIVINE NAME

The *Bibel in gerechter Sprache* raises at length an important issue: how should we translate the divine name YHWH (the Tetragrammaton, Greek for 'four letters') in the Hebrew Bible? We encountered this in Chapter 3 in connection with the Buber-Rosenzweig translation of the Bible, and in particular of Exodus 3, where it is given a folk-etymology linking it with the verb *hyh*, 'to be'. Like all Hebrew words, the name of Israel's special god was originally written with no vowels, so we cannot know for certain how it was pronounced. The best hypothesis is that it may have been 'yahweh', or perhaps 'yaho' or 'yahu': names that end in it seem to preserve the last of these, as in Yesha'yahu, 'Isaiah', 'YHWH saves'. But sometime in the last few centuries BCE the custom arose of not pronouncing the name at all. By then it was regarded as too sacred for utterance, and perhaps as risking a breach of the Commandment, 'You shall not take the name of YHWH your God in vain'. Jews started instead to say *adonai*, 'my Lord'. Once vowels came to be written in the biblical text, well into the Common Era, in the form of dots and dashes above and below the consonants, the vowels of *adonai* were added to the consonants of YHWH, as a reminder that it was *adonai* that should be said or sung. (Much later some Christians started to read the impossible word this produced as YEHOWA, i.e. Jehovah, but this is a form that never had any real foundation in antiquity beyond the page and has never been used by Jews.)

In Greek and Latin translations of the Hebrew Bible the word for 'Lord' was generally substituted for the form YHWH: *kurios* in Greek, *dominus* in Latin. The New Testament books, written in Greek rather than Hebrew, never use the name YHWH but always say 'Lord'. A few Greek manuscripts of the Old Testament retain the Hebrew letters, and we know early Christian writers were familiar with the Tetragrammaton, as they remark that the Jews called God PIPI, which, when written in Greek, looks quite like YHWH written in Hebrew. The tradition of using 'Lord' persisted in translations into European vernaculars and is still with us, though in print some way is usually found of signalling that YHWH occurs in the source text. In Luther Bibles the word *Herr*, 'lord', is printed HERR; in English the norm is also to use small capitals after the initial letter, thus: LORD.

Early Christians also used *kurios* to refer to Jesus: see 1 Corinthians 12:3, 'no one can say "Jesus is Lord" except by the Holy Spirit'. The word was also used in purely secular forms of address in antiquity, roughly equivalent to 'sir', but the use of the same term for both God and Jesus may well have encouraged the recognition of Jesus as divine at a time when his nature and status were still being worked out. If so, this would be an indication of the power translation can exercise over the development of a religion, for no comparable equivalence could so readily have been made if Christianity had remained a purely Aramaic-speaking religion. The word *kurios* had a breadth of applicability that extended to the Jesus the writers of the New Testament sought to describe; the Tetragrammaton emphatically did not. It is a reminder that Christianity emerged across linguistic borders, in dialogue with a Scripture that was known in a translated form – and that this may have opened some possibilities while foreclosing others.

Among Jews avoidance of speaking the divine name has resulted in a number of different devices alongside the use of *adonai*. One is to use the expression 'the name', in Hebrew *ha-shem*; another is to combine this form with *adonai* to produce *adoshem*. On paper, observant Jews will sometimes write the four consonants YHWH but without vowels, and likewise, when writing in English sometimes G-d or G'd.

In modern times Christians and non-religious Bible readers have sometimes used 'Yahweh', but this is now often avoided as potentially offensive to Jews. The Jerusalem Bible introduced it into the translation, even in the Psalms, which some groups then sang: the word was thus freely pronounced in worship for the first time in a couple of millennia. But this has slipped out of use, and the Revised New Jerusalem Bible has reverted to LORD. The dithering about the issue does, however, highlight an important question. Given that no modern Christian thinks of God as Yahweh, then using that word implies that we are concerned with the god worshipped in ancient Israel *as distinct from* God as we actually believe him to be today. The rendering 'Yahweh' tips us back into the ancient world in a suddenly quite distanced way: it is a very formal-equivalence way of dealing with the divine name. Forms such as 'Lord' and its equivalents in other languages have the effect, which many would regard as desirable, of equating the God of the Hebrew Bible with the God of the New Testament and with the God Jews and Christians worship now. Interestingly Ecclesiastes, probably from the third century BCE, does not use the Tetragrammaton at all but only 'God', Hebrew *elohim*; and Esther and the Song of Songs also do not use it. Where it does occur in other late books, to insist on 'Yahweh' in a translation may thus be a falsification of the impression it would actually have made on a contemporary reader, who would have been saying 'Lord' by then in any case.

Other ways of dealing with the divine name include phrases such as 'the Eternal', which was popularized in the mid-twentieth century in Britain by Moffatt and is also used by some Jews, sometimes with the addition 'blessed be he', *barukh hu*, or (as so often in the book of Isaiah) 'the Holy One', with the same addition. There is also a written abbreviation *y-y* in Hebrew letters. As we saw in Chapter 3, Buber and Rosenzweig used capitalized pronouns – HE, THOU, ME – to hint at God's ineffability. With reference to Exodus 3:14 (KJV: 'I AM THAT I AM'), where the name YHWH is connected obscurely with the Hebrew verb 'to be', *hayah*, some people also use I AM THERE or simply I AM.

How then should a modern Bible handle this issue, which is such a sensitive one? The *Bibel in gerechter Sprache* has adopted an ingenious device. It uses all the possibilities in one book or another, according to the preference of the individual translator; but as a header to every left-hand page it lists various alternatives, so that anyone reading the text in public can substitute their own preferred option. (This comes with a warning that a rehearsal before reading aloud is strongly recommended.) As always with translation, there is no one perfect solution, but this hands the decision over to the reader in quite a neat way. In seeing the realization of the text as a co-operation between translator and reader, just as a musical score requires a conductor and an orchestra, as well as an audience, to realize it, this reflects a rather postmodern approach to textual meaning and identity. It is also, however, a very practical suggestion, recognizing that people's sensitivities differ and that different situations may call for different treatment, perhaps especially in public worship, with its innate fluctuations in tone and register.

It has not been usual to transfer any of this to the New Testament, since Christians have no reservations about saying 'God'. David Bentley Hart, however, in his translation of the Gospel according to John, deals with the variation between *ho theos* ('the God') and *theos* ('God' or 'god') by rendering *ho theos* as GOD and *theos* as GOD if he thinks it too means the one God, or as 'god' if he thinks it refers to a subordinate divine being.* Thus

> In the origin there was the Logos, and the Logos was present with GOD, and the Logos was god; This one was present with GOD in the origin. All things came to be through him, and without him came to be not a single thing that has come to be. In him was life, and this life was the light of men. And the light shines in the darkness, and the darkness did not conquer it. There came a man, sent by GOD, whose name was John.

> (John 1:1–6)

---

* In fact Hart's distinction between GOD and GOD is even more complicated than this: see his note to the translation of this passage, *The New Testament*, p. 168.

These distinctions would not be perceptible if the passage were to be read aloud, but Hart explicitly states that his version is not meant for liturgical use, only for private study. The typographical devices do, however, alert the reader to some of the complexity of the prologue to John. The Word, incarnate in Jesus Christ, was divine in some sense yet not simply identical or interchangeable with God – the later doctrine of the Trinity is an attempt to cope coherently with this paradox. John's shifting use of *theos* and *ho theos* hints at it without solving the puzzle. Few translations of John point to it as ingeniously as Bentley Hart does through these typographical variations.

7
Words and Meanings

Translators don't differ only when it comes to stylistic matters – sometimes they disagree about the actual meaning of the words in the Bible, in view of the distance separating us from the biblical authors. Especially where there is a sharp divide between the two Testaments, there are important divergences of opinion about what truly significant words mean. Let us take three: soul, salvation and faith.

SOUL

> For whosoever will save his life shall lose it; but whosoever shall lose his life for my sake and the gospel's, the same shall save it. For what shall it profit a man, if he shall gain the whole world, and lose his own soul? Or what shall a man give in exchange for his soul?
>
> (Mark 8:35–7, KJV)

> 'For those who want to save their life will lose it, and those who lose their life for my sake, and for the sake of the gospel, will save it. For what will it profit them to gain the whole world and forfeit their life? Indeed, what can they give in return for their life?'
>
> (Mark 8:35–7, NRSV)

This saying of Jesus appears clear in meaning in the King James Version: those who sacrifice their life for Jesus' sake will not lose their soul. The New Revised Standard Version is more puzzling: those who give up their life will retain their life – implied perhaps also in the beginning of the KJV translation, but then explained in terms of losing or keeping one's soul. Confusingly, the same word – the Greek *psyche* or *psuche* – is translated both 'life' and 'soul'.

The New English Bible (followed by the Revised English Bible) goes further still, and renders the word as 'self':[1]

> 'Whoever cares for his own safety is lost; but if a man will let himself be lost for my sake and for the Gospel, that man is safe. What does a man gain by winning the whole world at the cost of his true self? What can he give to buy that self back?'

Why has the second meaning, 'soul', dropped out of the NRSV and almost all modern translations, to be replaced by 'life' or 'self'? Do Christians not believe in souls any longer?

Broadly speaking, the answer to this question is that they do not.[2] There is something approaching a consensus in theological thought in all the Churches that denies the existence of an entity called the soul as a part or element in the human person, which leaves the body at death yet, as earlier generations believed, can pass into the heavenly realm, since either it is immortal or God can immortalize it. Rather, it is usually said, human beings are psychosomatic unities, needing both physical and mental characteristics to be truly themselves. Christian tradition, indeed, as we find it in the creeds, speaks of the resurrection of the *body* rather than of the immortality of the soul, implying that God will revive those who have died rather than that they will live on after death through an inherent immortality – just as he raised Jesus, who had been dead in the tomb, and gave him a resurrection body, rather than simply confirming the immortality of his soul. But Christians have for most of their history combined this with a belief that there is a soul that endures when the body does not, and that passages such as Mark 8:35–7 refer to it.

In more recent times, however, many Christians have come to adopt the belief that a person is not a soul plus a body but rather an indivisible being, monistic rather than dualistic. This fits much better with the more materialist trend in modern science and philosophy, which asserts that consciousness is inseparable from embodiment: the mind cannot exist independently of the brain, according to this way of thinking, and hence the idea of the soul makes no sense. But in a quite remarkable shift, biblical scholars have come, since around the middle of the twentieth century, to affirm that the Bible actually shared this modern perception of human nature, which got lost through a dualistic Cartesian philosophy but can be rediscovered by careful attention to the meaning of biblical terms. *Psyche*, it is said, does not mean 'soul', seen as a separable part of the human make-up, but something like 'embodied life' – at least in the New Testament, which in this may well be at variance with usage in other Greek texts, and particularly with Greek philosophy of the Platonic kind.[3] When the New Testament speaks of a person's *psyche* it means that person's true self, just as the NEB renders it. It is not talking about some spiritual or mental component that could survive death.

Why was *psyche* thought not to mean 'soul' in the New Testament, when it does generally mean that in other Greek texts? One answer is perhaps that it was then believed that the 'psychosomatic unity' model was true, and therefore one would expect it to be taught in the New Testament. When we hold a belief strongly, we are predisposed to think that it is in the Bible. But there was also an empirical reason for seeing *psyche* as meaning embodied life or self, and that is that it was also being argued that such had been the teaching of the Old Testament, in its use of a Hebrew word that in some ways corresponds to *psyche*: the word *nephesh*.

In Genesis 2:7 we read in the NRSV that 'the LORD God formed man from the dust of the ground, and breathed into his nostrils the breath of life, and the man became a living being (*nephesh hayah*)', but the KJV has 'a living soul'. Clearly the man does not *have* a *nephesh*, but *is* a *nephesh*, and if we translate *nephesh* as 'soul', then man does not have a soul but is a soul – an embodied soul. This is part of what was sometimes called 'Hebrew totality thinking'.[4] Hebrew thinkers, it seemed, did not make the kind of mind/body distinctions we make. 'In Israelite thought man is conceived not so much in dual fashion as "body" and "soul", but synthetically as a unit of vital power or (in current terminology) a psycho-physical organism.'[5] The ancient Israelites, it was implied, had in a sense already arrived at the understanding of humans as psychosomatic unities that it has taken many centuries of modern thought to get back to.

This interpretation was persuasive to many biblical scholars and translators, and indeed, in the light of prevailing ideas about humanity, attractive; and it led to *psyche* in the above passage and in many other places in the New Testament being translated as 'life' or 'self' rather than 'soul'. There is, however, a basic mistake here. Even though *psyche* often corresponds to *nephesh*, *nephesh* has a much broader range of meanings than 'soul', and one of them is 'being' or 'living being', as the NRSV rightly perceives. In Genesis 2:7 it does not mean 'soul' at all. But how is the 'living being' constituted? As the result of God's making a physical body and then breathing into it 'the breath of life'. Now *nephesh* does not mean 'soul' here; but the 'breath of life' seems extraordinarily like a soul. The man, once made, may be a psycho-somatic unity, but that unity is constituted by the addition to the physical body of a divinely given breath – a breath that makes the difference between an inanimate and an animate being. Which is what is usually meant by a soul. 'Adam is fashioned out of mud, and God breathes into him the breath of life; he thus becomes an animate being, like any other animal. The passage is obviously dualistic: there are two ingredients in man, the mud and the breath.'⁶ Pursuing the meaning of the word *nephesh* is something of a wild-goose chase here. It can mean 'throat', 'appetite', 'corpse' and 'person' – as well as sometimes 'soul' (see Genesis 35:18, where Rachel's *nephesh* departs from her when she dies), though not in Genesis 2:7. (The use of the English word 'soul' to mean 'person' still occurs in expressions such as 'I didn't see another soul during my walk'.)

In several places in the Hebrew Bible it is clear that a human has both a physical and a spiritual component, often described as the spirit (*ruach*) rather than the *nephesh*, though the latter word does occur in that sense occasionally. Ecclesiastes 3:21 asks, 'Who knows whether the human spirit goes upwards and the spirit of animals goes downwards to the earth?', which implies that all animate beings are made up of body plus spirit. Similarly, when the dry bones in Ezekiel 37 are to return to life, this is effected by God bringing his spirit or wind or breath (all *ruach* in Hebrew) into them, thereby reanimating them. Ezekiel 37 is a metaphorical story, really concerning the restoration of the conquered and dispersed nation, but the metaphor works only if living beings are composed of the breath of God in their bodily flesh. When Elijah restores a dead boy to life (1 Kings 17:17–23), 'the life of the child came into him again': an inanimate corpse becomes a living person once more. All this indicates a basically dualistic model for humanity: flesh plus spirit or soul.

The New Testament too can use *psyche* as a counterpoint or in contrast with words for 'body', the classic place being Matthew 10:28, where Jesus says: 'Do not fear those that kill the body but cannot kill the soul; rather fear him who can destroy both soul and body in Gehenna [NRSV hell].' (Gehenna, originally the name of a smouldering rubbish tip outside Jerusalem in the Valley of Hinnom – Hebrew *ge hinnom* – came to be a place where the dead could be punished or annihilated, the nearest to a belief in hell that Judaism in this period came.) Whether the one to be feared here is God or the devil is unclear, but what is perfectly plain is that soul and body are distinguished. Interestingly, modern translators generally leave this contrast uncorrected by the totality theory, no doubt seeing that it does not fit and cannot be made to.

Accordingly, 'soul' should probably be used much more freely for both *nephesh* and *psyche* than has become common in modern translations. In the passage quoted at the beginning of this chapter, the rendering 'soul', as in the KJV, is probably right: there is nothing any of us can give in exchange for our soul, conceived of as a fundamental component of us that lives beyond death, rather than as a synonym for 'life'. The Hebrew Bible also implies that there is part of us that survives death, even though it is usually seen as attenuated and uninteresting, going down into the underworld (Sheol). Only in later books such as Daniel do the dead have any hope of a real future. But whatever the fate of the soul may be, there is one, and this was certainly widely believed by the time of Jesus and the writers of the New Testament.

One implication, as it happens, is that the gap between Hebrew and Greek thought on this matter is probably less wide than it is often presented. In the movement after the Second World War often dubbed the 'Biblical Theology Movement', largely an Anglophone and, indeed, North American phenomenon, the contrast between the two was presented very starkly. The New Testament, it was argued, even though it was written in Greek, was closer to the Hebrew mode of thinking, and in particular adhered to the totality idea of the human person.

James Barr showed that the contrast often resulted from comparing two unlike things: popular attitudes reflected in the Hebrew Bible, and the sophisticated thinking of Greek philosophers. If we go back beyond the philosophers, for example to Homer, we find ideas of life and death similar to that in the Hebrew Bible, with 'shades' surviving death but confined to Hades, a realm very like Sheol, where nothing happens and there is no longer any true life.

If, on the other hand, we go forward to the Jewish literature produced in the last couple of centuries BCE, we find it is much more like Greek philosophy. The book Wisdom of Solomon, probably from the first century BCE, reflects on the immortality of the human soul: 'The souls of the righteous are in the hand of God, and no torment will ever touch them' (Wisdom 3:1). Probably this was a borrowing from the philosophers, but that was only possible because there was not felt to be a contradiction between their thought and the Hebrew tradition. The perception that Hebrew and Greek thought are radically different, and that Christians should follow the Hebrew style, persists, however, especially in sermons. It can be useful in combating a particular kind of antisemitism, but has little foundation in biblical study. In particular, the New Testament should not be interpreted with a starting assumption that it is closer to a 'Hebrew' world-view – which in the case of the human person is then taken to mean the totality theory – than to Greek cultural norms: *psyche* is probably 'soul' rather than 'life' or 'self'.[7]

Thus a seemingly small point of translation can lead into a wide-ranging issue in the interpretation of biblical thought and culture. For those whose faith is influenced by the Bible, the question of whether it encourages belief in a soul or only in a 'self' is not a trivial matter, though for my part I do not think that the biblical picture is necessarily determinative: what is being discussed here is what the Bible takes as given, rather than what it overtly teaches. But even for those with a secular interest in the thought of ancient Israel, it is a significant issue. Does the Bible align with a typical modern philosophical view of the human person, or is it closer to an idealist position in which the soul is critical to human identity? It would be good to know, and that is only possible if we have a correct perception of the meaning of the terms involved. My own belief is that the psychosomatic unity model of the human being does not do justice to the biblical picture in either Testament.

SALVATION

Christianity is generally understood as a religion of salvation. To what extent Christians understand salvation as involving a life beyond death for the individual varies, but all versions of the faith have a central emphasis on human rescue from an undesirable plight, as God overcomes the power of sin and death through the cross and the resurrection of Jesus Christ. When words from the semantic field of 'salvation' occur in the Greek New Testament they refer to this supernatural gift of life beyond death and destruction, whether that is meant literally ('heaven') or metaphorically (a new world order). When Paul says that in the end 'all Israel will be saved', it is unclear whether he means that every Jew, as well as Gentile believers in Christ, will be raised from the dead, but he certainly means that some desirable change will come upon them for ever, reversing present conditions of suffering and hardship.

Certain strands of Judaism in the time of Jesus believed firmly in a coming divine transformation – what Jesus called the coming of the 'kingdom of God', that is, God's reasserted rule over all things. The writers of the New Testament shared this belief, and in addition thought that it had already been inaugurated in the resurrection and ascension of Jesus after his death on the cross. Belief in 'salvation' in this sense was part of the intellectual world the first Christians inhabited, and it is therefore correct to translate Greek *soteria* as 'salvation'. It may not have had exactly the same connotations for them that it has for modern Christians (which vary greatly in any case), but it is certainly in the right area. When in Acts 2:47 we read that 'day by day the Lord added to their number those who were being saved', the text surely implies a supernatural salvation. It is part too of Orthodox Jewish belief, though less emphasized and elaborated than in Christianity.

The books in the Hebrew Bible were nearly all written by a couple of centuries before the time of Jesus and his disciples, and for the most part they do not yet contain a hope for salvation, in the sense that

Greek *soteria* bears in the New Testament and subsequent Christian discourse. The latest book, Daniel, in its chapter 12, predicts the resurrection of at least some of those who 'sleep in the dust', but no earlier book clearly envisages that kind of salvation. The ideas recorded in the Hebrew Bible concern 'salvation' only in the sense of rescue from imminent peril, deliverance from enemies, divine action keeping people from dying in the first place – not a new life lying beyond the grave. We noted in Chapter 1 that the Septuagint, a translation in the period closer to the time of Daniel, tends to introduce the notion of post-mortem salvation into the Psalms, but that in origin they speak only of God 'saving' individuals from sinking down to Sheol even when they already have 'one foot in the grave', not bringing them back from it once they are actually dead. Texts that Christians have for centuries read around Eastertide as prophesying their own resurrection, made possible through Jesus, normally had originally a much less otherworldly concern: the rescue of the nation from its enemies and from harsh conditions of life. Take, for example, Isaiah 65:17–25:

> For I am about to create new heavens
> > and a new earth;
> the former things shall not be remembered
> > or come to mind.
> But be glad and rejoice for ever
> > in what I am creating;
> for I am about to create Jerusalem as a joy,
> > and its people as a delight.
> I will rejoice in Jerusalem,
> > and delight in my people;
> no more shall the sound of weeping be heard in it,
> > or the cry of distress.
> No more shall there be in
> > it an infant that lives but a few days,
> > or an old person who does not live out a lifetime;
> for one who dies at a hundred years will be considered a youth,
> > and one who falls short of a hundred will be considered accursed.
> They shall build houses and inhabit them;
> > they shall plant vineyards and eat their fruit.

They shall not build and another inhabit;
>   they shall not plant and another eat;
for like the days of a tree shall the days of my people be,
>   and my chosen shall long enjoy the work of their hands.
They shall not labour in vain,
>   or bear children for calamity;
for they shall be offspring blessed by the LORD –
>   and their descendants as well.
Before they call I will answer,
>   while they are yet speaking I will hear.
The wolf and the lamb shall feed together,
>   the lion shall eat straw like the ox;
>   but the serpent – its food shall be dust!
They shall not hurt or destroy
>   on all my holy mountain,

>   says the LORD.

>   (NRSV)

At first glance 'new heavens and a new earth' sounds like a major cosmic change, and recalls Revelation 21:1. But on closer inspection it is clear that the real force of the passage is a transformation of the natural order into what is in effect merely an improved version of it. People will still die, for example; they will live longer, but are still mortal, and some may be unlucky enough not to enjoy the full benefits of these new conditions and fall short of a hundred-year lifespan. The passage is not about the hope of heaven, but about a transformation in earthly conditions, with all inconveniences and injustices ironed out, and wild beasts tamed. This is usual in prophetic predictions of a glorious future. The sublime passages in Isaiah 40–55, many famous from Handel's *Messiah*, are similarly about earthly hopes: a return of Jewish exiles to the land of Israel and the reconstruction of Jerusalem. Christians have allegorized all this and made it apply to the heavenly Jerusalem, but on the face of it, at least, this is a misunderstanding of the prophecies' original import.

'Salvation', as understood by the writers of the New Testament and by Christians the world over since, thus does not really appear in the Hebrew Bible. But there are words traditionally translated as though it did. The Hebrew *yeshuʿah* is normally rendered 'salvation', but it should mostly be understood as deliverance or rescue. The corresponding verb, *yashaʿ*, similarly means to vindicate someone or save them from a threatening or difficult or dangerous situation, rather than to save them in the sense of freeing them from damnation. Thus in Isaiah 52:10, 'all the ends of the earth shall see the salvation (*yeshuʿat*) of our God' (NRSV) means that everyone will see God saving Israel from its plight by ending its exile in Babylonia and restoring the sacked Jerusalem. The word 'salvation' may not be the right term here, and the REB, surely correctly, renders 'deliverance'. Compare also Isaiah 30:15, 'in returning and rest you shall be saved; in quietness and in trust shall be your strength' (NRSV), where the sense is that the nation will be delivered from its enemies if it trusts quietly in God and does not take military action. The verse is not in origin a contribution to Christian theology or spirituality but rather to the foreign policy of a country in a crisis, and the REB again translates appropriately 'in calm detachment lies your *safety*, your strength in quiet trust'. We return to this verse below.

Language that we usually think of as being about salvation has a different meaning in the Hebrew Bible from the one it has in the New Testament. This needs to be indicated in any translation, as pointed out by an important article in the 1980s entitled ' "Salvation" is Not of the Jews',[8] using the phrase from John 4:22 ('salvation is from the Jews' – 'of' the Jews' in the KJV) and inverting it to make the point that salvation in its New Testament sense is not a Jewish concept. In fact, as we have seen, such ideas were in the mix in the Jewish world in New Testament times among some groups – Christians did not invent them – though Orthodox Judaism did not in the end develop them as Christianity did. But they do not occur in the Hebrew Bible to any significant extent: there, 'salvation' means 'deliverance from enemies', and is not metaphorical or allegorical in character. 'Save us, we pray' (Hebrew *hoshiaʿ-na*, 'hosanna', as in Psalm 118:25) means 'rescue us [from our foes]'. Old and New Testaments do not – where this issue is concerned – form a single document, but mean different things by the terms we commonly translate as 'salvation'. Even language about deliverance in a purely this-worldly sense is not evenly distributed in the Hebrew Bible. It is far more common in the Psalms, where it normally concerns deliverance from enemies or from illness, than in the

Pentateuch or even the prophets. And this comparative absence from the core books of Judaism tallies with and partly explains the fact that the religion as we now encounter it is not much focused on salvation, as Christianity is, but far more on loyalty to God's law and prescribed way of life.[9] Robert Alter accordingly tends to render 'salvation' words in the Hebrew Bible as 'rescue', 'deliverance' and the like, and this is truer to the general sense of the thought of ancient Israel as captured in the Bible.

FAITH

A similar difference between the Testaments, and between Greek and Hebrew, can be found in language concerned with faith or belief. A concern for the theme of faith in the Hebrew Bible or Old Testament would be unlikely to arise at all if it were not for the history of the Bible's reception, and specifically its use in formulating Christian doctrine, where it is the New Testament that has been most important. Faith has long been a central concept in Christianity, and the Old Testament, as part of the Scriptures of Christians, has been an important source of sayings containing the word 'faith' – or words that can be translated as 'faith', to be more accurate. These sayings have been pressed into service in expounding what Christians believe about the centrality of faith in Christian theology and the Christian life. Before we can ask what the Hebrew Bible in itself has to say about faith, and how words from that semantic field should be translated, a certain amount of reception history is therefore necessary.

Among the central Old Testament texts that have been identified as bearing on the question of faith, the most important by far has been Habakkuk 2:4, which in traditional translations (e.g. KJV) reads 'the just shall live by his faith'. This is the text at the heart of Martin Luther's doctrine of justification by faith, by which he claimed that 'the Church stands or falls'. Faith is here opposed to 'works', meaning, in Luther's context, not so much general moral behaviour but the special 'good works' that Catholics in his day were invited to perform: religious customs such as fasting, pilgrimages and attendance at various liturgical rites. For Luther, these were a distraction, shifting the core of Christian faith from an internal disposition of the heart towards God to external observances that were supposed to be able to aid the believer on the way to salvation. Famously, one of the things he most vehemently opposed was the sale of indulgences, resting on the idea that one could achieve, if not salvation, then certainly remission of years in purgatory by contributing to the Church's coffers.

By contrast, for Luther salvation was the result not of what we do, but of the grace of God; it was a gift, not a reward. This could then be generalized into the more far-reaching notion that it is not our conduct at all that generates salvation, but only the grace of God – which precedes all human deeds, good and bad. Indeed, good deeds are in themselves no better than actual sins, so incapable are they of producing salvation. Salvation, definitely meaning here salvation from being damned, not deliverance from enemies, is God's free gift. It is received, not worked for. But the faculty through which we receive it is faith, by which sinful humans become, at the same moment, those whom God has justified – that is, counted as if they were righteous. The individual saved by God is at once sinful and justified, *simul justus et peccator*.

For Luther, Habakkuk 2:4 summed up this central truth about the nature of Christianity. In this text, on his reading, it is through faith rather than through works that the righteous live. Understandably, in some of his followers this led to antinomianism – the belief that nothing the justified sinner went on to do could affect their salvation, and hence that no moral norms any longer held sway over Christians. Luther himself did not draw this conclusion: for him, faith is worked out in action even though having priority over it. Through faith we receive the righteousness God imparts, and this then makes it possible for us to live moral lives; God does not wait until we are righteous to bless us, because if he did, he would have to wait for ever. We cannot earn our salvation: we are so marred by sin that we would never be capable of it. This sounds pessimistic. But the good news of the gospel is that we do not need to earn salvation. God imparts it freely, and all we have to do is to receive it. We do this by turning to God in faith. Another key Old Testament text for Luther was Genesis 15:6: '[Abraham] believed the LORD, and the LORD reckoned it to him as righteousness.' Abraham was not chosen and blessed by God because he did good deeds, but simply because he believed.

Luther's development of this doctrine in the late-medieval period was a theological innovation, but these texts had been used before him for a related purpose by Paul, and it is from Paul that Luther derived his theory of justification by faith. In Romans 4, Paul discusses at length the text from Genesis 15:

> What then are we to say was gained by Abraham, our ancestor according to the flesh? For if Abraham was justified by works, he has something to boast about, but not before God. For what does the scripture say? 'Abraham believed God, and it was reckoned to him as righteousness.' Now to one who works, wages are not reckoned as a gift but as something due. But to one who without works trusts him who justifies the ungodly, such faith is reckoned as righteousness.

> (Romans 4:1–5 NRSV)

It is not what Abraham did after he was called by God, but the faith he had when God called him in the first place that made him righteous in the eyes of God. As Paul observes in the earlier letter to the Galatians (3:11), 'it is evident that no one is justified before God by the law; for "The one who is righteous will live by faith"', quoting Habakkuk again, as he also does later in Romans 1:17, where he says that in the gospel message 'the righteousness of God is revealed through faith for faith; as it is written, "The one who is righteous will live by faith."'

Paul's context was, however, very different from Luther's. The works of 'the law' which Paul was concerned with were not the buying of indulgences but the distinctive practices of Judaism. Both Galatians and Romans in slightly different ways are concerned with the question of whether one must be a Jew before one can be a Christian: whether observance of the detail of the Jewish law is incumbent on non-Jewish converts to the Christian way. Against powerful voices in the early Church, Paul maintained that this was not necessary. Romans is concerned throughout with this problem, a problem highly specific to the first-century Church and entirely different from those confronting Luther. What Paul seeks to show is that the basis on which Christians are accepted by God is not their adherence or non-adherence to the Jewish laws (by which he means not general moral laws such as the Ten Commandments, but the minutiae of ritual observance), but their willingness to believe in God through Jesus. Jesus, rather than the Torah of Judaism, is the route to salvation, and Jesus can be received only through faith, that is, through acceptance of him as the Saviour. Good behaviour then of course follows – Paul is as keen as Luther would be to oppose antinomianism – but God's act of justification precedes it. Consequently Jewish Christians can claim no priority over Gentile Christians, since for everyone, Jew and Gentile alike, it is faith rather than the works prescribed in the Torah that is the criterion of membership of the people of God.

In the past it was usual to read Paul through somewhat Lutheran eyes, and to interpret faith here in highly psychological terms, which is arguably how it is to be interpreted in Luther: a movement of the mind towards God, rather than external deeds. But since the 1980s what is now called the 'New Perspective on Paul'[10] stresses the importance of the context in which Paul was teaching, and the issue of the relation between Jews and Gentiles in the Church as the key to understanding him. For Paul faith does not mean primarily a psychological state, but trust expressed in action – the action of joining the Christian community and taking on its acceptance of Jesus as Lord and Saviour. Faith certainly has a psychological component, since it proceeds from what Paul calls the heart – a term which in his vocabulary includes what we should call the mind. But this is part of the whole package of becoming a Christian, which also involves ethical conduct and above all active membership of the Christian community.

Paul, according to adherents of the 'New Perspective', is not talking to individuals about their interior life, but to communities about what it is that holds them together. Steadfast trust in the promises of God expresses itself in Christian living, and it is that whole complex of things that for Paul is what 'faith' in practice amounts to. The contrast is not between faith and action, but between faith as faithful adherence to the Christian gospel, and works as continuing adherence to the Torah – the defining community mark of Judaism. Abraham is crucial here because he believed God, that is, entrusted his life and conduct to God, before the Torah was given. True, he received one of the signs of the Torah, circumcision, but he received it as a token of the faith he already possessed, in virtue of which he was already 'justified', rather than as the precondition of justification. His example proves that it cannot be only those who submit to the yoke of the Torah who will be saved, since he is said in Genesis 15 to have been justified through his faith in God centuries before the Torah was given to the Jewish people through Moses.

What we see in Paul is thus the sense of faith as meaning not simply intellectual assent to certain propositions – such as those that would later come to form part of the Christian creeds – but trusting self-commitment to the promises of God, which results in certain sorts of action. For him, this means primarily the kinds of action that mark out the Christian from society at large. And in the idea of 'trusting self-commitment' we come closer to the meaning of faith as it is in the Hebrew Bible than many modern Christian notions of it as a kind of intense belief, or assent to a series of propositions about God. But even Paul, in the first century, probably over-psychologizes what is meant by the various terms we can translate as 'faith' in the Hebrew Bible. There the focus is much more on action than on thought, as we shall see.

'Believe' in Biblical Hebrew is *he'emin*, the so-called Hiphil or causative form of the verb *'aman*, from which derives the familiar word Amen, meaning 'let it be established'. The use of the causative would make one expect that the form *he'emin* would mean 'cause someone else to believe', but in fact the verb does not occur in the simple non-causative form anyway. The normal sense of *he'emin* appears to be 'place one's confidence in' something or someone. So what Abraham did in Genesis 15 was to trust that God would carry out what he had promised – to make his descendants as numerous as the stars in the night sky and grant to them the land around him – and it was this trust that caused God to regard him as righteous. The corresponding noun is *'emunah*, which means faithfulness or trustworthiness. In Habakkuk 2:4 the meaning of the Hebrew is therefore that the righteous will 'live', i.e. prosper and do well, on account of their trustworthiness, reliability or steadfastness. Nothing is being said about faith in the sense of belief or assent. In a way the verse means almost the opposite of what Paul and Luther took it to mean, in that it is through actions which exemplify trustworthiness that the righteous will prosper. Similarly the verse is not saying anything about 'salvation' in the sense of an individual's eternal destiny, but about the way their life will be successful and fulfilled because they are reliable – this meshes with what was said above about the language of 'salvation'. It is the kind of verse that would be at home in a book such as Proverbs, stressing the success of those whose conduct can be counted on.

From the point of view of the Hebrew Bible – taken on its own terms and without regard for its reception history – neither the Genesis nor the Habakkuk reference is the most interesting for our theme. More revealing of faith as conceived biblically are a couple of places in the book of Isaiah. The first is in Isaiah 7:9. By general consent this is an oracle of the prophet Isaiah from the period between 735 and 732 BCE. At this time the people of Israel were divided into two kingdoms, the larger northern kingdom, known as Ephraim or, confusingly, as Israel, with its capital at Samaria, and the small southern kingdom, Judah, with its capital at Jerusalem, ruled over by kings descended from David. The northern kingdom had formed an alliance with Aram (Syria), its capital then as now at Damascus, to attempt to subjugate Judah and replace its king with a puppet. Judah under King Ahaz was at a loss to know what to do, since its army was certainly not able to resist the alliance, and one plan, which in the end Ahaz opted for, was to appeal to the Assyrians to the east to intervene, by sending tribute to them. The result would inevitably be, and was, that Judah became a kind of Assyrian vassal, but Jerusalem would be spared siege and conquest and the line of David would continue to rule.

Isaiah's advice, presented as a directive from God, was that Ahaz should do nothing. Judah had simply to wait for God to intervene and crush the alliance. In practical terms, he may have thought that the Assyrians, seeing a threat to their dominance of the region arising to the west, would take steps to crush it even if Judah did not ask them to, so that Judah would be spared and yet retain its independence. Whatever his political judgement may have been (and some think he was in fact a royal counsellor), Isaiah's prophecy opposed all action by Ahaz on *theological* grounds. He announces, 'Because Aram – with Ephraim and the son of Remaliah – has plotted evil against you, saying, Let us go up against Judah and cut off Jerusalem and conquer it for ourselves and make the son of Tabeel king in it; therefore thus says the Lord GOD, It shall not stand, and it shall not come to pass'; and he continues, 'If you will not believe [*he'eminu*] you shall not be established [*te'amenu*]', using first the active and then the passive form of the verb *he'emin*. The NRSV renders it 'If you do not stand firm in faith, you shall not stand at all' in an attempt to capture the pun: the sense is that those who do not rely on God will not be held firm by him. One German commentator gives it as '*Haltet ihr nicht Stand, so habt ihr nicht Bestand*.'[11] What God will do to the nation corresponds in some way to what they do in relation to him: confidence in what is truly trustworthy is rewarded with solid assurance and preservation. In both halves of the verse, then, the verb is clearly to do with reliability, solidity, confidence, trustworthiness.

This is matched by a later oracle, found in Isaiah 28:16, where God says that he is laying a reliable foundation stone in Jerusalem, the city of David, with the inscription 'One who trusts/believes [*ma'amin*, the participle from *he'emin*] will not panic.' The individual, or by extension the nation, that is quietly confident will not be rocked by anxiety. This probably reflects the period in the 700s BCE, when Judah was faced with the much greater threat of the Assyrians themselves, who in 701 would actually invade and lay siege to Jerusalem. Against the frenzied diplomatic activity that went on in these years as the smaller Syro-Palestinian states tried to prop each other up and to get help from Egypt – the rival superpower to the west, though it proved an unstable and unsatisfactory ally – Isaiah again urged the then king, Hezekiah, and his counsellors to pursue a strategic neutrality, almost to the point of pacifism, and simply wait for God to act. We do not know in detail what the outcome actually was: the Assyrians seem to have extracted a large tribute from the Judaeans, but they did not sack Jerusalem, and there are (probably legendary) accounts of how they withdrew suddenly and unexpectedly. (This is the story behind Byron's poem 'The Destruction of Sennacherib', beginning 'The Assyrian came down like the wolf on the fold'; see 2 Kings 18–19 for the biblical account, which may contain duplications.) 'Belief' is here again equivalent to 'trust'.

Did Isaiah's call for 'faith', in the sense of trust and confidence, come out of the blue, or did it have a basis in older tradition?[12] Such appeals to have faith do not occur anywhere else in the Hebrew Bible. But some scholars have suggested that the call to trust in God had its original social context in the sorts of rousing speeches made by generals, or in ancient Israel perhaps by prophets or priests, before battles: what is referred to in German scholarship as a *Kriegsansprache*, a 'war address'. In Deuteronomy 20:3–4 we read, 'before you engage in battle, the priest shall come forward and speak to the troops, and shall say to them: "Hear, O Israel! Today you are drawing near to do battle against your enemies. Do not lose heart, or be afraid, or panic, or be in dread of them; for it is the LORD your God who goes with you, to fight for you against your enemies, to give you victory."' In terms of content, such speeches are the opposite of what Isaiah said, since he was warning against taking military action; but formally they are very similar, and they share the sense that confidence is justified because God is truly trustworthy.

There is in fact another tradition in the Hebrew Bible which is closer to Isaiah's oracles, and that is found in the story of the victory over the Egyptians at the Red Sea following the exodus. Here the people are told they will not need to fight at all, since God will destroy the Egyptians himself without human aid: 'Moses said to the people, "Do not be afraid, stand firm, and see the deliverance that the LORD will accomplish for you today; for the Egyptians whom you see today you shall never see again. The LORD will fight for you, and you have only to keep still"' (Exodus 14:13–14). This is more or less what Isaiah is urging in his own era.

We could look beyond the Hebrew Bible for other possible origins of Isaiah's form of prophetic speech, to royal oracles of salvation for the king in times of national danger in other nations in the ancient Near East. In one such oracle, delivered to Esarhaddon, the seventh-century Assyrian king, the goddess Ishtar tells him, 'For days to come and for eternal years I have established your throne beneath the heavens . . . Fear not, O king! I have not rejected you.' The oracle has its parallel in Genesis 15, which begins, 'The word of the LORD came to Abram in a vision, "Do not be afraid, Abram. I am your shield."' Isaiah might thus be using a form that assures Ahaz of the security of his throne and his dynasty, and telling him that he must have confidence in the power of the God who promises these things to bring them about.

However, neither of these ancient parallels is quite equivalent to Isaiah's message. Isaiah is not saying, in either crisis, that there is no *need* to fear; rather that deliverance is *conditional* on not fearing: 'if you will *not* believe, you will not be established'.[13] By doing nothing, Ahaz, or in the later Assyrian crisis Hezekiah, is to affirm that the initiative is God's, and that God can be trusted. This involves intense psychological activity, it might be said, but total abstention from any physical activity such as mobilizing an army or building defences. The German scholar Egon Pfeiffer summed up what 'faith' in this sense meant for Isaiah as follows:

> The defining mark of faith in the Old Testament is a reciprocal relationship between activity and passivity. Faith is passivity, in so far as the human person acknowledges that God achieves everything, and draws from this the appropriate conclusion . . . The active side is apparent in the sense of 'holding as secure' – the person relies on the security, faithfulness, and reliability of God, and lives accordingly.[14]

In principle 'living accordingly' could mean either engaging or not engaging in military activity, since one might say that such activity is acceptable provided it is undertaken in complete submission to the will of God. But in practice it is pretty clear that Isaiah thought faith – that is, adherence to the belief in a reliable and dependable God – actually ruled out taking political and military steps to safeguard Judaean independence.[15]

All this is fully confirmed by a third passage in Isaiah which does not use any word that could be translated as 'faith', but which in other respects clearly belongs alongside the two verses under discussion. We examined it in the previous section. Here again is Isaiah 30:15 (and 30:16):

> For thus said the Lord GOD, the Holy One of Israel:
> In returning and rest you shall be saved;
> > in quietness and in trust shall be your strength.
> But you refused and said,
> 'No! We will flee upon horses' –
> > therefore you shall flee!
> and, 'We will ride upon swift steeds' –
> > therefore your pursuers shall be swift!

This too refers to the period of alliances with Egypt, in which negotiation to secure military help had replaced, as Isaiah saw it, the real need, which was for 'quietness and trust'. He goes on in chapter 31 to condemn 'those who go down to Egypt for help and who rely on horses, who trust in chariots because they are many and in horsemen because they are very strong, but do not look to the Holy One of Israel or consult the LORD' (31:1). What is wrong with this is summed up very simply in verse 3: 'The Egyptians are human, and not God; their horses are flesh, and not spirit.' To trust in them is therefore to trust is what is not ultimately trustworthy. This, then, is also a chapter about faith in the sense that word bears in the thought-world of the Hebrew Bible: trust in what is faithful and reliable.[16]

So far we have seen that the word usually translated as 'believe', *he'emin*, has as its main meaning reliance on the reliable – for the writers of the Hebrew Bible, especially on God. Are there any places where faith in the sense of assent to certain propositions is meant? The verb *he'emin* is used in a perhaps slightly more intellectual sense in 2 Chronicles 20:20. This passage appears to depend on some of the material in Isaiah. Preparing for a battle against the Moabites and Ammonites in Transjordan, King Jehoshaphat of Judah, who reigned in the ninth century, is here portrayed as saying to his troops, 'Listen to me, O Judah and inhabitants of Jerusalem! Believe in the LORD your God and you will be established; believe his prophets.' 'Believe in the LORD' involves the kind of trust already discussed, but 'believe his prophets' seems to mean 'believe what his prophets tell you', and is thus closer to belief in the sense understood by Christians (and English-speakers more generally, I would argue) today.

A further possibility is Psalm 116:10, which literally appears to say 'I believed (*he'emanti*) and I said, "I am greatly afflicted"', translated by the NRSV as 'I kept my faith, even when I said, "I am greatly afflicted"', which is certainly a plausible rendering of an obscure verse. Following common emendations it could mean 'I believed that I would perish, and I said, "I am greatly afflicted"', in which case *he'emin* would have the sense of thinking something to be true. But that is it. These cases aside, I do not know of anywhere where the verb has a clearly intellectual sense.[17]

It is, in fact, hard to find anywhere in the Hebrew Bible where there

is much emphasis on what is believed to be the case as religiously important. So far as the language is concerned, *he'emin* as we have seen does
not really correspond to most uses of the English verb 'believe'. Is there
anything that does? The nearest is probably the expression 'to say in
one's heart', sometimes abbreviated simply to 'to say', which does have
roughly the same force as 'believe' in the sense of 'think to be the case'.
There are many instances of it in the Psalms. It is mostly, or perhaps even
exclusively, used when the belief in question is erroneous. The classic
example is Psalm 14 (of which Psalm 53 is a duplicate), which begins
'Fools say in their hearts, "There is no God."' The Psalm immediately
proceeds to the practical consequences of such an erroneous belief,
going on to mention what is nearly always in the Hebrew Bible taken to
be the result of dismissing God, namely moral misconduct: 'They are
corrupt, they do abominable deeds; there is no one who does good.'

Another example of false belief can be found in Isaiah 40:27, a passage reflecting on the despair of Judaeans after the exile of many to
Babylonia in the sixth century BCE:

> Why do you say, O Jacob,
>   and speak, O Israel,
> 'My way is hidden from the LORD,
>   and my right is disregarded by my God'?

The prophet goes on to reassure those who think this way that God is
in fact strong and willing to rescue them:

> Have you not known? Have you not heard?
> The LORD is the everlasting God,
>   the Creator of the ends of the earth.
> He does not faint or grow weary;
>   his understanding is unsearchable.
> He gives power to the faint,
>   and strengthens the powerless.

Thus what the audience believes about God is shown to be mistaken,
and they are encouraged to have 'faith' in much the same way as we
saw in the earlier chapters of the book of Isaiah, that is, to put their
trust in God. The Babylonian conquerors also hold erroneous beliefs,
as we read in chapter 47:7, where Babylon is addressed:

> You said, 'I shall be mistress for ever',
> so that you did not lay these things to heart
> or remember their end.

No doubt if it is wrong to 'say' false things 'in one's heart', then it is good to 'say' true things, that is, to have correct beliefs. But I know of no occasion where anyone in the Hebrew Bible is actually commended for 'saying in their heart' what is true. We thus have the rather peculiar situation that false belief is condemned but right belief is never explicitly praised, and can only be said to be commended by inference. This means that faith in the sense of right belief is little stressed as a virtue in the Hebrew Bible – a huge contrast with the New Testament. Of course there are various propositions about God that people in ancient Israel in various periods did in fact assent to: for example, that God is one, as is expressed in the nearest thing to a creed in the Hebrew Bible, the so-called Shema ('Hear, O Israel: The LORD is our God, the LORD alone . . .') in Deuteronomy 6:4–9; or that God guided the people of Israel from Egypt into the Promised Land; or that it is God who gives fertility and prosperity. But there does not seem to be any great premium placed on overtly affirming these things or making declarations about them. A possible exception is what Gerhard von Rad in the middle of the last century referred to as the 'cultic credo' in Deuteronomy 26, where we read:

> When you have come into the land that the LORD your God is giving you as an inheritance to possess, and you possess it, and settle in it, you shall take some of the first of all the fruit of the ground, which you harvest from the land that the LORD your God is giving you, and you shall put it in a basket and go to the place that the LORD your God will choose as a dwelling for his name. You shall go to the priest who is in office at that time, and say to him, 'Today I declare to the LORD your God that I have come into the land that the LORD swore to our ancestors to give us.' When the priest takes the basket from your hand and sets it down before the altar of the LORD your God, you shall make this response before the LORD your God: 'A wandering Aramean was my ancestor; he went down into Egypt and lived there as an alien, few in number, and there he became a great nation, mighty and populous. When the Egyptians treated us harshly and afflicted us, by imposing hard labour

on us, we cried to the LORD, the God of our ancestors; the LORD heard our voice and saw our affliction, our toil, and our oppression. The LORD brought us out of Egypt with a mighty hand and an outstretched arm, with a terrifying display of power, and with signs and wonders; and he brought us into this place and gave us this land, a land flowing with milk and honey. So now I bring the first of the fruit of the ground that you, O LORD, have given me.' (Deuteronomy 26:1–10)

This can be called a declaration of faith. But it is isolated in the Hebrew Bible and far from characteristic of what we might think of as its culture. Overall, it seems that faith, in the senses in which we usually use the term today, is not very important in the Hebrew Bible. Right action is much more important than right thought, and though wrong thought is often condemned, this is precisely because it can lead to wrong action. Belief in the sense of trust is certainly much stressed, and Isaiah is a central witness to this, as are the Psalms: 'Trust in the LORD, and do good; so you will live in the land, and enjoy security', says Psalm 37:3. But belief in the sense of intellectual affirmation of certain theological propositions is essentially absent – to that extent the clichéd contrast between Christian orthodoxy and Jewish orthopraxy, whether or not it reveals anything of the difference between the two religions nowadays, does speak to a contrast between the Old Testament and the New. There is little in the Hebrew Bible that corresponds to Paul's dictum, 'if you confess with your lips that Jesus is Lord and believe in your heart that God raised him from the dead, you will be saved' (Romans 10:9) – not only because 'salvation' in the sense of an individual eternal destiny is mostly missing from the Hebrew Bible, but also because credal affirmation is a very low priority within it. To return to our starting point: justification by faith in the Lutheran and even in the Pauline sense is not really affirmed in the Old Testament, and certainly not in the two passages where Christians are most apt to find it, Genesis 15 and Habakkuk 2.

This should presumably make us wary of using the words 'faith' and 'belief', and their related verbs, in translating the Hebrew Bible. Robert Alter renders Isaiah 7:9 'If you trust not, you shall not hold firm'; Isaiah 28:16 'he who trusts shall have nothing to fear'; and Habakkuk 2:4 'the righteous man lives through his faithfulness'. These are all valid and indeed valuable correctives to the traditional translations that use 'faith' and 'believe' with an implication of intellectual assent. They might alert us too to the possibility that 'faith' in the New Testament may at least sometimes mean faithfulness rather than the assent of mind and heart, though the intellectual sense is much more prevalent there. The classic place is the Letter to the Hebrews, which stresses that faith involves right belief: 'without faith it is impossible to please God, for whoever would approach him must believe that he exists and that he rewards those who seek him' (Hebrews 11:6). The element of trust is not lacking, but the stress falls on having a right belief. The two Testaments are clearly divided on this issue.[18]

We have taken three words, or semantic areas, from many possibilities, to indicate how biblical translation requires a knowledge not only of the biblical languages but also of the intellectual milieu in which they were used. Sometimes an obvious equivalent in English (or whichever language is the target) does justice to the source text, as is the case, in my view, with the word 'soul' in many occurrences of *nephesh* in Hebrew and of *psyche* in Greek. At other times, as is true with words commonly translated 'faith' or 'believe', the correspondence is more inexact: 'believe' in the Hebrew Bible seldom means 'hold to be the case' and more often 'have faith in'. In the New Testament both senses occur with the Greek verb *pisteuo* and the noun *pistis*. 'Salvation' is arguably a distorting rendering of Hebrew *yeshu'ah* and at least sometimes of Greek *soteria*, as there is a development from a reference to earthly opponents, from whom the Psalmist particularly asks to be 'rescued' – 'saved' in that sense – to a belief in an otherworldly or more cosmic deliverance, from sin or death, for which the word 'salvation' is normal in Christian discourse.

Translators need to know the whole context of the texts they are translating, and cannot proceed in any wooden or purely formal way. Sometimes, as the discussion of 'faith' in particular has shown, this may involve deep immersion in the history and social setting within which words were used in the various cultures represented in the Hebrew Bible and the New Testament, where they overlap as well as where they starkly diverge. Biblical translation is in this respect no different from translation of any other ancient text: the rendering needs to rest on historical and cultural as well as lexical knowledge.

So much should be obvious to any experienced translator today. But applying this lens to the Bible also throws up broader challenges, particularly for Christians, though ones which help us to understand the relation of the Bible to the two faiths that claim it as their own. Some of the most profound and influential theological developments in Christianity seemingly hinge on what could be labelled mistranslations or misunderstandings. Habakkuk 2:4 originally meant approximately the opposite of what Paul and Luther thought it did. If the validity of a theological position is assumed (as many might think) to depend on a historically informed reading of Scripture, then the doctrine of justification by faith lacks a secure foundation. Perhaps the problem lies with that assumption, then, and the expectation that this scriptural quotation was not merely illustrative of some truth or a stimulus to the thinking of both men but rather literally and simply determinative of it. The Bible is so complex, and contains so many conflicting voices, that a claim to propound its teaching is always selective. Paul and Luther alighted on a text that was not intended to mean what they made of it; and that is fatal if we believe that all doctrine must derive unequivocally from Scripture. But not, I think, if we recognize that the Christian faith is only partly biblical. There are texts in the Bible that conflict with some Christian teaching, and conversely some Christian beliefs that find only a tenuous support from Scripture. Justification by faith is a theological claim rooted in the interpretation of the nature and message of the Christian gospel in its totality, and neither stands nor falls by the meaning of Habakkuk 2:4, even if that text – interpreted entirely against its original meaning – provided some impetus for it. The Bible and the faiths it feeds are not identical, though the disparity is seldom quite so stark as here. The apparently small question of how the Hebrew word '*emunah* should be translated thus provides a window on to some of the most significant themes in Christianity, and ultimately on to Christian understanding of the nature and authority of the Bible.

It illuminates too the frequent lack of consonance between the Hebrew Bible and the New Testament. Some scholars have been keen to insist that the latter, though written in Greek in the first century CE for a largely non-Jewish Christian readership, is somehow of one mind with the Hebrew Bible, thinking 'Hebrew' thoughts and sharing the same mindset as authors operating in another language family and at many centuries' remove. This is convenient for anyone wishing to treat the Bible as a single unified whole, with consistent thought-forms throughout. We have seen, however, that this is far from true. The words translated 'salvation' in Hebrew and Greek respectively have very different meanings, and modern translations sometimes succeed in registering this discrepancy, as can be seen in Robert Alter's renderings. Biblical concordances, especially if working exclusively with an English version and not attending to the original languages, easily create the misleading impression that the Hebrew Bible and the New Testament use the same words. They don't. What is more, as we saw with words translated 'soul', neither Testament is always internally consistent in its use of terms, since both are made up of many books written over a long period. This is particularly true of the Hebrew Bible, whose latest books can share concepts with the New Testament rather than with older ones. In Daniel, for example, salvation includes individual resurrection just as in the New Testament, but this isn't true for most of the other books of the Hebrew Bible.

The diversity and lack of coherence in the Bible, and even within its constituent parts, has been one of the fundamental findings of the critical approach to Scripture that was spearheaded by the Enlightenment, and which held sway for several centuries among biblical specialists in Europe. Times have changed, though, and more recently some have made a new case for unity, seeing the biblical books as joined together by just the kind of linkages – and hence consistency of meaning across times and cultures – that critical study has long denied. The next chapter takes this up – and the challenge it poses to the thesis just put forward.

8

The Bible as a Web

LEITWORT AND TYPE SCENE

The operas of Richard Wagner (1813–83) are marked by frequent use of the *Leitmotiv*, a musical phrase that designates a particular character or situation and recalls it to the audience's mind each time it recurs. The *Leitmotiv* is usually very short – just a few notes – but distinctive enough to be unmistakable. When we hear it we think immediately, 'Ah, Siegfried.'

The German writer Thomas Mann (1875–1955) adopted the idea of the *Leitmotiv* in some of his fiction. Thus in his novella *Tonio Kröger* there is a recurring phrase, 'we aren't gypsies in a caravan', which recalls the bourgeois background of the protagonist and his respectable family. The *Leitmotiv* is a device that imparts structure to the story and marks out a recurring theme. It also memorably features in Mann's great reworking of the biblical story of Joseph and his eleven brothers.[1]

Martin Buber and Franz Rosenzweig proposed that the Hebrew Bible uses such a method to knit together its narrative. They referred to the existence of the *Leitwort*, 'guiding word', in the text. Much as with a *Leitmotiv*, a *Leitwort* calls to mind earlier incidents or conversations in the text, and often helps to indicate that texts suspected of being assembled from fragments or from diverse sources do in fact cohere. Buber wrote: 'By *Leitwort* I understand a word or word root that is meaningfully repeated within a text or sequence of texts or complex of texts; those who attend to these repetitions will find a meaning of the text revealed or clarified, or at any rate made more emphatic.'[2]

An example[3] is the Hebrew expression *lekh lekha*, 'take yourself off' or simply 'go' – literally in Hebrew 'go for yourself' – which occurs twice in the story of Abraham in Genesis (Genesis 12:1 and 22:2), but is otherwise very rare in the Hebrew Bible and appears nowhere else in the Pentateuch. The first occurrence marks Abraham's call to go out from his homeland to the land of Israel, the second to go to Mount Moriah and there sacrifice his beloved son, Isaac – the two most momentous events in Abraham's life. Because we have registered the strange expression *lekh lekha* at the beginning of the story, we notice it when it occurs again in Genesis 22 and expect that something equally important is about to happen, as indeed it then does. Abraham is a man with a mission: how ironic, then, that the mission seems to lead to the death of his much-loved son. As we know, the story ends happily with Isaac saved, but this little Hebrew phrase alerts us, by its unusual character, that we are about to encounter some major event. Buber and Rosenzweig accordingly translate the *Leitwort* in the same way in both places, as *Geh vor dich hin* – roughly 'Go on before yourself'.

Everett Fox picks out the theme of *seeing* in the Abraham story as described in Buber's essay 'Abraham the Seer'. Abraham is promised all the land that he will see (Genesis 12:1), God is seen by him (12:7), and he is again told he will possess the land he sees (13:15). His concubine Hagar addresses a 'God of Seeing' (16:13), and finally in Genesis 22, the 'Binding of Isaac', God will 'see to' providing a sacrificial lamb, and Abraham sees the ram that will substitute for Isaac, and is seen by God. The place is therefore called 'YHWH will see', that is, provide. This is a typical *Leitwort* principle at work in the text.

The *Leitwort* can be illustrated from a much more complex example. Generations of Bible readers have been puzzled by Genesis 38, the story of Judah and Tamar, which looks like an interpolation in the story of Joseph. The account of Joseph's adventures otherwise runs continuously from Genesis 37 to 50, and is a remarkably coherent tale. In chapter 37, Joseph's envious brothers abandon him to be taken to Egypt by a passing troop of foreigners, but tell Jacob, their father, that a wild animal has eaten him, producing his long-sleeved robe (the KJV's 'coat of many colours') stained with goat's blood as evidence. The story resumes in chapter 39 with Joseph's deeds in Egypt. But in chapter 38 we have what seems a wholly unconnected story about Joseph's brother Judah, who has a daughter-in-law twice over, Tamar. After the death of her two husbands, Er and Onan, Judah promises to give Tamar another of his sons as a husband, but fails to do so. So Tamar contrives to sleep with Judah himself, disguising herself as a prostitute, and extracts from him a staff, a signet ring and a cord by way of a pledge that he will send her a baby goat in payment. When she becomes pregnant and he is about to have her executed for adultery, she produces the pledges and he recognizes that he is the one to blame.

What has this to do with the story of Joseph? Apparently nothing – though it is worth noting that what we think of as 'the Joseph story' is in fact described in Genesis itself (37:2) as 'the story of the family of Jacob'. But Robert Alter has argued, following rabbinic comments in the fifth-century CE Great Midrash on Genesis (*Bereshith rabbah* 84:19), that the two stories are stitched together through the common theme of recognition: Jacob's recognition of the robe as evidence of his son's death, and Judah's recognition of the pledges as evidence of his own guilt. 'Recognize', a legal term rather than a causal one, is the *Leitwort* binding the stories together. Genesis 38 not only allows a pause in the account of Joseph in Egypt, but also illustrates the same theme; and the verb should therefore be translated in the same way in both places, as against, for example, the NRSV, which has 'recognize' in the first occurrence (Genesis 37:33) and 'acknowledge' in the second (Genesis 38:26).

Here the principle of the *Leitwort* has potentially wide-ranging significance not only for translation but also for theories about the origins of the text, as we shall see. First, though, it is worth asking what we are actually asserting by saying that Genesis 12 and 22, or 37 and 38, are 'linked' by a *Leitwort*. There are three main possibilities, which the apparently innocent question of how the text should be translated forces us to consider. Two will concern us in this section, the third in the next.

The most obvious explanation of these overlaps in vocabulary and theme is that there are distinct authors at work here, and one was familiar with the work of the other and quoting from or at least alluding to it. We could imagine that the author of Genesis 38 had read Genesis 37, perhaps in an earlier version of the Joseph story, and decided to insert the story of Judah and Tamar before chapter 39 because it was clear that the theme of legal recognition was central to both tales. Similarly the Genesis 22 writer knew about the command to Abraham to 'take himself off' to Canaan, and told the story of the near-sacrifice of Isaac in such a way that the reader would recall that first momentous event in Abraham's life.

This would be of a piece with a general tendency of later biblical authors to allude to or quote earlier ones. Similar activity is very obviously going on all over the New Testament. Paul, for one, quotes extensively from the Old Testament Scriptures: see, for example, Romans 9–11, where there is a string of references to passages about the salvation of the Gentiles, as Paul interprets them.

But even within the Hebrew Bible itself there are clear cross-references. Sometimes they are obvious and explicit, as with the reference in Daniel 9:2 to the prophecy 'in the books' by the prophet Jeremiah that the exile would last seventy years, reinterpreted to mean seventy 'weeks of years', that is, 490 years. Thus also Joel 3:10, 'Beat your ploughshares into swords, and your pruning-hooks into spears', surely refers to, and reverses, Isaiah 2:4, 'they shall beat their swords into ploughshares, and their spears into pruning-hooks'. There are now many studies of such inner-biblical cross-references.[4] We may make a distinction between direct quotation and allusion, but in either case the translator is likely to want to show recognition of the phenomenon. I suggested in Chapter 5 that the book of Revelation might be translated in a slightly archaizing style, as also the first two chapters of Luke, and this would mark our recognition that both works allude to (while seldom actually quoting) many Old Testament passages.

So much for conscious reference to one text by the author of another. There can also be unconscious echoes, where the author is subliminally influenced by another text without necessarily being aware of this. An extended example of this might be Romans 1:18–32. Here Paul argues that sin follows a certain pattern. First, individuals cease to acknowledge God, even though he can be recognized from the evidence of the created world. Secondly, they start to worship idols instead, lifeless images of things created by God, from animals and birds to human beings. Thirdly, they then start to commit sexual sins. And fourthly, they fall into every other type of sin, of which Paul produces an exhaustive list (Romans 1:29–31). Now this passage may be entirely of Paul's making, but it bears a strong resemblance to Wisdom of Solomon 13–14 (one of the deuterocanonical or apocryphal books, which Paul almost certainly knew). This follows essentially the same sequence, and it is reasonable to think that it was in the back of Paul's mind, even though he does not quote it. In the same way, the author of Genesis 22 might have recalled *lekh-lekha* from Genesis 12 without referring to it consciously or deliberately.

These two possibilities, an author's conscious or unconscious use of one passage in another, are easily comprehensible and present no particular problems for any reader, on the contrary deepening our understanding of the text. We have been talking, however, as though passages occurring later in the book of Genesis must depend on ones appearing earlier, and with a book written in linear fashion by a single author, in the way a modern writer would probably work, this would be a fair assumption. But this is not necessarily the case with biblical texts. Genesis 12 and 22 are reckoned by many scholars to come from different underlying sources, and the relative dates of these is undetermined. Genesis 22 could well be earlier than Genesis 12 in origin. In any case they are almost certainly not from the same hand – there is no one 'author' of Genesis. Similarly Genesis 37 and 38 could be from different authors, joined together as we know them by a 'redactor' or editor in antiquity. In this case the rather deliberate parallel between the two 'recognition' scenes might count against the likelihood of dual authorship, but it would still be possible to think of the two scenes as in origin separate cases of a similar *type* of story, which we might call 'legal acknowledgement of an unwelcome fact'. Robert Alter has similarly argued that the Bible contains a number of what he calls 'type scenes' that display a similar pattern: in this he is drawing on a familiar category from the study of Homer. One clear example is the 'meeting at a well', found in Genesis 24, Genesis 29, Exodus 2 and, in the New Testament, John 4. The three Hebrew Bible examples lead to a betrothal. Type scenes include 'the annunciation . . . of the birth of the hero to his barren mother; the encounter with the future betrothed at a well; the epiphany in the field; the initiatory trial; danger in the desert and the discovery of a well or other source of sustenance; the testament of the dying hero'.[5]

Now, Alter conspicuously does not argue that the author of one of these type scenes was familiar with the others, in the sense that there is either conscious or even unconscious allusion. It cannot be shown that Exodus 2 depends on Genesis 24, or indeed vice versa, on the literary level. Alter's point is not about compositional practice or technique, but about a relationship objectively existing between several texts irrespective of their authors' intentions or designs. Whatever was meant, or even subconsciously assumed, by the authors, there is an observable parallel among these type scenes. This raises the possibility that texts can interconnect unbidden, even by chance. And that gets us into theories of intertextuality, a third way of understanding cross-referencing among texts on the *Leitwort* or type-scene level.

INTERTEXTUALITY

Intertextuality is a theory about the interrelation of texts and, indeed, all cultural products, including works of art and music. The term appears to have been coined by Julia Kristeva (b. 1941), a Bulgarian scholar and critic working in Paris, developing insights of Mikhail Bakhtin (1895–1975) in innovative ways in the 1960s and 1970s.[6] The theory was extended further by Roland Barthes and Jacques Derrida. As it has entered the lexicon of poststructuralist discourse, intertextuality is an idea about the interrelationship of *all* texts – not simply of certain specific texts – which are seen as forming an interlocking mesh or web. As Kristeva put it, describing one of Bakhtin's ideas, it is a 'conception of the "literary word" as an *intersection of textual surfaces* rather than a *point* (a fixed meaning), as a dialogue among several writings'.[7] Or again, 'in the space of a given text, several utterances, taken from other texts, intersect and neutralize one another'.[8] The task of the philosopher of intertextuality is not to reconstruct the 'intertexts' – the texts on which a given text draws – except as illustrating the truth of these definitions. The task, rather, is to reflect on what the whole concept implies about human culture in general.[9]

The theory essentially states that all texts form an interconnecting web, so that anyone writing something supposedly new is in fact simply adding one more element to what is already there; and, conversely, the meaning of what they write is determined by its place in the web, not by their intention or the decisions of the reader. Thus Kristeva 'defines intertextuality as the sum of knowledge that makes it possible for texts to have meaning'.[10] Reality is a '*texte générale*'. This is not far in practice from the proposal by Harold Bloom, from the (apparently) vastly different American critical tradition, to the effect there are no texts, only relations between texts.[11] There are also strange affinities with T. S. Eliot's theory that the literary works in a 'canon' form an order among themselves, and when a new (important) work is written, it both derives its meaning from the rest of the canon and yet changes the overall meaning of that canon.[12] Except that in Kristeva's theory there is no question of 'great' works, as there was for Eliot (and is for Bloom). In Kristeva, the matter is understood much more democratically, and the 'intertexts' of any given piece of writing reach beyond the world of 'high' literature to encompass all the products of human culture, with all the texts ever written and all the social conventions ever established. Bloom thinks that major writers rebel against their own 'belatedness',[13] which supposes that authors have intentions when they write, in a very pre-postmodern way. Yet he goes on, in an idiom closer to Kristeva, 'belatedness seems to me not a historical condition at all, but one that belongs to the literary situation as such'. This leads him at once to mention Jorge Luis Borges, who observed, paradoxically, but from this point of view truly, that writers 'create their own predecessors'.[14]

The only role of biblical study within the framework of a theory of intertextuality would be to provide examples of how texts interconnect. Biblical scholars, however, have been attracted by intertextuality not as a name for a literary and cultural theory but as a possible *technique* for identifying the dependence of one text on another – strictly speaking, a misreading of Kristeva's point. Thus Alter's idea that the biblical text includes type scenes which by their resemblance interact with each other can be described, in a loose use of the term, as an intertextual interpretation. What matters here is that it does not imply that any author intended the parallels among the different type scenes. The stories of the meeting at the well, for example, do not need to be arranged in chronological order so that we can decide which depends on which. They are interrelated simply by appearing in the same Bible, and features of one can illuminate the others. This is an example of 'the death of the author', as articulated by Roland Barthes. Once the text is written, its meaning and interpretation no longer depend on its author, but are determined simply by its place in the web of other writings.

As one biblical scholar writes, 'To the Bible scholar, intertextuality is nothing new . . . The way in which Jewish works of the Second Temple period and the New Testament used the Old Testament forced exegetes to address the issue of intertextuality long before this post-modern shibboleth was created.'[15] Indeed, as another comments, the third-century Origen is a pre-eminent example of a scholar in whose work 'scripture is interpreted by scripture',[16] and this to many seems a clear case of intertextuality – reading one text in the light of another. In biblical studies today the term is widely used to cover all cases of interrelation between texts in the Bible, and hence to include what has more traditionally been referred to as 'Scripture citing Scripture', 'inner-biblical interpretation' and the 'reception' of earlier biblical texts in later ones. Though the term is certainly seen by some scholars as modish, its use is now widespread, and attractive to many biblical specialists. Important contributions were made as early as the 1980s, particularly in the work of Richard B. Hays[17] on Paul, and others have picked up where he left off.[18] A working definition of intertextuality in the sense most biblical specialists have adopted is provided by Peter D. Miscall: ' "Intertextuality" is a covering term for all the possible relations that can be established between texts.'[19] This is by no means what the term meant when Kristeva first introduced it into literary theory, but it is what many biblical specialists have come to understand by it.

The implication of this for translators is that parallels among similar texts exist even if they are not interrelated through actual influence in one or other direction, and that these have meaning. They are part, as it were, of the grammar of the biblical narrative, and should be so presented. This in turn implies something about the nature of the Bible as a whole, which sees the finished form as transcending the individual parts and cohering at a supra-literary level, and it leads to our next topic.

THE BIBLE AS A SINGLE WHOLE

The kind of reading championed by Alter means that Bible-reading starts to look rather like what in Jewish Studies would be called mid-rashic interpretation. A *midrash* (plural *midrashim*) is a sequential commentary on a given biblical book, and a number of midrashim have come down from late antiquity and the Middle Ages. Their most salient characteristic is the way they combine passages and words from all over the Hebrew Bible without any attention to the dates of the different biblical books being drawn on, or to their differences of genre. Any verse, sentence, phrase or even individual word in the Bible can illuminate any other. To put it in Kristevan terms, any text is an intertext for any other text, without any concern for its origins or original meaning. The Bible is seen as a tissue of interconnected sayings and ideas, in which chronological order matters not at all. Here are some examples from the *Mekhilta de-Rabbi Ishmael*, a third-century CE work which comments on the first half of the book of Exodus:

> 'It came to pass in the morning watch' (Exodus 14:24)
> You find that the prayers of the righteous are heard in the morning. Whence do we know about Abraham's morning? It is said: And Abraham arose early in the morning [Genesis 22:3; other examples taken from the past follow] ... Whence do we know about the mornings of the prophets destined to arise in the future? It is said: O Lord, in the morning thou shalt hear my voice; in the morning will I order my prayer unto thee, and will look forward [Psalm 5:3; other examples follow from passages taken to be predictions]. Whence do we know about the mornings of the world in general? It is said: They are new every morning; great is thy faithfulness [Lamentations 3:23].

Alter's readings could be called mildly midrashic in this sense, seeing parallels and interrelations between the different biblical texts, read as if they were all contemporary with each other. He is not at all unaware of historical developments and the work of the biblical authors, but he tends to resist 'archaeological' work on the text that delves down to find its supposedly original form and looks for different strata within the Bible. He is more interested in the surface similarities among diverse parts of Scripture. He treats the Hebrew Bible as in that sense a single document, with an interrelation between all its parts. It is rather as though, while recognizing that the corpus of Shakespeare's plays is full of diversity and variety, we were nevertheless to look for connecting themes and turns of phrase across the whole, and to be quite prepared to quote later plays as though they were a point of cross-reference for earlier ones.

All this implies that the Bible is a single whole – which is what most people think anyway, if they have never undertaken any critical study of it. But this 'pre-critical' conception of Scripture here returns in a 'post-critical' form, as what Paul Ricoeur called a 'second naïveté'. It was an attitude that was shared by many students of the Bible well before the theory of intertextuality. Buber and Rosenzweig explicitly espoused it:

> The historicist vision discovers both in the book as written and in the book as read a multiplicity of centuries, of writers, of readers. The vision that seeks to regard the book, not from outside, but in inward related-ness and belonging, will find the unity of the book as written and the unity of the book as read equally evident.[20]

> The Bible seeks to be read as One Book, so that no one of its parts remains self-contained; rather every part is held open to every other.[21]

Buber and Rosenzweig often characterize the biblical editor or redac-tor, generally referred to as 'R', as *rabbenu*, Hebrew for 'our teacher', because it is at the final redactional level – the one we possess – that the Bible communicates its message. Alter sums the matter up so far as the Pentateuch is concerned:

> The Torah is manifestly a composite construction, but there is abun-dant evidence throughout the Hebrew Bible that composite work was fundamental to the very conception of what literature was, that a pro-cess akin to collage was assumed to be one of the chief ways in which literary texts were put together. What we have, then, in the Five Books is a work assembled by many hands, reflecting several different view-points, and representing literary activity that spanned several centuries. *The redacted whole nevertheless creates some sense of continuity and development, and it allows itself to be read as a forward-moving pro-cess through time and theme from book to book, yielding an overarching literary structure we can call, in a singular version of the title, the Torah.* The Torah exhibits seams, fissures, and inner tensions that cannot be ignored, but it has also been artfully assembled through the ancient editorial process to cohere strongly as the foundational text of Israel-ite life and the cornerstone of the biblical canon.[22]

This sense of the unity of the Bible underlies much translation. Arguably it is an attitude that can be found in the attempt of the Revised Version in the 1880s to use the same English word for the same Hebrew or Greek one, thereby treating the Bible as if it were a single self-consistent text. Translators are not alone in this. On the whole it is only biblical scholars who seriously treat the Bible as a collection of disparate books: most readers, religious or not, think that one part can indeed illuminate others, in a somewhat midrashic, non-historical way. Hence the popularity of biblical concordances, which list every occurrence of a given word and thus enable readers to criss-cross the text without paying any attention to the particularities of the different books in which the words appear. The historical approach to translation commended in the previous chapter – in which each text is seen as an individual work that may bear witness to a different stage in the development of biblical language and literature – is radically incompatible with this way of proceeding. Formal-equivalence translations tend in the direction just outlined: we have already seen that John Goldingay follows the principle of using the same word for at least technical theological terms throughout the Hebrew Bible in *The Old Testament for Everyone*. His translation presupposes that the Hebrew Bible is essentially a single text.

The KJV deliberately does not use the same word for the same word:

> Wee have not tyed our selves to an uniformitie of phrasing, or to an identitie of words, as some peradventure would wish that we had done, because they observe, that some learned men some where, have been as exact as they could that way . . . But, that we should expresse the same notion in the same particular word; as for example, if we translate the Hebrew or Greeke word once by Purpose, never to call it Intent; if one where Journeying, never Traveiling; if one where Thinke, never Suppose; if one where Paine, never Ache; if one where Joy, never Gladnesse, &c. Thus to minse the matter, wee thought to savour more of curiositie then wisedome, and that rather it would breed scorne in the Atheist, then bring profite to the godly Reader. For is the kingdome of God become words or syllables? why should wee be in bondage to them if we may be free, use one precisely when wee may use another no lesse fit, as commodiously?

The translators even argue wittily that they are giving many words their due by including them in the translation of the Bible, almost as if they were people:

> If wee should say, as it were, unto certaine words, Stand up higher, have a place in the Bible alwayes, and to others of like qualitie, Get ye hence, be banished for ever, wee might be taxed peradventure with S. James his words, namely, To be partiall in our selves and judges of evill thoughts.[23]

Underlying the approach to translation that leads to uniformity of phrasing is a particular theological understanding of the Bible as a single and unified Scripture for the Jewish and/or Christian community. This idea is spelt out in great detail in the work of Brevard S. Childs, a twentieth-century biblical scholar in the USA, and of those who have broadly followed in his footsteps such as the British scholar R. W. L. Moberly and the American Christopher R. Seitz. Each has his own nuance, but they and a good many other Old Testament scholars agree in seeing the Bible as a unified canon within the practice of Jews and Christians, and indeed go beyond the Hebrew Bible to include the New Testament within this overarching structure. Childs sums the matter up as follows:

> The modern theological function of canon lies in its affirmation that the authoritative norm lies in the literature itself as it has been treasured, transmitted and transformed ... The term canon points to the received, collected, and interpreted material of the church and thus establishes the theological context in which the tradition continues to function authoritatively for today.[24]

This is approximately what Christians have traditionally believed about the Bible. It is the reason why inconsistencies between or within biblical books have presented such a problem to believers, and why they have often looked for ways to reconcile them. Take the parade example of the two different accounts of creation, in Genesis 1:1–2:3 and Genesis 2:4b–25. They envisage many differences in the order of the events, for example, whether man and woman are created together after the animals (Genesis 1:26–8) or the man is created first, then the animals, and then the woman (Genesis 2:15–24). Much ink has been spilt arguing that the two accounts are really compatible, and the motive behind this is usually the conviction that the Bible is one, and must therefore speak with a single voice. The scholars just mentioned are not so unsophisticated as to deny the existence of incompatible doublets such as this within the Bible, but they do think that it possesses a unity that transcends them.

A more 'critical' way of thinking about inconsistencies accepts that they may be real, not to be explained away or smoothed out. It is the acceptance that inconsistencies really are present in the biblical text that led, among other things, to the hypothesis that the Pentateuch is the product of weaving together four originally independent 'sources' (conventionally labelled J, E, D and P).[25] Whether this picture is partly or wholly true, if we accept that there are inconsistencies, these need to be reflected in translation. For example, one strand in Genesis speaks of 'establishing' a covenant, and another of 'cutting' a covenant, and this difference needs to be registered by the translator. It is arguable that any translation, and especially a formal-equivalence one, needs to be sensitive to these stylistic differences and not iron them out so that they become invisible to the readers who know no biblical languages, which is nearly all of them. There will be more to say about 'critical' hypotheses and how they might affect translation in the next chapter.

My present purpose, however, is not to adjudicate between a critical and a unitary reading of the Bible, but simply to point out how much this issue is intertwined with the way the text is translated. The translation of the text as a unity, by always using the same word in English for the same word in Hebrew or Greek, tends to reinforce the idea that the Bible is all of a piece; whereas differentiation between different passages and attention to the immediate context of a sentence, even though it seems incompatible with one elsewhere in the Bible, stresses the diversity and tension within the text. For the latter approach, not every word that occurs in more places than one is necessarily a *Leitwort*, and the Bible is not a web of intertextual relationships but rather a library of books, differing greatly in their subject and form.

It is worth noting in passing that the functional/formal equivalence distinction does not correlate exactly with this contrast. Formal equivalence may help to underpin a holistic view of the Bible by using the same word for the same word, but it may also, as we have just seen, emphasize the diversity within the text by insisting on mirroring the variation of words in the Hebrew and Greek even when this points away from any overall unity. Functional equivalence may similarly coexist either with a tendency to read the text as a coherent whole, or with a desire to capture the individual flavour of this or that book as a single work in its own right. The RV and KJV shared the same holistic view of the text, yet pursued different approaches, with the KJV varying words even when the same Hebrew or Greek word occurred – to that extent looking for functional equivalence – while the RV tried to keep the same word and thus had a formal-equivalence approach. This is a reminder that the formal/functional contrast is not the only significant difference between biblical translations.

Though it is felt most keenly in Christianity, the question of the unity of the Bible is a major theological issue for both the religions that hold it sacred, as well as for individual believers, and styles of translation both reflect and contribute to it.[26] An emphasis on intertextuality tends on the whole to support the idea that the Bible is a single work, however complex and variegated, and encourages translations that facilitate cross-reference and a holistic reading. Treating the Bible as a web of interconnections hangs together with many assumptions shared by most religious readers. Though, as we have seen, the idea of intertextuality developed in the often aggressively secular environment of literary theory, it has been attractive to many in the faith traditions of both Judaism and Christianity because it is so readily compatible with a belief that the Bible has a God-given unity. Many believers strongly wish to see the Bible as more than a mere collection of disparate books. They hold that, however it may have been compiled, it now forms a single work, since it is divinely given and God cannot be the source of contradiction. This belief can influence translators, leading them to reconcile conflicts and disagreements between different books, or within them. Equally, translations can in turn encourage readers to overlook such problems, and thus promote the sense that the Bible is a unity. Few readers, including translators, approach the Bible without expectations about its religious value: most want it to be self-consistent, so that it will support and nourish faith more effectively. Translation may seem a religiously neutral activity, but in reality it is one – and not the least significant – arena in which thinking about the status of the Bible is worked out.

9

Translation and Biblical Criticism

Translators are in general expected to render the text that lies before them, not to change it. But in the case of the Bible, matters are not so simple. The Bible exists in many divergent manuscripts, so that translators must decide which to follow, and the text can sometimes be uneven, with hints of underlying complexities in its composition that show through in the original wording and may need to be reflected in the translation. In this chapter we look at four examples of these complications.

1 SAMUEL 13:1

Saul was one year old when he became king, and he reigned for two years over Israel.

So runs the Hebrew text of 1 Samuel 13:1, in my literal translation. Considering that much of 1 Samuel relates Saul's military exploits, marriage and extensive issue, there is surely something wrong here. The King James Version ingeniously translates it 'Saul reigned one year; and when he had reigned two years . . . ', but that is not what the Hebrew says. (Goldingay similarly renders 'Sha'ul had been one year reigning and he reigned two years over Yisra'el.') Nor does it say, as the New English Bible renders it, 'Saul was fifty years old when he became king, and he reigned over Israel for twenty-two years', with a footnote indicating that these are 'probable readings' while not citing any evidence. The Revised English Bible changed this to 'Saul was thirty years old when he became king, and he reigned over Israel for twenty-two years', citing 'some Greek manuscripts' (unspecified) for 'thirty' and again describing 'twenty-two' as 'probable reading'. In the Revised New Jerusalem Bible, we find 'Saul was ... years old when he became king, and reigned over Israel for ... and two years', with a footnote: 'The Hebr. has "Saul was one year old ... and reigned over Israel for two years", which is absurd; the true figures have been lost.' The New Revised Standard Version has 'Saul was ... years old when he began to reign; and he reigned for ... and two years over Israel', noting that in the case of 'one' 'The number is lacking in the Heb text (the verse is lacking in the Septuagint)', and in the case of 'two' '*Two* is not the entire number; something has dropped out.' The Good News Bible translates speculatively 'Saul was thirty years old when he became king, and he ruled over Israel for forty-two years' – 'forty-two' is based on the evidence of Acts 13:21, which says that Saul ruled for forty years. Finally, the Jewish Publication Society's Tanakh says 'Saul was ... years old when he began to reign, and he reigned two years over Israel', avoiding the absurdity of Saul's ruling as a baby but leaving 'two years' as it is, even though the events described in the Bible imply a considerably longer reign.

Alter explains what may be going on here: 'The Masoretic Text, notoriously defective at this point, says "Saul was a year old ... and two years he reigned." This whole sentence is absent from the Septuagint, leading one to suspect that the redactor here stitched into the narrative a textual fragment in which there were lacunae in the numbers that he did not presume to fill in.'[1]

It is a small matter, of little concern to all but a few. It raises at a microcosmic level a major issue in biblical translation, however. Should translators simply render the Hebrew, even if the result is (as it is here) an absurdity, or should they change the text before translating it? If the latter, should they consult other ancient versions such as the Septuagint or Vulgate (or other ancient manuscripts, such as the Dead Sea Scrolls if they contain the text in question), and if so, how much weight should they give to this evidence? Should they be willing to reconstruct out of their own minds a probable change ('emendation') to the text they have before them, and if so, how should they indicate that they have done so?

There is obviously a sliding scale in such matters. A modern translator faced with a text that reads 'The European Union is a confederation confederation of sovereign states' will not pause long before deleting one of the 'confederation's as a mere typo (known in technical terms as dittography, accidentally writing something twice). Given as the source text 'The European Union is a of sovereign states', the translator will need to think more. Something has clearly dropped out, but what is it? Some work may be needed before the translator can be sure whether the original was supposed to have 'confederation', 'union', 'group', or some other word in that general semantic range, and much may hang politically on which word is chosen. If the whole document repeatedly uses one of these words rather than another, however, the translator may feel able to proceed, but may need to consult someone in an official position to authorize the chosen word, or check with the author, if the author is known and contactable. If it looks as though a whole paragraph or section has been omitted, because the argument does not run smoothly, then the translator may look at the same document in another language – all EU documents are produced in multiple languages – to see what may have accidentally dropped out. Occasionally mere common sense will result in a small change, too. Thus if the text speaks of 'the importance of environmental conversation', the translator might guess that the original had been 'conservation' – but such conjectural emendation would need to be very tightly controlled. The aim is to render the text as originally intended, and various sorts of evidence might help in that task.

Where the Bible is concerned, all these approaches are used in the method of study known as 'textual criticism', the attempt to reconstruct earlier versions of the text where it is damaged or distorted ('corrupt' in the technical jargon). Textual critics identify places, such as the passage about Saul, where there appear to be problems about what the text says, or where it does not make sense, and then seek to improve it. They may draw on manuscripts other than the one that lies at the base of the *Biblia Hebraica Stuttgartensia*, the standard Hebrew Bible (see the next chapter), or on ancient translations such as the Septuagint and Vulgate, or they may appeal to common-sense explanations of how the text came to be corrupt and how it might be restored to an earlier and better state.

All these approaches are exemplified in the catalogue of 1 Samuel 13:1 above. There is some appeal to other manuscripts, though these are not identified, and some to the Septuagint, which lacks this problematic verse altogether. But for the most part conjectural emendation has been used, producing numbers that seem plausible or, in the case of the Good News Bible, chime with the New Testament – evidence that the GNB operates with a belief that the Bible is ultimately a single self-consistent work, as discussed in the previous chapter, a belief characteristic of the evangelical constituency for which the translation is intended and from which it derives.

Textual criticism is a sophisticated and well-developed field of study. It is even more essential for the New Testament than for the Hebrew Bible, since there is no established text of the New Testament but rather a plethora of different manuscripts which form recognizable families, whereas there is a widely accepted Hebrew text based on the St Petersburg (formerly Leningrad) Codex from the eleventh century CE. But even with the Hebrew Bible there are important differences between manuscripts, and between them and the ancient translations into Greek, Latin, Syriac and many other languages, as surveyed in Chapter 1. The biblical texts found among the Dead Sea Scrolls since the middle of the twentieth century have increased the evidence of textual variation, despite the fact that their text is often very close to later manuscripts. It is clear, for example, that the Dead Sea group's manuscript of Jeremiah was shorter than the one known to us, and closer to the version in the Septuagint. The question of which version of Jeremiah ought to be preferred by translators is a live one, and there is a case for following the Septuagint, as there is in general – see the next chapter.

But there is room also for conjecture, as has happened in the case of 1 Samuel 13:1. Since the age of Saul at his assumption of the kingship ('one') and the length of his reign ('two years') as given in the Hebrew not only cannot *be* correct but also cannot, surely, have been *believed* to be correct by any scribe, emendation is called for. Probably the most satisfactory solution is to indicate in a note that there is a problem, and print an ellipsis as the Revised New Jerusalem Bible does. But if one wishes to provide some actual number, then the best that can be managed is probably inspired guesswork, which seems to be how the New English Bible translators arrived at Saul coming to the throne at fifty and reigning for twenty-two years, in which the only part of the Hebrew text to survive is 'two'. Not very inspired, to my mind, since the stories about Saul suggest he was far less than fifty when he became king, but certainly guess-work. (The Revised English Bible's 'thirty' seems a more plausible age for accession, but again is largely a guess, though it appeals to 'some Greek manuscripts'.)

The larger question, however, is this: should translators emend the text at all? In extreme cases such as this one, it is hard to see how they can avoid it. Yet the translator is presumably not in the business of deciding how old Saul actually was when he became king or how long he actually reigned – historical questions outside their remit. The translator's job is to translate the text. Yet what is the text? It is a shifting entity, a moving target. We can see this from a more complex example, taken from the next chapter of 1 Samuel.

1 SAMUEL 14

Saul has directed his army not to eat until after a forthcoming battle (14:24). His son Jonathan fails to hear the order, however, and consumes some honey. As a result things go badly wrong in the Israelite camp. James Barr picks up the story:

> Saul resorted to lots to determine, by a process of elimination, who was responsible. The first choice was to be between the royal family (Saul and Jonathan) on the one side and the people of Israel on the other. Compare now the difference between AV [i.e. KJV], which follows the traditional Hebrew (Masoretic) text, and RSV, which follows the Greek (Septuagint).

1 Sam. 14.41:

AV

Therefore Saul said unto the LORD God of Israel, Give a perfect *lot*. And Saul and Jonathan were taken; but the people escaped.

RSV

Therefore Saul said, 'O LORD God of Israel, why hast thou not answered thy servant this day? If this guilt is in me or in Jonathan my son, O LORD, God of Israel, give Urim; but if this guilt is in thy people Israel, give Thummim.' And Jonathan and Saul were taken, but the people escaped.

The text followed by RSV (which accords with the translation in the Septuagint) makes good sense of the incident. Saul is using the double lots, Urim and Thummim, one negative and one positive. His prayer to God makes clear what the question is, and gives a very credible account of the procedure, and certainly not one that the Septuagint translators would have invented. There is little doubt that the text followed by RSV is the correct one. The Greek was correctly translated from a Hebrew which we no longer possess. The Hebrew text dropped out most of two sentences through a common copying error (the copyist's eye slipped from the first 'Israel' to the second and he missed out what lay between). The piece lost disappeared from the entire tradition of the Hebrew Bible: though we possess a multitude of manuscripts, none of them have the lost portion of text.[2]

Barr is surely right in saying that the RSV follows the 'correct' text, that is, the text that the author of Samuel originally wrote. But is that what the translator is meant to be translating? Not all translators think so. I note that the NRSV follows the lead of the RSV, as do the RNJB (which does not even footnote the verse) and Alter, but the JPS Tanakh stays close to the Hebrew and merely indicates the Septuagint reading in a note. Goldingay remains entirely faithful to the received Hebrew text and renders 'give Thummim' as 'Grant the truth' (*thummim* in other contexts can mean 'perfection'). Underlying the difference between the majority who follow the Septuagint, and the minority position of the JPS and Goldingay, there is a whole clash of translation philosophy and, perhaps, of theories of biblical authority and inspiration. The majority who follow the Septuagint think that the translator's job is to render what the text originally said, so far as this can be reconstructed, irrespective of the traditional wording. The (more conservative) minority holds that the text is authoritative as it stands, and must be translated without emendation. Not surprisingly, the minority tends also towards formal equivalence, the majority towards functional, though the correlation is not complete.

Further examples of texts where the Septuagint probably preserves an earlier text than the Hebrew are Hosea and Ezekiel; and indeed there is scarcely a book in the Hebrew Bible where the Greek translation does not at some points reflect an older text than our printed Hebrew Bibles, based on the St Petersburg Codex. There have been fashions in translation practice where all this is concerned. Broadly speaking, until the work of Moffatt in the 1920s translators followed the Hebrew pretty closely and did not emend. Then until the early 1970s the trend was to emend rather freely: NEB marks the high-water mark of emendation, with many conjectural renderings. Since then the pendulum has swung back in a more conservative direction, with the Masoretic Text reasserting itself.[3] A case can be made on both sides. The Bible is a classic work in its received form, and it is necessary to have a translation of it as it stands. Yet it is also useful to discover its underlying origins and development, and for that a translation that indicates how it was probably worded originally is also valuable. It might be felt, however, that one cannot well combine the two tasks in one translation. Most existing translations are a compromise, following the traditional text unless there is a problem, but in that case turning to the ancient versions and to conjectural emendation. The result is a translation of a Hebrew Bible that in a sense does not actually exist. But perhaps we have to live with that.

JOHN 1:12–14

The case of the New Testament is rather different, as there has never been an official text. There is the so-called Textus Receptus ('received text'), which is the text that was in common use from Reformation times onwards. It was established by Erasmus (1466–1536) in 1516 on the basis of various medieval manuscripts, and printed in several editions by the French printer Robert Estienne ('Stephanus'; 1503–1559). This is the text that underlies Luther's Bible, Tyndale and the King James Version, but no one ever decreed that it was to be regarded as authoritative. Where the Hebrew Bible is concerned, the Masoretic Text has the weight of tradition behind it in Judaism, but the Textus Receptus of the New Testament has only a long tradition of use, and no modern translator would think of translating it: all modern New Testament translations rest on emendation through the study of multiple manuscripts. In practice, most New Testament scholars have for many years used successive editions of the Nestle-Aland Greek New Testament (*Novum Testamentum Graece*), a product of the Institute for New Testament Textual Research, founded at the University of Münster by Kurt Aland, which is now in its twenty-eighth. It, also, is in a sense a Bible that does not exist, since it is a 'critical' text, that is, one based on collating different manuscripts and sometimes even conjectural emendations. Even so, New Testament translators often also make their own decisions about the text before they translate it, so that there is probably no version that is an exact translation even of Nestle-Aland, let alone of any actual New Testament manuscript.

In the case of the New Testament, as with the Hebrew Bible, doctrinal considerations can help to dictate decisions about which text to translate. A clear example occurs at the beginning of John's Gospel. We read in the NRSV:

> But to all who received him, who believed in his name, he gave power to become children of God, who were born, not of blood or of the will of the flesh or of the will of man, but of God. And the Word became flesh and lived among us.
>
> (John 1:12–14)

John seems to speak of the spiritual rebirth, a rebirth unlike their original fleshly one, of those that believe in the Word of God, who became incarnate in Jesus. But a few ancient translations (in Latin and Syriac), and quotations in the early Christian writers Tertullian and Irenaeus, have:

> But to all who received him, who believed in his name, he gave power to become children of God; who *was* born, not of blood or of the will of the flesh or of the will of man, but of God. And the Word became flesh and lived among us.

Here it is the Word who had no normal human birth but was born of God alone. This is, most scholars think, a reference to Jesus' conception by a virgin, commonly referred to as the virgin birth – the doctrine that he had no human father, but was 'conceived by the Holy Spirit and born of the Virgin Mary', as the Christian creeds express it.

For a textual critic, the question is: how to decide? Which is the original reading or closer to it? Most would argue as follows: no one faced with a text that affirms the virgin birth of Jesus would have changed it into a statement about the rebirth of believers, since they would be appearing thereby to deny a central plank of Christian doctrine. It is much likelier therefore that the first reading set out above is older, and that it has been tinkered with to produce a witness to what was later considered orthodox Christian doctrine. The alteration represents what Bart Ehrman calls the 'orthodox corruption of Scripture',[4] the theory that 'scribes occasionally altered the words of their sacred texts to make them more patently orthodox and to prevent their misuse by Christians who espoused aberrant views'.[5]

In this instance there is anyway overwhelming evidence from all Greek manuscripts in favour of the first rendering above.[6] But even without this, we should still probably prefer it, on the grounds that it is more likely to have been changed into the second version than vice versa – though this did not prevent the Catholic Jerusalem Bible from printing 'was born' without indicating in a note how fragile that reading is. The same doctrinal pressure that resulted in the singular translation in the first place was probably still operating on the translators in the 1960s. The Revised New Jerusalem Bible adopts the translation 'were', as do other modern versions, but it still adds a note: 'If this mss reading is correct it refers to the divine origin of the children of God. However, there are also arguments in favour of the alternative mss reading, "who was born", referring to Jesus' divine origin.' We are not told what these arguments are.

GENESIS 11–12

In the nineteenth century textual criticism of the kind we have been looking at was often known as 'lower' criticism, to distinguish it from another, more speculative approach generally called 'the higher criticism'. This was the attempt to reconstruct the history of the biblical text, not in order to discover the oldest wording, but to establish by what stages it had come into existence. It was more or less what is now often called 'source criticism' or 'source analysis', and looks into the underlying material that the biblical authors are thought to have worked with. In the case of study of the Pentateuch, where the term is most often encountered, this means the process that led scholars to think that these books are a compilation from four underlying sources, traditionally known, as we have seen, as J, E, D and P – the so-called Documentary Hypothesis (see the previous chapter). These sources display different styles in the Hebrew, and this will emerge in any competent translation. For example, almost any English version will make it possible to spot the difference of style between the repetitious and formulaic accounts we find in parts of P and the livelier style of other strata in the text, however we account for this. The difference can easily be seen in the following two examples:

> Then Moses said to Aaron, 'Say to the whole congregation of the Israelites, "Draw near to the LORD, for he has heard your complaining."' And as Aaron spoke to the whole congregation of the Israelites, they looked towards the wilderness, and the glory of the LORD appeared in the cloud. The LORD spoke to Moses and said, 'I have heard the complaining of the Israelites; say to them, "At twilight you shall eat meat, and in the morning you shall have your fill of bread; then you shall know that I am the LORD your God."'
>
> In the evening quails came up and covered the camp; and in the morning there was a layer of dew around the camp. When the layer of dew lifted, there on the surface of the wilderness was a fine flaky substance, as fine as frost on the ground. When the Israelites saw it, they said to one another, 'What is it?' [Hebrew *man hu*, which passed into Greek as *manna*]. For they did not know what it was. Moses said to them, 'It is the bread that the LORD has given you to eat.'
>
> (Exodus 16:9–15)

> On the day the tabernacle was set up, the cloud covered the tabernacle, the tent of the covenant; and from evening until morning it was over the

tabernacle, having the appearance of fire. It was always so: the cloud covered it by day and the appearance of fire by night. Whenever the cloud lifted from over the tent, then the Israelites would set out; and in the place where the cloud settled down, there the Israelites would camp. At the command of the LORD the Israelites would set out, and at the command of the LORD they would camp. As long as the cloud rested over the tabernacle, they would remain in camp. Even when the cloud continued over the tabernacle for many days, the Israelites would keep the charge of the LORD, and would not set out. Sometimes the cloud would remain for a few days over the tabernacle, and according to the command of the LORD they would remain in camp; then according to the command of the LORD they would set out. Sometimes the cloud would remain from evening until morning; and when the cloud lifted in the morning, they would set out, or if it continued for a day and a night, when the cloud lifted they would set out. Whether it was two days, or a month, or a longer time, that the cloud continued over the tabernacle, resting upon it, the Israelites would remain in camp and would not set out; but when it lifted they would set out. At the command of the LORD they would camp, and at the command of the LORD they would set out.

(Numbers 9:15–23)

However the stylistic differences here are explained (and most commentators regard both as different strata of P), there is no difficulty in seeing that they are real. One passage is a story, the other a summary, long-winded and repetitious, of a recurring procedure. This will emerge from any translation.

There are also, however, places where the sources disagree on matters of fact, and then the question for the translator is how far the disagreement should be rendered in the translation and how far reconciled. Again the decision taken about this can become a yardstick of both the translator's attitude towards the status and authority of the text and that of their intended readers.

For example, Genesis 11:22–12:4 reads as follows in the NRSV:

When Serug had lived for thirty years, he became the father of Nahor; and Serug lived after the birth of Nahor for two hundred years, and had other sons and daughters.

When Nahor had lived for twenty-nine years, he became the father of Terah; and Nahor lived after the birth of Terah for one hundred and nineteen years, and had other sons and daughters.

When Terah had lived for seventy years, he became the father of Abram, Nahor, and Haran.

Now these are the descendants of Terah. Terah was the father of Abram, Nahor and Haran; and Haran was the father of Lot. Haran died before his father Terah in the land of his birth, in Ur of the Chaldeans. Abram and Nahor took wives; the name of Abram's wife was Sarai, and the name of Nahor's wife was Milcah. She was the daughter of Haran the father of Milcah and Iscah. Now Sarai was barren; she had no child.

Terah took his son Abram and his grandson Lot son of Haran, and his daughter-in-law Sarai, his son Abram's wife, and they went out together from Ur of the Chaldeans to go into the land of Canaan; but when they came to Haran, they settled there. The days of Terah were two hundred and five years, and Terah died in Haran.

(chapter 11:22–32)

Now the LORD said to Abram, 'Go from your country and your kindred and your father's house to the land that I will show you. I will make of you a great nation, and I will bless you, and make your name great, so that you will be a blessing. I will bless those who bless you, and the one who curses you I will curse; and in you all the families of the earth shall be blessed.'

So Abram went, as the LORD had told him; and Lot went with him. Abram was seventy-five years old when he departed from Haran.

(chapter 12:1–4)

Thus in Genesis 12 we read that Abram was seventy-five years old when he left Haran, but this sits uncomfortably with the end of the preceding chapter, where Abram's father had Abram when he himself was seventy (Genesis 11:26), and died in Haran at 205 (11:32). This implies that Terah was still alive, aged 145, when Abram departed for Canaan. Yet the narrative seems to suggest that Abram left for Canaan after Terah's death. To avoid the clash, some versions, including King James, render the verb in 12:1 as pluperfect: 'The Lord had said to Abram . . .'. This solution of the problem survives also in the New International Version, and there again the motivation is probably to avoid any suggestion that the text is inconsistent. The 'critical' solution is simply to postulate that Genesis 11 and Genesis 12 derive from two different sources, thereby relieving us from the expectation that they should be compatible: Genesis 12 begins the story of Abram and probably comes from J, while the notes about the ages and lifespans of Abram's various ancestors in Genesis 11 come from P, probably a later source interested in such matters, as J was not. The KJV was unaware of that explanation; the NIV panel must have been aware of it but rejected it, most likely on the doctrinal grounds that there can be no inconsistencies in the Bible.

The Hebrew of 12:1, however, reads 'And the Lord said to Abram', using the normal narrative form of the verb, not the form that is usually used to designate what we would call a pluperfect. So in more conservative renderings a theory about the inner consistency of the biblical text here trumps the normal grammatical meaning. Usually one would expect the translator to render what the text appears to say and imply, and not to attempt a reconciliation with other passages. This is similar to the case of 1 Samuel 13:1 (Saul's age when he became king), but here the problem is not at the level of textual criticism (what the text originally said) but at the 'higher-critical' level (there is an inconsistency in the text).

This kind of translation therefore has possible effects on our understanding of Biblical Hebrew grammar and syntax. If the KJV/NIV translation is accepted, then it provides evidence that this particular verbal form (technically known as *wayyiqtol*) can indicate the pluperfect, and this would then come to figure in books on the Hebrew language. But the existence of this piece of evidence depends not on a study of Biblical Hebrew but on a particular theory about the nature of the Hebrew Bible as self-consistent. There are in fact rare places where the form used here does signify something like a pluperfect,[7] but the verb in Genesis 12:1 reads more naturally as a simple past. It would not have occurred to anyone to render it with a pluperfect if there had not been a clash with the previous chapter. This is thus a place where a theological conviction (the belief that there are no inconsistencies in the Bible) has prevailed over a natural reading of the text. The innocent reader of the NIV will generally be quite unaware of the theological niceties that lie behind its translation at this point, a translation that affects the statistics of the use of the various verb forms in the Hebrew Bible by appearing to offer support to the idea that this particular form can be pluperfect in meaning.

Translation is never neutral. Yet in a case such as this, the choice of translation correlates with, or is even driven by, particular convictions about the character of the Bible. Those who have a strong belief that the Bible is always self-consistent will tend to translate so as to make this apparent, in the process skewing, as it will seem to the detached observer, the facts of Hebrew grammar and syntax. Theological stances on the Bible's status and character thus affect, and are registered in, decisions about seemingly specialized, perhaps even trivial, questions of linguistics that will appear to most as purely factual and without bearing on matters of faith. What is at stake, it seems to me, is whether these decisions help to produce the Bible as we would like it to be, rather than as it actually is. As noted at the end of the first chapter, the Bible and its faiths are not identical, and translation is one of the primary sites where the difference between Scripture and religious beliefs is negotiated.

10

Which Bible?

THE GREEK BIBLE

Translators of the New Testament don't have to ponder which books to translate. Its contents have been fixed since the fourth century, when Athanasius' Festal Letter of 367 listed exactly the books we now have, even though details of the text remained fluid and have never acquired an official form. The Old Testament is a different matter, however. The Hebrew text is indeed fixed, more firmly than that of the New Testament, in the form of the Masoretic Text. This is enshrined in the St Petersburg Codex from the eleventh century CE although, as we have seen, translators sometimes feel free to emend it. This text is published as *Biblia Hebraica Stuttgartensia*, the edition all biblical scholars use, though that is slowly being replaced, book by book, by *Biblia Hebraica Quinta*. But alongside the Hebrew text there is also the Greek translation, the Septuagint, which contains several additional books (known to Protestants as the Apocrypha and to Catholics as deuterocanonical) and also has very different versions of some of the books it shares with the Hebrew, such as Esther, Daniel and Jeremiah – not just textual variants in individual verses, but large additions that transform the whole book. Greek Esther, for example, has prayers uttered by Esther, where the original Hebrew book notoriously contains no single mention of God. The Septuagint, with its descendant the Latin Bible, is thus not simply a translation of the Hebrew, but includes material that never existed in Hebrew at all. The Wisdom of Solomon, for example, was composed in Greek, and there was never a Hebrew version. Even where they are translations from the Hebrew, books in the Septuagint are sometimes clearly based on a different Hebrew text from the one that has come down to us. In any case it has its own kind of authority as the Old Testament accepted and revered by most early Christians, including the authors of the New Testament, who normally quote it without attempting to correct it from the Hebrew. The question therefore arises: should Christians revive the ancient tradition – which has never died out in the Eastern Orthodox Churches – of regarding the Greek Old Testament as the true Christian Bible? Should translations for Christian use therefore be renderings of the Greek rather than of the Hebrew?[1]

This would mark an enormous shift for Protestants and Catholics alike, and may seem a shocking suggestion. It would appear to undermine at a stroke the insight, crucial in modern interfaith dialogue, that Jews and Christians share the Scriptures of the Hebrew Bible, even though they of course differ where the New Testament is concerned, and we shall come back to this problem at the end of the chapter. Catholic Bibles, however, already include translations of the books that are only extant in Greek, such as (again) Wisdom of Solomon. With the book of Sirach (Ecclesiasticus) it is normal to translate the Greek version, but to include material from the Hebrew text where that is now known, producing a hybrid rendering. Lutherans and Anglicans also sometimes use Bibles that include the deuterocanonical/apocryphal books, translated for the most part from the Greek.

Setting the deuterocanonical works aside, the Greek Old Testament contains passages that differ in their teaching and implications from the Hebrew text of the main body of the Bible. The Greek translators were generally aiming at a faithful translation of the Hebrew, so that we cannot really speak of a distinct 'theology of the Septuagint'.[2] But it does sometimes reflect – unconsciously, on occasion – ideas circulating in the types of Judaism prevalent when it was made, not in the earlier times when most of the Hebrew Bible itself was composed. Its existence helps us to understand both Judaism and Christianity better, by providing a bridge between the Hebrew Bible and the New Testament. In part this is because it contains the deuterocanonical books, which were mostly written after the Hebrew Bible was nearly complete, during the last two centuries BCE, in what is now usually called the Second Temple period. But in a way the whole Septuagint is a document of this period, in that even the books that derive from an earlier time in their original Hebrew guise – the bulk of the Hebrew Bible – have often been translated into Greek in such a way as to communicate ideas that were not current for the original Hebrew writers. A useful guide here is Philip Jenkins's *Crucible of Faith*,[3] which points out how many of the ideas crucial in the New Testament derive not from the mainstream traditions of thought present in the Hebrew Bible, but from the intellectual and cultural atmosphere of the Hellenistic world in which Jews lived in the final years before the time of Jesus and, later, the destruction of the Second Temple. Examples of such late-flowering ideas are: the last judgement, heaven and hell, the existence of many angels and demons, and the immortality of the soul. Some of these ideas occur in the Septuagint, in passages translated from the Hebrew Bible as well as in the deuterocanonical books, where they are more markedly present. But they do not occur in the main body of the Hebrew Bible itself, and can be at most glimpsed in its latest books.

As we saw in Chapter 2, the Greek translators often introduced more ideas into the text about the end-time and about resurrection.[4] This can be observed in the Psalms, but also in the Greek version of Sirach, which is markedly more eschatological (that is, more concerned with speculation about the end-time) than the Hebrew original. At Sirach 7:17 the Hebrew has 'the expectation of mortals is worms', pointing to a common fate in the grave for all humanity, whereas the Greek reads 'the punishment of the ungodly is fire and worms', a reference to a post-mortem judgement on the wicked.

Similarly, there is an increase of 'Messianic' references. It is well known that Messianism is at most a fleeting presence in the Hebrew Bible, and even where it occurs it normally takes the form of predictions about a coming king of an earthly, even if exalted, kind. But in the Greek we find the idea of the Messiah's name existing before creation ('his name shall endure longer than the sun', Psalm 71:17 LXX; 'his fame', Psalm 72:17 Hebrew), and even of the Messiah himself as a quasi-angelic being who existed before his birth on earth ('from the womb, before the morning-star, I brought you forth', Psalm 109:3 LXX; 'from the womb of the morning, like dew, your youth will come to you', Psalm 110:3 Hebrew, referring to the king).[5] Whether or not there may have been Christian influence on those renderings in the course of the Septuagint's transmission, which in due course involved Christian as well as Jewish scribes, they certainly fit happily together with Christian ideas of the pre-existence of Christ, and take on a different meaning from the one they had in the original Hebrew.[6]

Returning to the theme of the fate of non-Jews, an interesting example is discussed by Timothy Michael Law.[7] In Acts 15:16–18, we read that at a council of the apostles in Jerusalem James cited Amos 9:11–12 – in Hebrew, a prophecy that one day a restored kingdom of Judah will once again dominate other nations ('the remnant of Edom and all the nations who are called by my name', NRSV). But James cites it in the Greek rendering, 'in order that those remaining of humanity, and all the nations upon whom my name has been called, may seek me out' – which prophesies salvation for the Gentiles rather than Israelite domination of them. This fits perfectly with the message of Acts that salvation is offered to non-Jews, but it depends on seeing the Greek rather than the Hebrew text as authoritative. Indeed, it implies that it was the Greek that was so regarded by James and the other apostles – surely rather unlikely, as they were Aramaic-speakers who, it is generally assumed, read the Bible in the related language, Hebrew, not in Greek.

Examples of this kind suggest that the Septuagint is for Christian purposes more useful than the Hebrew. One could reason that Christian writers who stressed the divine inspiration of the Septuagint were arguing correctly, given their starting point: God had revealed more about his coming Messiah and his achievements in the Greek than in the Hebrew Scriptures on which it rested. Law points out that the Septuagint's use of *christos* (Anointed One, Messiah) and also of *pneuma* (spirit) were often gifts to the imagination of Christian writers, who took them in a Christological and Trinitarian sense much harder to extract from the original Hebrew. Thus at Lamentations 4:20 'the breath of our nostrils, the LORD's anointed, was taken' clearly refers to the Judaean king, probably Jehoiachin, taken into exile in Babylon in the 590s BCE. But in the Greek version it is *christos kuriou* ('the Christ of the Lord') who was 'taken', which Christian writers readily interpreted as a reference to the arrest and passion of Jesus.[8]

Thus the Greek Old Testament coheres better with the New Testament than does the Hebrew Bible, being closer to it in time and accordingly also in its theological slants. A classic case is the prophecy in Isaiah 7:14, where the Hebrew has simply *'almah,* 'young girl', but the Greek *parthenos,* 'virgin'. It has been argued that had Matthew not known the Old Testament in Greek, the idea of the virgin birth would never have arisen.[9] This argument seems to me faulty, since this text was not commonly regarded as a prediction of the birth of the Messiah in pre-Christian Judaism in any case, so can only have been identified and used as such by someone who already believed that Jesus had been born of a virgin. Law agrees, but shows that the Greek translation was none the less significant:

> It is possible, indeed quite likely, that Matthew had already known a tradition of the virgin birth of Jesus. But the Gospel writer's argument that this man is the promised Messiah could not have been made without a citation from the Jewish scriptures. It would have been one thing for Matthew to say, 'This Jesus was born of a virgin according to an oral tradition', but for him to have had a text from the Jewish scriptures, provided by the Septuagint, meant that he could ground the tradition of the virgin birth in a real prophetic utterance.[10]

If the Greek Bible had not been Matthew's reference point, this would have been impossible. Reading the Hebrew Bible in Greek made Christian beliefs, certainly linked to some contemporary Jewish ideas but not genuinely to be found in Jewish Scripture, 'biblical' and helped early Christians to develop their own distinctive beliefs in a way inconceivable had they remained wedded to the original Hebrew. Some beliefs that became central to Christianity, such as Paul's defence of justification by faith, worked well in Greek but would have been less successful – perhaps even impossible – if his word for 'faith' had been the Hebrew *'emunah,* concerned as we saw with steadfastness rather than with intellectual or spiritual assent.

Similarly, Proverbs 8:22 was a crucial text in debates in the fourth century CE about the divine status of Jesus. Here personified Wisdom says: 'the LORD created me [Greek: *ektisen me*] as the first of his works'. Once Wisdom is understood as a reference to the divine Word or Logos incarnated in Christ, then the verb becomes essential to showing that the incarnate Word was nevertheless created by God, and was not God himself. This was the case argued in the fourth century CE by the Arian faction, while the group that would come to be seen as orthodox, led by Athanasius, contended that the verb did not have that meaning. It did not occur to either side to mention that the verse was a translation, though that would have helped the orthodox cause, since the Hebrew reads *qanani*, 'possessed me' or 'acquired me' rather than 'created me'. All agreed that the authority was the Septuagint, to the point that the matter was simply not raised. The Greek Old Testament *was* the Bible.

So it can be argued that the Bible that was authoritative for many, if not all, early Christians, including the New Testament writers, was the Septuagint. They appeal to it not only for its general themes, which are usually the same as the Hebrew, but for specific teachings and wordings that often differ from those in the original. And, to recall the three semantic areas examined in Chapter 7 (soul, salvation and faith), the Greek Old Testament is often much closer to New Testament meanings than is the Hebrew – not surprisingly, since like the New Testament it was produced in a context shaped by the Hellenistic culture of the Mediterranean world that had come into being after most of the Hebrew Bible was already written. The New Testament is in important ways continuous with the Greek translation of the Hebrew Bible, rather than with that Bible in its original Hebrew (and Aramaic). The apocryphal/deuterocanonical books provide a kind of bridge between the ancient Israel of the Hebrew Bible and the Judaism of the time of Jesus and Paul, and the transition from the Old to the New Testament is smoother if those books are regarded as part of the biblical canon.

In a translation intended for Christian use, therefore, a case can be made for rendering the Greek version of the Old Testament as the base, rather than the Hebrew. Many of the early Christians' arguments about the meaning of the Old Testament make sense only if the text being used is the Greek. Like the *Letter of Aristeas* and the Jewish author Philo (*c.*20 BCE–*c.*50CE), many Christian writers also believed that the Septuagint was a divinely inspired translation.[11] Even Jerome seems to have subscribed to this, at the very same time as he insisted on going back to the *hebraica veritas*, the 'Hebrew truth'. The prestige of the Septuagint for early Christians is undeniable; it was after all from the Greek, not the Hebrew, that most other Christian translations of the Old Testament were made.[12]

It can be argued that to discuss the Old Testament on the basis of the Greek rather than the Hebrew is and always was flawed. To do so is to oppose Jerome and the Protestant Reformers who defended the 'Hebrew truth'. Yet if we follow them, we decisively cut ourselves off from the vast majority of thinkers in the early Church, a point that I believe biblical scholars who work from the Hebrew rather than the Greek (that is, most of us) do not always take into adequate account. If, on the other hand, we abandon the trend in most modern scholarship and biblical translation of treating the Hebrew as authoritative, and instead emphasize the Greek, a different sort of chasm opens up. With the Greek Old Testament as our canon of Scripture, the Hebrew has no particular privilege. At one level this does not matter, any more than it matters that most Christians refer to a Bible in their own language, rather than in its original ones. But it means accepting many of the interpretative translations within the Septuagint itself, even though they are known not to be rendering the original meaning of the underlying text. It is rather as though we were to defend the King James Version against the original biblical text of which it is a translation. (There are indeed those who do this, but they are not regarded as serious by most of those who study the Bible – rather as 'King James fundamentalists'.[13])

A modern critical scholar might argue that the discord between (Hebrew) Old and (Greek) New Testaments is profitable, and in any case historically accurate: they are the documents of what became two different though related religions. But from the point of view of Christian theology we might think that the combined Old Testament and New Testament of the Greek Bible are a better 'fit', and so more appropriate for Christian use. Of course this could become part of a 'supersessionist' claim, thoroughly appropriating the Old Testament for Christian use and wresting it away from Judaism. But it need not be supersessionist: it could be simply a factual recognition that the Hebrew original does not have the same authoritative status for Christians as it has for Jews. It is the Hebrew Bible in Greek translation, along with the deuterocanonical books, that is the Old Testament for Christians – so it might be argued.

This case is set out persuasively by Hartmut Gese.[14] Gese claims that for Christians the Old and New Testaments, both in Greek, form a single closed corpus of religious tradition, since the Christians who produced the New Testament also decided on the contents of the Old. The Hebrew canon is a later entity, formed when Jewish authorities *removed* the purely Greek ('apocryphal' or deuterocanonical) books from Scripture (a distinctly minority view, but defended strongly by Gese). The Septuagintal canon is a Christian canon; Christians affirmed the Hellenistic version of the Scriptures and had no interest in accepting only books extant in Hebrew, since they were overwhelmingly Greek-speakers anyway. Accepting the Hebrew canon means creating a gap between the Old Testament and the New, whereas with the Greek canon there is a smooth continuity from one to the other: the deuterocanonical books symbolize and represent the fact that tradition continued from ancient Judaism into the Christian movement. The two-Testament Bible, with the Greek canon of the Old Testament, fits the Christian way of telling the story of salvation much better than if we replace the Septuagintal Old Testament canon with the shorter Hebrew one. In any case, Hebrew Bible plus New Testament constitutes a Bible that didn't exist until the Reformation: the ancient Christian Bible, whatever Jerome might have preferred, was always the Greek Scriptures of both Testaments (or a translation of them, for example into Latin), and this necessarily included the deuterocanonical books. Judaism and Christianity appeal to different forms of the Scriptures they partly share.

Gese's arguments support the Septuagint canon as a symbol of continuation, but also of change, in Jewish religious tradition during what used to be called (from a Christian perspective) the 'intertestamental' – now usually 'Second Temple' – period. This change in some ways prepared the ground for Christianity – for example, in a heightened eschatology and emphasis on human sin and the need for salvation from it, including the coming of the Messiah, central themes in Christian belief that have receded in many types of Judaism. To do Gese's points justice we should really need to include some of the other Jewish works from the Second Temple period, for example early texts among the so-called Pseudepigrapha such as 1 Enoch. As James Barr argued, the deuterocanonical books may *symbolically* 'point to' the continuity of tradition between the Testaments, but do not represent all the literature that existed in that period, much of which never became canonical yet which is equally part of the continuity of religious tradition.[15] But Gese does at least show up the lacuna between the Hebrew Bible and the New Testament if those two collections are regarded as the only Scriptures. With the deuterocanonical books included, the transition from one to the other is much easier.

It may follow that the Septuagintal canon does more justice to the logic of the New Testament, and that this why early Christian writers adopted it over the other possibilities available in their day. Another reason was of course that all the Old Testament books, not only the deuterocanonicals, were equally extant in Greek, and Greek-speaking Christians simply did not discriminate among them. They were probably for the most part unaware that Jews had a different canon, at least until Melito of Sardis, in the second century CE, went on a fact-finding tour of Palestine and discovered that the Jews there were using a shorter canon than Christians.

If we are looking for a unified theology of both Testaments, seen as a single work and forming a 'web' (as described in Chapter 8), then Gese is probably correct in thinking that the Septuagint canon makes this a much easier task to accomplish. Whether his ideas work on the historical level is less clear. As Barr argues, for a historical evaluation of early Christian thought the disjunction between the Testaments is probably as important as the continuity:

> [T]he coming of Christ into the world is not just a step upward in an already existing process of revelation; nor is it a new or final interpretation of a revelation previously given; nor is it an intellectual solution in which all the pieces of a puzzle suddenly come together into one pattern. It may be some of these things incidentally and in part, but in principle it differs in that with the coming of Christ there is a new substance of revelation, something that was not there before, even if intimations and premonitions of it are to be seen all through earlier times. The New Testament events are not just a completion of the Old, or a completion of a preceding continuum of tradition, or a fulfilment or final interpretation of these, but a new substance of divine presence that had not been (fully?) there before, and one which does fulfil the Old Testament but is not fully explained by being taken as such a fulfilment.[16]

Christians differ in how strongly they stress the element of newness Barr points to, as against the continuity with the Old Testament, which all continue to affirm. But, as Barr goes on to argue, the relationship is at best an uneven one: there are elements in the Old Testament that scarcely appear in the New (creation, covenant) and ideas in the New Testament that are only weakly attested in the Hebrew Bible (eschatology, Messianism). Accepting the Greek canon of the Old Testament makes the unevenness slightly less marked, but there is still a gap and, if Barr is right about the essential newness of the substance of what is affirmed in the New Testament, it is a gap that is bound to remain whatever one's conclusions about the canon.[17] Judaism and Christianity share much, more than either faith has usually recognized, and can be considered siblings. But they are not twins.

Nevertheless an approach such as Gese's suggests that it is worth thinking again about the status of the deuterocanonical books of the Old Testament, and carrying out a re-examination of the Protestant canon.[18] This was also suggested by Hans Hübner in his *Biblical Theology of the New Testament*.[19] Hübner argued that what matters for understanding early Christianity is not the Old Testament in itself, in the sense of the Hebrew Scriptures as found in Hebrew manuscripts and in printed Hebrew Bibles, but the Old Testament *as received in the New*. For practical purposes that means the Septuagint, since most quotations of the Old Testament in the New are taken from the Septuagint rather than translated directly from the Hebrew. Some New Testament works are modelled on the Septuagint: recall the discussion of Luke 1–2 in Chapter 5. However we understand the origins of the Septuagint – and no one doubts that it was a Jewish translation – this was the 'Old Testament' for almost all early Christians, from Paul, just two decades after Jesus, onwards. This may surprise some, given that Christianity was a Jewish sect and that Jesus and his immediate disciples almost certainly spoke Aramaic and probably read the Scriptures in Hebrew (those of them who were literate, that is). Yet the great majority of Jews in the first century already lived outside Palestine, in the overwhelmingly Greek-speaking world, and for them the Bible meant the Septuagint. The ecumenical mindset that reminds us that Jews and Christians 'share' the Old Testament can mislead us into forgetting that there was hardly ever, if at all, a time when it was the Hebrew Bible in its original languages that was authoritative for Christians. Their Bible was always the Greek Bible. We shall return to this point at the end of the chapter.

The Septuagint thus provides a kind of missing link between the world of the Hebrew Bible and that of the New Testament. It is easy to see why Gese argues that it is the Septuagint that should be Christians' 'Old Testament', as it was for the New Testament writers and the authors of the 'patristic' age (the first few Christian centuries), and remained, albeit in a Latin translation, throughout late antiquity and the Middle Ages. It is still fully authoritative in the Orthodox Churches that use Greek. An early-modern Christian preference for the Hebrew Bible was driven less by religious motives than by a desire to return *ad fontes*, 'to the sources' – a Renaissance, rather than strictly a Reformation, imperative. Theologically, a case can be made for retaining the ancient emphasis on the Greek version of the Old Testament as a more appropriate background to the New, given that it was Hellenized Judaism in its various forms in the first century that formed the hinterland to early Christianity, rather than the religion of a still more ancient Israel such as we see embedded in the Hebrew Bible. Christians today, anxious to avoid the antisemitism of their forebears, often stress that what they call the Old Testament was the matrix for Jesus and the early Church and so is indispensable. They are correct, but we also need to recognize that, almost from the time of Jesus and his very first disciples on, it was the Old Testament *as read in Greek* that provided that matrix.

All this argues that for a Christian theological use of the Bible a translation of the Septuagint, rather than of the Hebrew Bible, is highly serviceable, perhaps even preferable. The Hebrew Bible in its original languages, Hebrew and Aramaic, is critical for Judaism, but for Christians it is significant as the text *underlying* their Old Testament, rather than their Old Testament itself. For scholars, and those interested in the religious thought and history of ancient Israel, it is of course vital, and translations of it need no justification. But a Christian 'Holy Bible' containing the New Testament really demands the Septuagint as its Old Testament.

Translations of the Greek Old Testament do exist. A nineteenth-century version by J. C. L. Brenton takes the style of the King James

Bible as its model, but there is also a much more recent one by Nicholas King in colloquial English,[20] and a committee-produced *New English Translation of the Septuagint (NETS)*,[21] which takes the NRSV as its basis for style and presentation. A large scholarly edition is appearing book by book in a French series, La Bible d'Alexandrie, with French translation and notes.[22] In German there is the *Septuaginta Deutsch*,[23] and in Spanish *La biblia griega Septuaginta*.[24] But these are all regarded as of interest to scholars, not promoted as the Old Testament for Christians in general. (An exception is *The Orthodox Study Bible*,[25] designed for use by members of Orthodox Churches, which presents a translation of the Septuagint alongside the KJV New Testament – reflecting the fact that Greek-speaking Orthodox Christians continue to regard the Septuagint as their canonical Old Testament.) At least as an experiment, *NETS* could be used for readings in church in Anglophone settings, conveying to English-speakers a better sense of the Bible as it was known by the writers of the New Testament than can be gained from the usual translations of the Hebrew.[26]

Thinking about biblical translation, as we have seen in this chapter, can lead to new, far-reaching ideas about what the canon is and how it relates to the faith. Practically speaking, I do not imagine that my thoughts will inaugurate a sea-change in translation practice or liturgical principle, and no one will now start to downgrade the Hebrew text within Christian biblical study. But it is hard to avoid the conclusion that thinking through the matter consistently might very well take some in that direction. It was the Hebrew Bible as received in early Christianity – and that means in Greek – that was important for most generations of Christians until the Reformation, and its replacement since then by the Hebrew original is not obviously the right course. No Christian Church has ever declared the Hebrew text rather than the Greek to be canonical, and lists of the books that are officially Scripture, which exist in many decisions of Church councils and committees, do not specify a language, except Latin in occasional Catholic teachings. For scholarly study all versions of the Bible are relevant and none is uniquely important, but for use in the Church the case for reinstating the Greek Old Testament cannot be easily dismissed.

In recent times, as we saw, it has become commonplace to emphasize that Jews and Christians 'share' the Hebrew Bible, despite the obvious disagreement over the status of the New Testament. This, alongside robust condemnations of antisemitism by many Churches, has significantly improved relations between the two faiths, helping to replace polemic with dialogue and mutual understanding, while keeping at bay the ancient but ever-present threat of Marcionism – the belief that the God of the Old Testament is not the God of the New, but a hostile and angry deity Christians should reject. This new-found respect for Judaism is something to be nurtured, and nothing said here is meant to undermine it. Joint study of the Scriptures, both in academia and in practices such as 'scriptural reasoning', which sees non-specialist Jews and Christians explore the texts together, deepens this sense of shared ownership. It also reveals, however, just how differently the two read the Scriptures they both revere – so much so that it sometimes feels as if they are, after all, different texts. The two religions do not arrange the books in the same order, nor do they foreground the same themes when interpreting them. And though most Protestants agree with Jews about the contents of the Bible, despite ordering and interpreting them differently, Catholic and Orthodox Christians follow the practice of virtually all Christians until the Reformation in treating as Scripture the deuterocanonical books. These books make a more than trivial difference to the overall thought-world of the Old Testament, slanting it more towards the intellectual and spiritual culture of the Second Temple period. That is, towards the ideas that would become important to Christians, such as resurrection, the existence of angels and demons, and expectations of an imminent end to the present world order.

In this chapter we have added a further qualification to any simple belief that a common Scripture creates a unity between Judaism and Christianity, a 'Judaeo-Christian tradition'. To accept the Old Testament as Scripture, yet to hold that its canonical form should follow the shorter Jewish canon and be in the Hebrew language, is to break with Christian assumptions that were universal from Paul to Luther and distinguished the two faiths more sharply than this idea of a common tradition allows. And to suggest that the Old Testament is more authoritative for Christians in a Greek translation than in its original languages is to tap into a reverence stretching back to Philo and other early Jewish and Christian writers who saw the Septuagint as divinely inspired (see Chapter 1). It is worth recalling too that the words of Jesus, almost certainly uttered in Aramaic, are regarded by Christians as having authority even though they were transmitted solely through a Greek translation in the Gospels, and are no longer extant at all in their original language. Translation thus goes back to the very beginnings and heart of the Christian movement. It has been central in communicating its message, and even in shaping what that message is. The Septuagint is in places a rereading of the Hebrew Bible – though we have seen that translation inevitably involves an element of rereading, even in the exceptional cases where an equilibrium between source and target is achieved (see Chapter 4). 'What was originally expressed in Hebrew does not have exactly the same sense when translated into another language', as the Prologue to Sirach puts it. It is the translated Hebrew Bible that influenced early Christian beliefs. The Greek version did not directly contradict its Hebrew source – to suggest that would be to mischaracterize their relation – but as a translation it could not be identical with it either. It reflected the ideas of the age and culture that produced it, just as translations always have, and still do.

Conclusion: Purpose and Power

In most acts of translation there is only one source text, but many possible renderings. One purpose of this book has been to show that, when it comes to the Bible, there can be no one ideal version – no holy grail for the translator, waiting to be discovered. Another has been to capture the significance of translation, for some of these imperfect versions have been as important in their effects as the source texts themselves – on occasion even more so.

Here I should like to develop both these strands with the help of Reiß and Vermeer's *Towards a General Theory of Translational Action*.[1] This work sets out what the authors call a *Skopos* theory of translation, in which the Greek *skopos* refers to what they otherwise label the 'purpose' (German *Zweck*) of translation. The intent is not so much to set out a programme or manual for translation, but to analyse how it works in general and to account for its many and varied purposes. There are three terms Reiß and Vermeer use that introduce a good deal of clarity into the discussion here: adequacy, genre and purpose.

ADEQUACY

The word 'accuracy' is often applied to this or that biblical translation to commend it as better than others. We saw that the Revised New Jerusalem Bible is said in its Preface to be more 'accurate' than its predecessor, the New Jerusalem Bible – meaning that it is more literal, adheres more closely to biblical modes of expression, exhibits (in the jargon) more formal equivalence. But 'accuracy' in this sense is hardly a neutral term, presupposing as it does that a translation closer to the original is innately superior and truer, whereas we have seen that in many cases a freer rendering can actually be more accurate. It can often convey the sense of the original in the target culture better than a version that strives to match it word-for-word. 'Accuracy' as generally used also tends to imply that there is one ideal version, if only we could find it.

Reiß and Vermeer propose replacing 'accuracy' with 'adequacy'. No translation can ever be perfect, but some are more adequate than others when measured against various criteria, only one of which is verbal closeness to the source text. Of course there can be translations that are inaccurate – wrong or bad. A version of John 1:1 that ran 'In the beginning the Word did not exist' would be simply a mistake. But technically competent translations vary in their adequacy. In Chapter 4 we saw examples of translations, both of the Bible and of other texts, that are very adequate indeed, and some are formally but others functionally equivalent, in some cases a mixture of the two. Adequate translations include more features of the original text than inadequate ones, but principally are fitter for the desired purpose.

On such criteria most published translations of the Bible may be judged adequate. They normally rest on sound and wide scholarship and are made by competent readers of the text able also to write good English of various types and registers. All will contain occasional inaccuracies, where the translators have slipped up, and most have their share of idiosyncratic or even mistaken renderings, but few will seriously mislead anyone. Each of course trumpets its own superior merits in its Introduction, but that is to be expected. Hardly any are genuinely defective. This may disappoint any reader who was expecting this book to end with a firm endorsement of one particular version or a blanket dismissal of all extant ones, but true inadequacy is blessedly rare.

GENRE

The second term to attend to is genre, or possibly text-type (for present purposes the distinction between the two terms is not very significant).[2] Paying attention to the genre of a text is, as we have seen, important. A saga or legend does not call for the same kind of translation as a novel, and hymns are different (even if in some cases subtly) from lyric poems. The tendency to translate all the biblical books in a uniform style, regardless of their varied genres, is arguably a defect in adequacy. Looking at the Flood narrative we saw that any determination of its genre is likely to influence the style of translation. Those who see it as a legend will perhaps use a style familiar from folklore, while anyone who thinks of it as historical reportage might use one more like that of a newspaper report. Translators are obliged to take a stance on this if their renderings are to be adequate, and some modern versions fail this test in places, for example by treating all the 'historical' books of the Old Testament, and the Gospels and Acts, as if they were the same kind of material – thus failing to distinguish legends such as the stories of Elijah and Elisha and perhaps the birth stories in Matthew and Luke from 'novelistic' narratives as seen in the story of David and his court, and annalistic reports found in some of the accounts of the later kings of Israel and Judah.

Genres in every culture operate with certain conventions, and the translator has to decide whether to retain the conventions exemplified in the source text or to assimilate them to those of the target culture. Reiß and Vermeer illustrate this with the conventional way of wording a notice of someone's death in a newspaper in the English- and German-speaking worlds respectively. English papers list the name of the person who has died under the general heading 'Deaths', with the date, but seldom include the word 'died', which conversely always occurs in the German equivalent. The translator in either direction has to decide whether to include the word or not: one way signals that the text is foreign, the other assimilates it to the target context. Here, focused on a single word, is the essence of the decision between formal and functional equivalence.[3] The Bible throws up thousands of similar examples of genre conventions different from Anglophone ones, which is part of what makes translating it such an interesting, but also such a challenging, task.

The genre question arises quite acutely with the letters of Paul. They are indeed letters, but of what sort? The modern tendency has been to translate them in a somewhat informal style, seen at its peak in the Jerusalem Bible, or in J. B. Phillips's work *Letters to Young Churches*, both conveying a certain freshness and directness. On the other hand it may be felt that Paul was writing rather formal missives – they are long by the standards of his day – that were meant to be kept and pored over, just as they have been, by succeeding generations. That is to understand them as a kind of treatise, a 'letter' in name only, perhaps something more like a modern papal encyclical. In that case a more formal diction would be expected. In support of this view, we could note that the letters themselves often use complicated language, with long sentences and highly technical vocabulary. A simplified version, such as that in the Good News Bible, does not capture this at all. Of course, it does not attempt to do so, since it is intended to give the essence of Paul's teaching for readers and hearers with a restricted English vocabulary, and in that task it succeeds. Whether versions in both styles convey essentially the same 'information' is a matter of debate between the Nida approach (the Greek is simply a vehicle for transmitting ideas) and the Alter stance (every word counts and there must be no dumbing-down). There is much to be said on both sides, as we have seen.

Genre issues can arise even with a short text. Reiß and Vermeer give as an example the sentence 'He was a good citizen and a gentleman, who always kept himself in good shape until he was run over by a car.'[4] If this occurred in a funeral eulogy, a translator would rightly render 'kept himself in good shape' in some other way ('paid attention to his health and fitness', for example) to avoid the unintentional humour. But if it was intended as a joke, some way would have to be found of retaining the reference to shape in the target language, or devising some other way to make the joke work. Both translations would be accurate and adequate, but the genre identified would determine which should be used. In the Bible we sometimes lack information about genre, however, and have to do the best we can to find appropriate renderings despite our ignorance. For some, the Bible as a whole is a kind of genre – the word of God – and this justifies a uniform style throughout; but this comes to grief on the specificity of the individual books, even though it is carried through in a classic translation such as the King James Version.

What to do when the source text belongs to a genre that no longer exists or has currency? The prophetic oracles, for example, belong to a now defunct form. Some roughly equivalent genre can be sought, though there simply may not be one. The alternative – normally the preferred approach – is to translate rather literally and thereby invent a new genre in the target language. This is an example of the translation affecting or enhancing the target culture in the way that the 'hermeneutical' tradition of translation encourages. The Bible as a whole has had a major impact on the religious and literary culture of the West through translations, introducing such genres as not only the prophetic oracle but also the Gospel and the apocalypse. It is not so much particular translations that have had this effect, as in exaggerated claims made for the King James Version, but the entire tradition of the translation of biblical books into other languages.

PURPOSE

The third, and most significant, term in Reiß and Vermeer's argument is purpose (*skopos*). The adequacy of a translation cannot be judged unless we know what it is *for*. To revert to the obituary example: in a novel we would probably assimilate a death-notice to the prevailing conventions of the target culture, since otherwise the reader would tend to be puzzled and think some special point was being conveyed through the unexpectedly unfamiliar conventions. But if we were using the obituary, as in this book, as an example of the ways in which German conventions differ from British ones, a literal translation would obviously be needed – and would include, in the German, the rather complicated features of Germanic obituaries, and in the English the comparative terseness and matter-of-fact quality of Anglophone ones.

An example on a larger scale given by Reiß and Vermeer focuses the question of the purpose of translations more clearly:

> an election campaign speech can be translated as such (if the English-speaking US presidential candidate wants to address Spanish-speaking Puerto Ricans), as a piece of information about a campaign speech (in order to inform Spanish newspaper readers of what the American candidate has to say) or as teaching material for the study of American

rhetoric in an English language class; it can also be culturally trans-
ferred (e.g. toning down US American sentimentalism [*sic*] for German
readers, etc.)[5]

Unless the purpose of a translation is known, none can be made. We
have seen that there is often a tension between an evangelistic purpose
in biblical translation, as is true of versions indebted to Nida, and a literary interest in transmitting a classic to a discriminating readership, as
with Alter. Both aims cannot be satisfied by the same translation: one
concentrates on communicating the message, understood as extractable
from the words, the other focuses on conveying the style and verbal skill
of the biblical writers. No single translation can accomplish both, though
competent translators may try to attend to both in some measure.

Mapping biblical translation in Chapter 2, we saw that there were
other possibilities beyond formal and functional equivalence. One
takes formal equivalence to an extreme, word-for-word point, whereas
another pushes functional equivalence in the direction of a text
inspired by, but not in any normal sense equivalent to, the source.
Thus there are at least two extreme and two more centrist types.

Reiß and Vermeer, however, identify five types of translation, and
this typology is also useful. At one extreme is an interlinear gloss, useful for learning a new language. As they point out, such a method 'was
used for early translations of the Bible, where translators regarded
each word, and the order in which words occurred in the text, as
"sacred" and therefore inviolable'.[6] We saw that Jerome, who in general opposed word-for-word translation in favour of sense-for-sense,
excepted biblical translation from this rule because he believed that in
the Scriptures even the order of words was a 'mystery' that had to be
replicated (though in reality he did not at all practise what he preached,
but rendered the Bible into normal, though highly 'biblical', Latin).
Incidentally, the interlinear gloss is about the only kind of translation
that is reversible, in that one can reconstruct the underlying source
text from it: no other type of translation allows this.

The second type Reiß and Vermeer identify is a 'literal' translation.
This is one that respects the norms and rules of the target language
but is meant mainly for language learners who need to know which
word of the translation corresponds to which in the source text. An

(at least theoretical) commitment to literal translation in this sense motivates the desire to use the same word in the target language for the same word in the source text, which we have seen was attempted in the English Revised Version in the 1880s, and in our own day is carried out fairly consistently by Goldingay in *The Bible for Everyone*. To some extent some more extreme 'imitative' translations such as Buber-Rosenzweig and Fox might belong to this type, in that they treat the exact wording of the biblical text, and even in some measure the word order, as needing to be captured in German or English; the same can be said of Chouraqui's French version. This is formal equivalence with a vengeance. It is vulnerable to the criticism that it gives the false impression that the original text was written in a strange and obscure style, when in fact it was in the normal Hebrew, Aramaic or Greek of its own day ('Plato was modern to Plato'). On the other hand, it shows the reader not acquainted with the original language how the text is articulated, and seeks to avoid a too-quick 'modernizing' of it, or its over-ready assimilation into current culture. Against the naïve assumption that the Bible was written 'for us' it emphasizes that it comes from a distant and foreign environment.

A third translation type is described by Reiß and Vermeer as 'philological'. This is what many would think of as simply 'a translation' – one that retains the contours of the original in a way that successfully 'foreignizes' the rendering of it, yet is in normal idiomatic English (or whatever the target language may be). The result does not feel like a text originally composed in the target language, but it is fully comprehensible in it. Probably most biblical translations that have endured, or are likely to endure, fall into this category. The Hebrew Bible's narratives do not sound like a modern novel or a modern historical account, and Paul does not sound like a modern preacher: distance is preserved. Yet the text is not obscure or impossible to understand. In English this kind of translation starts with Tyndale and continues through the King James Version down to the New Revised Standard Version of our time. The original shines through the translation, but without any excessive sense that the English is unnatural or forced. Most moderate kinds of formal-equivalence translations, as surveyed in Chapter 3, would come under this heading.

Fourthly, there is what Reiß and Vermeer call 'communicative' translation, where the aim is to convey the same information as in the source but in such a way that the target language is used to produce a native-sounding text. This roughly corresponds to functional equivalence in Nida's sense. The fact that it is more or less the norm in commercial translations provokes Venuti's accusation of 'colonialism' and his attacks on the idea of the invisibility of the translator. In Bible translations, the New English and Revised English Bibles, along with the Jerusalem and New Jerusalem Bibles, belong here, as does Wright's New Testament in *The Bible for Everyone*. We saw both the advantages and the drawbacks of this approach in Chapter 2.

Finally there are 'creative' translations. This is the term Reiß and Vermeer use for cases in which translators have to integrate an unfamiliar type of text, or terms and concepts that do not yet exist in the target culture, into their rendering, perhaps forging a new type of language in the process – the parade example would be Luther's reshaping of German through his translation of the Bible. We could also call translations creative when they produce a degree of equivalence that perfectly balances source and target, as in the examples of outstanding translations quoted in Chapter 4. Here the aim or purpose is to produce a rendering that is both adequate and, beyond that, results in a piece of literature on a par with the source. In this aim the King James Version at its best works supremely well – sometimes even exceeding the original, as with Paul's letters, though equally at times lapsing into incoherence.

NO PERFECT TRANSLATION

No map of approaches to translation corresponds perfectly to the territory, but Reiß and Vermeer have produced one that classifies different types of rendering in a helpful way. By stressing the importance of the purpose or aim of a translation they avoid the sometimes pointless disagreements over which is the 'best' rendering of a source text, which bedevils much thinking about biblical translation. It always depends on what, and whom, the translation is intended for, and if this is ignored comparisons between different versions of the Bible can be between apples and oranges. The King James Version and the Good News Bible are both effective and adequate, but with different goals and audiences in mind. Children's Bibles are another obvious case where a rendering may be ideal for the intended readership but would seem wholly inappropriate if read aloud during a service at Westminster Abbey (though it could administer a useful jolt to any tired members of the congregation there).

Where does all this leave Eugene Nida's widely influential typology of formal versus functional equivalence? It remains a very useful shorthand for distinguishing between two broad categories of translations, those that (in Schleiermacher's formulation) take the reader to the text and those that bring the text to the reader, and its heuristic value has been evident throughout. Nida's aim in introducing the distinction was, however, to commend functional equivalence and discourage formal equivalence, at least for translations intended for those previously unacquainted with the Bible, and in missionary situations. In attending to the purpose of a translation, his typology runs parallel with that of Reiß and Vermeer, but where the Bible is concerned he is not much interested in purposes other than evangelism, which restricts the scope of his cartography and indeed inquiry.

My own thesis aligns with that of Reiß and Vermeer: there cannot be one correct translation of the Bible, or indeed of any text; all depends on the purpose. Undoubtedly there are bad translations, but they are of all types. English-speakers are fortunate to have many good ones, and have much to gain from knowledge of a number of them. The purposes of biblical translation may include study, liturgical reading, devotional use, evangelism and literary appreciation: each will have its own appropriate character, though all need to respect the original purpose of the writers as well, so far as this can be ascertained. Few manage to serve more than one purpose, and to fuse the source and the target texts together, but this, to return the quotation in Chapter 2 of Richard Hooker, is something 'we may rather wish than look for.'

THE POWER OF THE TRANSLATOR

When translation succeeds, it often seems invisible – sometimes to the point where readers forget that the version of the Bible they are most attached to is not the original. 'King James fundamentalism', which sees the KJV held as more inspired than its source – so much so any suggestion that it might need correcting in the light of the underlying Hebrew or Greek is resisted – is a minority attitude. The associated tendency to ground religious arguments in the exact wording of the translation preferred by the given community – whether the KJV or something more modern – as though this were the God-given text is less rare. Attending to the work of translators, the specifics of their historical context, beliefs and assumptions – including denominational commitments – as we have impedes such misuses of Scripture and the veneration of any particular version. All are necessarily provisional and approximate, as I hope to have shown.

The KJV's literary excellence is undeniable and we have seen many reasons to affirm it, but that cannot make it more canonical than the texts of which it is a translation. Those too are not flawless anyway, since they contain variant readings in different manuscripts, gaps and inconsistencies where passages have been miscopied, and linguistic obscurities in imperfectly known ancient languages. King James's three 'companies' of translators (in Oxford, Cambridge and Westminster) were devout and exceptionally learned, as most biblical translators have usually been, but they were not infallible. That they succeeded as much as they did is something to marvel at, not something to burden with expectations of inerrancy, and of conformity with what we believe and what we implicitly wish Scripture to be.

One of my aims in this book has been to show that the 'adequacy' (rather than perfection) of a translation is time- and context-bound, dependent not only on what is current in the translator's day, but also on subjective decisions that reveal their own personality and beliefs. The greatest translations of Scripture are still only *versions*, as the titles of many published Bibles remind us, and they reflect the translators' distinctive use of the target language and its possibilities as much as they reflect the contents and contours of the source texts. Think again of the superlative renderings discussed in Chapter 4. The translation of du Bellay's sonnet gives us this homesick poet in English about as exactly as imaginable, yet is also unmistakably Chesterton; and the elegiac Good Friday hymn is an extraordinarily accurate reflection of Peter Abelard's mood and theological interpretation of the doctrine of the atonement, yet could only be by Helen Waddell. Just so, passages in the KJV, or in successful modern versions such as the REB, can be instantly identified. They have their translators' fingerprints all over them. No rendering from one language into another can produce an exact equivalent of the original, and the translator cannot but intervene.

Invisibility or neutrality may be what many translators aim at, if they see themselves as humble servants of the text. But as we have seen, and as the Continental, 'hermeneutical' tradition maintains (often in contrast with the pragmatically oriented Anglophone one), all renderings of a text are marked by their translator's ideas and outlook. Biblical translations depend on a profound understanding of the source texts, and therefore require the translator to take up residence in the culture from which it comes and avoid distorting it; but they also demand rootage in the target language and its culture, and a distinctive manner of communicating in it. When Luther translated Habakkuk 2:4 as 'the just shall live by his faith', following Paul's lead, rather than 'by his faithfulness', which is closer to what the Hebrew means, his rendering was honest. His intention was to give (in Goethe's phrase) a 'plain' translation – not to embroider or manipulate the text, but merely to bring out a meaning not previously noticed. The result was also, as is clear to us now, distinctly Lutheran, with enormous consequences. It was to change the face of Europe.

Not even the most literal translation is neutral. All renderings of the Bible inflect the text. Formal equivalence transmits the text's meaning, as all types of translation aspire to, but often conveys in addition a sense that the text is foreign and oddly worded, which is not how it would have appeared to its original readers. Those repelled by this may turn for a cure to functional equivalence instead, only to find that it generates, conversely, a text that risks losing its grounding in an ancient culture. Even the best functional-equivalence versions speak clearly to us only at the price of falling out of their original context. There are occasional, dazzling renderings that somehow manage to give us both, but even they cannot substitute for the original – and our very admiration for the translator can prevent us from attending closely to the message of the text. Attempting to capture one language in another is an endlessly fascinating task, but never wholly successful.

Yet the translated Bible is no pale imitation. It has enormous power. It was through translation that Scripture's dominant ideas achieved currency not only in the two world religions that hold the Bible sacred but in Western culture at large, secular or not. In mediating ancient Israelite ideas, originally expressed in Hebrew, through the medium of Greek – the lingua franca of the Mediterranean world around the turn of the era – it was translators who provided the cultural matrix for both Christianity at its birth and for Judaism before the rabbinic era ('early Judaism' as it is now usually called). The Septuagint in some ways exerted greater influence then than the original Hebrew. For many Jews in Egypt in this period, it was the only point of access to the Scriptures, just as in the Middle East many of their co-religionists depended on an Aramaic rendering.

By the time of Jesus, Judaism – not only in the diaspora but even in the Jewish homeland – was heavily influenced by the Hellenistic culture common to all the Mediterranean world. The New Testament scholar Martin Hengel's dictum that in the first century CE 'all Judaism was Hellenistic Judaism' is an overgeneralization, but there is a core of truth in it. It has often been thought that it was Christians who first took the essentially Hebraic ideas of the Jewish Scriptures and Hellenized them, and Paul is frequently taken to be the main culprit.

The Septuagint gives the lie to this story. As we have seen, many of the ideas that distinguish the New Testament from the Hebrew Bible – angels and demons, eschatology and the afterlife – were not Christian inventions, but were already current in Judaism before Jesus was born. They can be found in the Septuagint, especially in the deutero-canonical books, which are Jewish in origin even though they were later rejected in Judaism and accepted only by Christians. The Septuagint, which expresses a Hellenistic way of understanding the Hebrew Bible, can be considered both an emblem and an agent of this influence. It imparted many new directions to the thought of Jews in the Second Temple period, not least to the small sect which very soon became a new religion, practised almost exclusively by Gentiles.

The nascent Christian movement, soon to consist overwhelmingly of Greek-speakers who knew no Hebrew, continued to recognize the Bible inherited from ancient Israel just as contemporary Jews did, even while additionally creating Scriptures of its own in the form of the

New Testament. These Christians affirmed the Septuagint – knowing it to be a Greek version of a largely Hebrew text, but believing or assuming it to be divinely inspired. They did not consciously articulate a claim to be appealing to the Greek *rather than* to the original Hebrew, since they perceived the Septuagint as The Bible, and with few exceptions took no interest in its underlying source. It was likewise through Greek that the Gospels transmitted the story and the sayings of Jesus, despite the fact that it was in Aramaic that his sayings had first been uttered and the story spread from mouth to mouth. The Greek-speaking converts who began to record it in writing were acting as translators of material that no longer survives in its original language at all.

This more than confirms that translation was central to Christianity from its earliest days. The curious dialectical and ambiguous relationship the religion has with the Hebrew Bible, redefined as the 'Old Testament' and radically reinterpreted as focused on Jesus and the Church, was formed through translation. Just the existence of a Greek version of the old Scriptures meant that a combination of the Old Testament with the New, which was in Greek anyway, could be understood as a single, continuous Bible, propounding the Christian message through all its parts. And translation, as we have seen, has a causative dimension. It helps to determine the way readers and hearers assimilate and react to the text. It can change perceptions of the text's original meaning and even reshape what the vernacular is capable of expressing, stretching its native vocabulary to encompass new concepts. These were the Scriptures of the writers of the New Testament. It was the Hebrew Bible *as translated into Greek* that provided the hooks, however precarious, on which the new religion could hang the developing theologies and doctrines that distinguished it from its parent.

At the time of the Reformation, Luther and the other Reformers likewise looked anew at the Scriptures they shared with the religious authorities of their day, whose readings they would come to disavow. The Bible was in a sense remade, its ancient terms taking on fresh significance as they became naturalized and understood in ways compatible with their new intellectual and spiritual setting. Inspiration for and vindication of new ways of reading the Scriptures, and the great upheaval these engendered, was found in translation into the vernacular, as each new rendering was in itself a fresh interpretation and a potential stimulus to further ones.

In the centuries since, innovative renderings of the Bible in many languages have similarly both reflected and helped to form new styles of religious faith and practice in many Churches, Protestant and Catholic alike, and in some varieties of Judaism, as more colloquial versions of biblical texts have come to be widely used in liturgy and beyond. Translation has been powerful as both an agent and an index of change in the two religions that regard the Bible, in its various forms, as a central part of their heritage. Much of the history of its reception is the history of its translation.

Notes

INTRODUCTION

1 See the discussion of biblical translations in Leonard J. Greenspoon, 'Jewish Bible Translation', in John Barton (ed.), *The Biblical World*, London: Routledge, 2002, pp. 397–412, and Henry Wansbrough, 'Christian Bible Translation', in ibid., pp. 413–26.

2 There is an enormous literature on translation theory and practice, some of which I shall refer to in detail. Good introductions are provided by Susan Bassnett, *Translation Studies*, London: Routledge, fourth edition, 2014; Matthew Reynolds, *Translation: A Very Short Introduction*, Oxford: Oxford University Press, 2016; and Daniel Weissbort and Astradur Eysteinsson (eds), *Translation – Theory and Practice: A Historical Reader*, Oxford: Oxford University Press, 2006. See also A. Lianeri and V. Zajko (eds), *Translation and the Classic: Identity as Change in the History of Culture*, Oxford: Oxford University Press, 2008, where the treatment of translations of classic texts has some parallels with the issues in translating the Bible. See also Gideon Toury, *Descriptive Translation Studies and Beyond*, Amsterdam and Philadelphia: John Benjamin's Publishing Company, revised edition, 2012. A defence of translators against the frequent accusation that they falsify the meaning of the original (summed up in the Italian pun *traduttore traditore*, 'the translator is a traitor') can be found in Mark Polizzotti, *Sympathy for the Traitor: A Translation Manifesto*, Cambridge, MA and London: The MIT Press, 2018. (I am grateful to Professor Tal Goldfajn for alerting me to this and other works on translation, and for very helpful discussions about translation in general.) Older studies include J.-R. Ladmiral, *Traduire. Théorèmes pour la traduction*, Paris: Payot, second edition 1994, and G. Mounin, *Les problèmes théoriques de la traduction*, Paris: Gallimard, 1963. On biblical translation in particular an important work is Timothy Wilt (ed.), *Bible Translation: Frames of Reference*, Manchester: St Jerome, 2003.

3 I was intrigued to read the following, from an experienced Bible translator: 'For the last almost fifteen years during which I have engaged in translation as my profession I have almost never thought theoretically about translation itself': Y. C. Whang, 'To Whom is a Translator Responsible – Reader or Author?', in Stanley E. Porter and Richard S. Hess (eds), *Translating the Bible: Problems and Prospects*, London and New York: Bloomsbury, 1999, pp. 46–63, p. 46.

CHAPTER 1

1 For more detail on all the developments described in this chapter see Bruce M. Metzger, *The Bible in Translation: Ancient and English Versions*, Grand Rapids, MI: Baker Academic, 2001.
2 Ezra 4:8–6:18 and 7:12–26, and Daniel 2:4b–7:28.
3 See Matthew Black, *An Aramaic Approach to the Gospels and Acts*, Oxford: Clarendon Press, third edition, 1967 (first edition 1946).
4 For a readable, thoughtful and up-to-date account of the origins of the Greek Bible see Timothy Michael Law, *When God Spoke Greek: The Septuagint and the Making of the Christian Bible*, Oxford: Oxford University Press, 2013. For a vastly more detailed study see Alison Salvesen and Timothy Michael Law (eds), *The Oxford Handbook of the Septuagint*, Oxford: Oxford University Press, 2021.
5 For a recent discussion see Benjamin J. Wright, *The Letter of Aristeas: 'Aristeas to Philocrates' or 'On the Translation of the Laws of the Jews'*, Commentaries on Early Jewish Literature, Berlin: W. de Gruyter, 2015; also Dries De Crom, 'The *Letter of Aristeas*', in Salvesen and Law (eds), *Oxford Handbook of the Septuagint*, pp. 121–34.
6 See Wright, *The Letter of Aristeas*.
7 See Abraham Wasserstein and David J. Wasserstein, *The Legend of the Septuagint: From Classical Antiquity to Today*, Cambridge: Cambridge University Press, 2006. There is also a very useful discussion in Brook W. R. Pearson, 'Remainderless Translation? Implications of the Tradition concerning the Translation of the LXX for Modern Translational Theory', in Porter and Hess (eds), *Translating the Bible*, pp. 64–84, which sets out the reception history of *Aristeas*.
8 The Jewish writer Philo (c.20 BCE–c.50 CE) thought the LXX inspired, indeed on a par with the Hebrew: the two versions were for him 'sisters'. See Hindy Najman and Benjamin J. Wright, 'Perfecting Translation: The Greek Scriptures in Philo of Alexandria', in J. Baden, H. Najman and

E. Tigchelaar (eds), *Sibyls, Scriptures, and Scrolls: John Collins at Seventy*, Leiden and Boston, MA: Brill, 2017, vol. ii, pp. 897–915.

9 See M. L. Klein, 'Converse Translation: A Targumic Technique', *Biblica* 57, 1976, pp. 515–37; R. P. Gordon, '"Converse Translation" in the Targums and Beyond', *Journal for the Study of the Pseudepigrapha* 19, 1999, pp. 3–21.

10 MacCulloch, *Reformation,* p. 73, following a suggestion by Bernard Cottret.

11 A recent discussion of Wyclif's translations and commentary can be found in Andrew Kraebel, *Biblical Commentary and Translation in Late Medieval England: Experiments in Interpretation*, Cambridge: Cambridge University Press, 2020.

12 For an interesting study of the Geneva Bible see S. Dean McBride Jr, 'Interpretive Reception of the Book of Exodus in the English Geneva Bible of 1560', in Barry R. Huff and Patricia Vesely (eds), *Seeking Wisdom's Depths and Torah's Heights: Essays in Honor of Samuel E. Balentine*, Macon, GA: Smith and Helwys, 2021, pp. 89–125, with some plates. See also Gerald Hammond, *The Making of the English Bible*, New York: Philosophical Library, 1983, pp. 89–136, and David Daniell, *The Bible in English: Its History and Influence*, New Haven, CT: Yale University Press, 2003, pp. 113–388. The Geneva Bible was what we should now call a study edition, with copious maps, introductions to the various books, charts and notes – none of which would appear in the King James Bible.

13 Metzger, *Bible in Translation*, pp. 76–7.

14 See *The Translators to the Readers: Preface to the King James Version of 1611*, CrossReach Publications, 2016, p. 54.

15 Ibid., pp. 45–6.

16 See Alan H. Cadwallader, *The Politics of the Revised Version: A Tale of Two New Testament Revision Companies*, Scriptural Traces 14, Library of Hebrew Bible/Old Testament Studies 637, London: T & T Clark, 2019.

17 The absence of the Apocrypha from most editions of the KJV that are readily available in the UK results ultimately from the decision of the British and Foreign Bible Society in 1826 to stop printing it, on religious grounds. Until then it had been normal for Bibles to include it, and readings from it were prescribed in the Church of England until the late twentieth century, when the custom arose of providing alternatives from the canonical Old Testament when the Apocrypha occurred in the Church lectionary. So far as I know, this momentous change took place silently and without debate.

18 Revised edition 1972; the first part to be translated, the epistles, appeared as *Letters to Young Churches* in 1947.

19 See E. V. Rieu, *The Four Gospels: A New Translation*, London: Penguin, 1953.

20 *The Jewish Study Bible*, ed. Adele Berlin and Marc Zvi Brettler, New York: Oxford University Press, second edition, 2014.

21 David Bentley Hart, *The New Testament: A Translation*, New Haven, CT and London: Yale University Press, 2017. Bentley and Wright have discussed their respective approaches online – see christianitytoday.com

CHAPTER 2

1 Martin Buber and Franz Rosenzweig, *Scripture and Translation*, transl. by Lawrence Rosenwald and Everett Fox, Bloomington and Indianapolis: Indiana University Press, 1994, p. 47. The quotation is from Rosenzweig's essay 'Scripture and Luther', published in 1926 as a pamphlet.

2 See the discussion in Flora Ross Amos, *Early Theories of Translation*, New York: Columbia University Press, 1920, Octagon Books, 1973, still an important book for pre-modern ideas about translation. On the Latin writers on translation see Astrid Seele, *Römische Übersetzer. Nöte, Freiheiten, Absichten, Verfahren des literarischen Übersetzens in der griechisch-römischen Antike*, Darmstadt: Wissenschaftliche Buchgesellschaft, 1995, helpfully reviewed by Bruno Rochette in *Revue belge de Philologie et de l'Histoire* 74, 1996, pp. 186–8.

3 Richard Hooker, *Of the Laws of Ecclesiastical Polity* V.19:2.

4 John Dryden, 'Preface to Ovid's Epistles', in W. P. Ker (ed.), *Essays of John Dryden*, vol. i, Oxford: Clarendon Press, 1900, p. 237.

5 L. G. Kelly, *The True Interpreter: A History of Translation Theory and Practice in the West*, New York: St. Martin's Press, 1979, p. 59. In biblical translation similar things might be said of the version by Pope's younger contemporary Edward Harwood, whose translation of the parable of the Prodigal Son begins 'A gentleman of a splendid family and opulent fortune had two sons. One day the younger approached his father, and begged him in the most importunate and soothing terms to make a partition of his effects betwixt himself and his elder brother.' (I take this example from Metzger, *Bible in Translation*, p. 83.)

6 Andrew Chesterman, *Memes of Translation: The Spread of Ideas in Translation Theory*, revised edition, Amsterdam and Philadelphia, John Benjamin's Publishing Company, 2016.

7 See also Lucienne Chan, 'La traduction littérale dans l'histoire de la traduction', unpublished dissertation, Ottawa 1987, supervised by L. G. Kelly, p. 87, who also makes the point that translations that are 'close' to the source text are described as literal by those who dislike them, since for many 'literal' has become a bad word in thinking about translation.

8 See ibid., p. 31, and Lawrence Venuti, *The Translator's Invisibility: A History of Translation*, London: Routledge, revised edition, 2018, p. 15.

9 Nida's works include *Message and Mission: The Communication of the Christian Faith*, New York: Harper & Brothers, 1960; *Language, Structure and Translation*, Stanford, CA: Stanford University Press, 1975; *On Translation: An Expanded Edition*, Hong Kong: City University of Hong Kong, 2006; and other works listed in other footnotes below.

10 Eugene Nida and C. Taber, *The Theory and Practice of Translation*, Leiden: Brill, 1969, p. 12, quoted in Roland Boer, 'The Dynamic Equivalence Caper', in *Ideology, Culture, and Translation*, ed. S. S. Elliott and R. Boer, Atlanta, GA: SBL Press, 2012, p. 15. Compare the Preface to the NIV, which is said 'to articulate God's unchanging Word in the way the original authors might have said it had they been speaking in English to the global English-speaking audience today'.

11 Boer, 'Dynamic', p. 19.

12 Eugene Nida, 'Principles of Correspondence', in Lawrence Venuti (ed.), *The Translation Studies Reader*, New York and Abingdon: Routledge, second edition, 2004, pp. 141–55, p. 146; originally pp. 156–71 of Nida, *Toward a Science of Translating*, Leiden: E. J. Brill, 1964.

13 Hilaire Belloc, 'On Translation', *The Bookman: A Review of Books and Life* 74:1, 1931.

14 Quoted in George Steiner, *After Babel: Aspects of Language and Translation*, third edition, Oxford: Oxford University Press, 1998, p. 351.

15 See David Bellos, *Is That a Fish in Your Ear? Translation and the Meaning of Everything*, London: Penguin, 2011, pp. 171–86.

16 This is an actual example, from a translation made for Sumatra in the seventeenth century by Albert Cornelius Ruyl: see ibid., p. 178.

17 A recent German translation aimed at young people, the *Basis Bibel*, operates like the Good News Bible with a restricted vocabulary, very useful marginal glosses on technical terms, and a rule that no sentence should exceed sixteen words or contain more than one subordinate clause. The effect is not surprisingly somewhat staccato, especially in Paul's letters

where there are often many subordinate clauses in the Greek, but highly comprehensible.

18 Eugene Nida, *Good News for Everyone: How to Use the Good News Bible (Today's English Version)*, London: Fount, 1977.

19 Anna Wierzbicka, *What Christians Believe: The Story of God and People in Minimal English*, New York: Oxford University Press, 2019. This is not a complete translation of the New Testament but does contain a good many passages, such as the one cited here, that follow biblical texts closely, and it is clear that it would be possible to translate the whole Bible using her word-stock, with the addition of course of a number of technical terms, as she herself argues.

20 I am grateful to Bishop Stephen Platten for pointing out this issue.

21 George Campbell, *A Translation of the Four Gospels with Notes*, London, 1789, 2 vols, vol. i, p. 344; cited in Kelly, *True Interpreter*, p. 149.

22 Campbell, *Translation*, vol. i, p. 341.

23 See Hans J. Vermeer, 'Skopos and Commission in Translation Theory', in Andrew Chesterman (ed.), *Readings in Translation Theory*, Helsinki: Oy Finn Lectura Ob, 1989, pp. 173–87; also in Venuti (ed.), *Translation Studies Reader*, pp. 191–202. For a fuller discussion see Katharina Reiß and Hans Josef Vermeer, *Grundlegung einer allgemeinen Translationstheorie*, Tübingen: Niemeyer, 1984; English version *Towards a General Theory of Translational Action: Skopos Theory Explained*, Manchester: St Jerome Publishing, 2013.

24 Words © 1962, Ren. 1990 Hope Publishing Company, 380 S Main Pl, Carol Stream, IL 60188.

25 Already in Eugene Nida, *Bible Translating: An Analysis of Principles and Procedures, with Special Reference to Aboriginal Languages*, New York: American Bible Society, 1947.

26 Naomi Seidman, *Faithful Renderings: Jewish-Christian Difference and the Politics of Translation*, Chicago and London: University of Chicago Press, 2006, p. 17.

27 See the detailed treatment in Dave Brunn, *One Bible, Many Versions: Are All Translations Created Equal?*, Nottingham: Inter-Varsity Press, 2013, which is discussed further in Chapter 3.

28 James Barr, 'Modern English Bible Versions as a Problem for the Church', *Quarterly Review* (United Methodist Church, Nashville, TN) 14/3, 1994, pp. 263–78; reprinted in John Barton (ed.), *Bible and Interpretation: The Collected Essays of James Barr*, 3 vols, Oxford: Oxford University Press, 2014, vol. iii, pp. 253–65, p. 265.

29 See Metzger, *Bible in Translation*, p. 71.

30 This point is also raised by J. W. Rogerson, 'The Old Testament Translator's Translation – A Personal Reflection', in Porter and Hess (eds), *Translating the Bible*, pp. 116–24.

31 James Barr, 'After Five Years: A Retrospect on Two Major Translations of the Bible', *Heythrop Journal* 15, 1974, pp. 381–405; reprinted in Barton (ed.), *Bible and Interpretation*, vol. iii, pp. 231–52, p. 246.

32 Robert Alter, 'Introduction to the Hebrew Bible', in his *The Hebrew Bible*, 3 vols, New York: W. W. Norton and Co., vol. i, p. xv.

33 Lawrence Rosenwald, 'Buber and Rosenzweig's Challenge to Translation Theory', in Buber and Rosenzweig, *Scripture and Translation*, pp. xxix–liv, p. xlviii.

34 Martin Buber in Buber and Rosenzweig, *Scripture and Translation*, p.28.

35 Franz Rosenzweig in Buber and Rosenzweig, *Scripture and Translation*, p. 60.

36 Barr, 'After Five Years', in *Bible and Interpretation*, vol. iii, p. 246.

37 A quotation from Norman Shapiro (source unspecified) in Venuti, *The Translator's Invisibility*, p. 1.

38 Henri Meschonnic, *Les cinq rouleaux*, revised edition, Paris: Gallimard, 1986, p. 11 (my translation).

39 Lawrence Venuti, 'Genealogies of Translation Theory: Jerome', *Boundary* 2 37/3, 2010, pp. 5–28; reprinted in Venuti (ed.), *Translation Studies Reader*, pp. 483–502, p. 483.

40 Compare the similar argument in Chan, 'La traduction littérale' and Seidman, *Faithful Renderings*.

41 Efraín Kristal, *Invisible Work: Borges and Translation*, Nashville, TN: Vanderbilt University Press, 2002, p. 14.

42 Ian Mason, 'Text Parameters in Translation: Transitivity and Institutional Cultures', in Eva Hajicova, Peter Sgall, Zuzanna Jettmarova, Annely Rothkegel, Dorothee Rothfuß-Bastian and Heldrun Gerzymisch-Arbogast (eds), *Textologie und Translation*, Tübingen: Narr, 2003, pp. 175–88; reprinted in Venuti (ed.), *Translation Studies Reader*, pp. 399–410, p. 401.

43 Mason, 'Text Parameters', p. 401.

44 See the discussion in Bart Ehrman, *Heaven and Hell: A History of the Afterlife*, London: Oneworld, 2020.

45 Alter, *Hebrew Bible*, vol. i., pp. xiii–xxxix. Cf. already the condemnation of 'explanatory translation' in Stephen Prickett, *Words and the Word: Language, Poetics and Biblical Interpretation*, Cambridge: Cambridge University Press, 1986, with reference to the Good News Bible.

46 Robert Alter, *The Art of Bible Translation*, Princeton, NJ and Oxford: Princeton University Press, 2019, pp. 62–3.

47 Sometimes there can be a certain crassness in functional-equivalence translations, as in the Jerusalem Bible's rendering 'sex is always a danger' in 1 Corinthians 7:1–2.

48 Cf . Chan, 'La traduction littérale', p. 38.

49 Paul Valéry, *The Art of Poetry*, transl. by Denise Folliot, New York: Vintage Books, 1961, pp. 170–71; quoted in Hans-Georg Gadamer, *Gadamer on Celan: 'Who Am I and Who Are You?' and Other Essays*, New York: State of New York Press, 1997, p. 3.

CHAPTER 3

1 See Chapter 1, and my discussion in John Barton, *A History of the Bible: The Book and Its Faiths*, London: Allen Lane, 2019; American edition *A History of the Bible: The Story of the World's Most Influential Book*, New York: Viking, 2019, p. 349.

2 Possibly the most extreme attempt to translate every word literally, including particles, is found in the work of J. J. Junckherrott (d. 1732), who also proposed that the 'root meaning' of words should always be indicated in the translation – in some ways an anticipation of Buber-Rosenzweig, see below. The result is more or less impenetrable German. See the discussion in Bruce Robert Macdonald, *Translation as Transcendence: Walter Benjamin and the German Tradition of Translation Theory*, Ann Arbor, MI: ProQuest Dissertation Publishing, 1984.

3 See Bellos, *Is That a Fish?*, p. 47.

4 The ancient translations such as the Septuagint are generally moderately literal in today's terms: see James Barr, *The Typology of Literalism in Ancient Biblical Translations*, Göttingen: Vandenhoeck & Ruprecht, 1979. It is probable that the translators proceeded a few words at a time, dividing the text into what linguists call (a technical term) 'chunks' rather than grasping a whole passage, and this almost inevitably leads to something like 'word-for-word' translation, though not necessarily in a slavish way. For the technique see Anneli Aejmelaeus, *Parataxis in the Septuagint: A Study of the Renderings of the Hebrew Coordinate Clauses in the Greek Pentateuch*, Helsinki: Suomalainen Tiedeakatemia, 1982: she calls it 'segmentation'.

5 John Dryden, Preface to *Ovid's Epistles* (1680), quoted in Venuti (ed.), *Translation Studies Reader*, p. 39.

6 Jerome, *Liber de optimo genere interpretandi* (*Epistula 57*), ed. G. J. M. Bartelink, Leiden: Brill, 1980, section V:2. See Venuti (ed.), *Translation Studies Reader*, pp. 21–30, esp. pp. 23–4.

7 Amos, *Early Theories of Translation*, Preface.

8 Barr, 'Modern English Bible Versions', p. 257.

9 Buber and Rosenzweig, *Scripture and Translation*, pp. 60 and 74; also Martin Buber, 'Zu einer neuen Verdeutschung der Schrift', 1954, transl. by D. Robinson as 'Martin Buber: On the Diction of a German Translation of the Scripture', *Translation and Literature* 2, 1993, pp. 105–10, p. 107: 'As if an authentic missive, an authentic saying, an authentic song could ever be reduced to a detachable What, and its How sloughed off.'

10 Alter, *Art of Bible Translation*, pp. 90–91. (Alter attributes the translation quoted to the Jerusalem Bible, but in fact it is taken from the first revision of the JB, the New Jerusalem Bible.) Alter also points to the modern tendency to use inappropriately precise technical terms instead of the often generic usages of the Hebrew: 'Another consequence of the impulse for clarification is to represent legal, medical, architectural, and other terms from specific realms of experience in purportedly precise modern technical language when the Hebrew by and large hews to general terms', ibid., p. 11.

11 Leora Batnitzky, 'Translation as Transcendence: A Glimpse into the Workshop of the Buber-Rosenzweig Bible Translation', *New German Critique* 70, 1997, pp. 87–116.

12 Revised New Jerusalem Bible, p. x.

13 Cf. Steiner, *After Babel*, p. 327.

14 Kelly, *True Interpreter*, p. 92.

15 Alter goes so far as to suggest that parataxis enshrines a particular world-view: 'parataxis is the essential literary vehicle of biblical narrative: it is the way ancient Hebrew writers saw the world, linked events in it, artfully ordered it, and narrated it', Alter, *Hebrew Bible*, vol. i, p. xx.

16 Vladimir Nabokov, 'Problems of Translation: *Onegin* in English', *Partisan Review* 22, 1955, pp. 496–512; reprinted in Venuti (ed.), *Translation Studies Reader*, pp. 113–25, p. 119.

17 See Chan, 'La traduction littérale', p. 20.

18 John Goldingay and Tom Wright, *The Bible for Everyone: A New Translation*, London: SPCK, 2018.

19 Goldingay, 'Preface to the Old Testament for Everyone', ibid., p. xi.

20 Wright, 'Preface to the New Testament for Everyone', ibid., p. 927.

21 'Supernatural man' works less well as a form of address at 2 Kings 4:40.

22 Sarah Ruden, *The Face of Water: A Translator on Beauty and Meaning in the Bible*, New York: Vintage Books, 2018.

23 Hart, *New Testament*, p. 578.

24 Francis Newman, *The Iliad of Homer*, London: Walton & Maberly, 1856, p. xvi; quoted in Venuti, *The Translator's Invisibility*, p. 101.

25 Everett Fox, 'The Book and Its Context', in Buber and Rosenzweig, *Scripture and Translation*, pp. xiii–xxvii.

26 Martin Buber and Franz Rosenzweig, *Die Schrift und ihre Verdeutschung*, Berlin: Schocken, 1936.

27 Fox, 'The Book', p. xiii.

28 André Chouraqui, *La Bible*, Paris: Desclee de Brouwer, 2003.

29 Meschonnic, *Les cinq rouleaux*, p. 11.

30 Ibid., p. 95.

31 Everett Fox, *The Five Books of Moses*, New York: Schocken Books, 1983. Fox has also translated the book of Samuel: *Give Us a King!: A New English Translation of the Book of Samuel*, New York: Schocken Books, 1995.

32 Fox, *Five Books*, p. xix.

33 Cf. Buber and Rosenzweig, *Scripture and Translation*, p. 138.

34 Another, recent imitative translation is by Edward L. Greenstein, *Job: A New Translation*, New Haven, CT: Yale University Press, 2019. This is clearly, and avowedly, in the tradition of Buber-Rosenzweig in its desire to let the Hebrew 'show through' the English.

35 Seidman, *Faithful Renderings,* p. 17, citing Edward L. Greenstein, 'What Might Make a Bible Translation Jewish?', in David M. Goldenberg (ed.), *Translation of Scripture*, Philadelphia: Annenberg Research Institute, 1990, p. 87.

36 Brunn, *One Bible, Many Versions*.

37 New International Version, p. xiii.

38 Venuti, *The Translator's Invisibility*, p. 125.

39 See Chan, 'La traduction littérale', p. 65, arguing that the speaker of the target language will wish to read the original if encouraged to do so by a 'literal' translation.

40 Walter Benjamin, 'The Translator's Task', in Venuti (ed.), *Translation Studies Reader*, pp. 75–83, p. 75; from German original, 'Die Aufgabe des Übersetzers', 1923, transl. by Stephen Rendall.

41 A useful study of Benjamin's ideas about translation is Macdonald, *Translation as Transcendence*. Macdonald brings out the kabbalistic background in some of Benjamin's arguments, as well as his interest in literalism. See also M. Ballard, *De Cicéron à Benjamin: traducteurs, traductions, réflexions*, Lille: Presses universitaires de Lille, 1992.

42 Compare Wolfram Eilenberger, *Time of the Magicians: The Invention of Modern Thought, 1919–1929*, London: Allen Lane, 2020, p. 213: 'For Benjamin, language is expressly not a *means* for conveying valuable information to others but a *medium* in which we become aware of

ourselves and all the things that surround us – recognizing both by nam-
ing them. We don't express ourselves through language, but language
expresses itself through us ... his argument was that language facilitates
not mundane communication but the revelation of being.' Eilenberger
draws parallels with Wittgenstein and Heidegger.

43 See Macdonald, *Translation as Transcendence*.
44 Benjamin, 'The Translator's Task', p. 81.
45 Batnitzky, 'Translation as Transcendence', p. 87.
46 See Georgia Warnke, 'Hermeneutics and Critical Theory', in Michael
    N. Forster and Kristin Gjesdal (eds), *The Cambridge Companion
    to Hermeneutics*, Cambridge: Cambridge University Press, 2019,
    pp. 237–59, p. 243.
47 See Seidman, *Faithful Renderings*, p. 197.
48 Kristal, *Invisible Work*, p. 21.
49 F. D. E. Schleiermacher, 'Über die verschiedenen Methoden des Über-
    setzens', transl. by Susan Bernofsky as 'On the Different Methods of
    Translating', in Venuti (ed.), *Translation Studies Reader*, pp. 43–63, pp.
    45–6.
50 Cf. Steiner, *After Babel*, p. 280: 'The evolution of modern German is
    inseparable from the Luther Bible, from Voss's Homer, from the succes-
    sive versions of Shakespeare by Wieland, Schlegel, and Tieck.'
51 Neil MacGregor, *Germany: Memories of a Nation*, London: Allen Lane,
    2014, pp. 101–4.
52 See C. S. Lewis, 'The Literary Impact of the Authorized Version', The
    Ethel M. Wood Lecture delivered before the University of London on 20
    March 1950, London, 1950; reprinted in *They Asked for a Paper*, Lon-
    don: Geoffrey Bles, 1962, pp. 26–50. Lewis argues strongly that much of
    the influence of the Bible is due to the original, not specifically to the
    translators. In any case versions before the KJV were determinative for
    many English writers – the Geneva Bible, after all, not the KJV, was the
    Bible of Donne, Herbert and Shakespeare, as remarked in Chapter 1.
53 On this example see Metzger, *Bible in Translation*, p. 92.
54 I am grateful to Professor Paul Joyce for this example.
55 David Damrosch, 'Translation and World Literature: Love in the Necrop-
    olis', Chapter 4 of David Damrosch, *What is World Literature?*,
    Princeton, NJ: Princeton University Press, 2003, pp. 147–69; reprinted
    in Venuti (ed.), *Translation Studies Reader*, pp. 411–28, p. 427.
56 Goldingay and Wright, *Bible for Everyone*, p. 928.
57 Steiner, *After Babel*, p. 282.
58 On this see Lewis, 'Literary Impact of the Authorized Version'.

59 Reiß and Vermeer draw attention to a paradoxical element in a more formal-equivalent translation: 'Thomas Carlyle's *History of Friedrich II of Prussia* is written in a Teutonic style, with very long and complex sentences . . . If this book were to be translated into German, the usual strategy to translate sentence by sentence would result in a stylistically unmarked text which perfectly conforms to the German style conventions for this genre. In order to render the specificity of Carlyle's style, the translator would probably have to adapt the text to Kantian ways of expression' (*Towards a General Theory*, p. 193).

CHAPTER 4

1 Damrosch, 'Translation and World Literature', p. 424.
2 Michel Foucault, 'Les mots qui saignent', *L'Express* 688, 1964, pp. 21–2, cited in Antoine Berman, 'La traduction comme épreuve de l'étranger', *Texte* 4, 1985, pp. 67–81, transl. by Lawrence Venuti as 'Translation and the Trials of the Foreign' in Venuti (ed.), *Translation Studies Reader*, pp. 240–53, p. 241.
3 Cf. Belloc, 'On Translation'.
4 Steiner, *After Babel*, p. 313.
5 Ibid., p. 314.
6 T. S. Eliot, 'Tradition and the Individual Talent' (1919), in *Selected Essays, 1917–1932*, London: Faber and Faber, 1932, second edition, 1934.
7 Steiner, *After Babel*, p. 401.
8 Ibid., p. 317.
9 See ibid., p. 423.
10 Ibid., pp. 438–40. I do not think this judgement on Müller is correct, which may be confirmed by the fact that other composers have also set his poems, but it is a widely held opinion. Incidentally, Müller was himself an accomplished translator, rendering medieval German poems into modern German, and also translating Greek texts.
11 Steiner, *After Babel*, p. 318.
12 Bellos, *Is That A Fish?*, pp. 197–8, gives the example of translation of novels from English into French that avoid 'fronting' ('Moi, je ne l'aime pas') to a degree that make them non-idiomatic overall even though in any given instance the non-fronted rendering can perfectly well be defended.
13 *The Collected Poems of G. K. Chesterton*, London: Methuen, seventh edition, 1939, p. 179.
14 Helen Waddell, *Mediaeval Latin Lyrics*, Harmondsworth: Penguin, 1964, pp. 178–9, from original publication of 1929.

15 See Batnitzky, 'Translation as Transcendence', p. 87.
16 Bellos, *Is That A Fish?*, p. 181.

CHAPTER 5

1 The reactions described here are those that came from literary reviewers, appealing mainly to aesthetic considerations. There are also religious groups that regard the KJV as divinely inspired: see my discussion of 'King James fundamentalism' in Barton, *History of the Bible*, pp. 466–7. As I illustrate there, some in the USA even think the KJV more inspired than the Hebrew and Greek texts from which it was translated, and therefore resist any proposal to change it in the light of knowledge of those texts. Hostile British reactions to the NEB, however, did not usually result from that kind of theological belief, which is rare on this side of the Atlantic.

2 In the JB 'the sound of a gentle breeze', in the RNJB 'a light sound of silence'.

3 Rosenzweig, 'Scripture and Luther', in Buber and Rosenzweig, *Scripture and Translation*, p. 53.

4 Ibid., p. 54.

5 Steiner, *After Babel*, p. 412.

6 Ibid., p. 365.

7 Ibid., p. 335.

8 Buber, 'Zu einer neuen Verdeutschung', p. 106.

9 Steiner, *After Babel*, p. 262.

10 Jerusalem Bible, p. vi.

11 NRSV, p. xv.

12 H. W. and F. G. Fowler, *The King's English*, third edition, Oxford: Oxford University Press, 1990 (first published 1906).

13 Alter, *Art of Bible Translation*, pp. 4–5.

14 See Ben Crystal and David Crystal, *Shakespeare's Words: A Glossary and Language Companion*, London: Penguin, 2004.

15 See Alter, *Art of Bible Translation*, pp. 5–6.

16 J. W. Goethe, *Dichtung und Wahrheit*, xi, cited in Buber and Rosenzweig, *Scripture and Translation*, p. 129.

17 Alter, *Art of Bible Translation*, p. 55.

18 See Barr, 'After Five Years', in *Bible and Interpretation*, vol. iii, p. 237. Barr comments that 'the philological novelties of the NEB have become something of a figure of fun among scholars, for all their deep respect for those who worked on the production of it. Competent scholars are left open-mouthed.'

19 Gerald Hammond already suggested in the 1980s that different styles would be appropriate for different biblical books. Some of the Gospel narratives, he argues, particularly in Mark and Matthew, are as paratactic as Old Testament stories and should be rendered in the same way, with many 'and's and no explanatory connectives ('then', 'hence', 'accordingly' and so on); whereas others, particularly in Luke, have a more complex syntax. This contrast is captured, he claims, in the KJV but not on the whole in modern translations. See Gerald Hammond, 'English Translations of the Bible', in Robert Alter and Frank Kermode (eds), *The Literary Guide to the Bible*, London: Collins, 1987, pp. 658–9.

20 Alter in fact does use archaism for ABH.

21 On all this see Steiner, *After Babel*, pp. 366–7.

22 On the translation of social dialects see Ineke Wallaert, 'The Translation of Sociolects: A Paradigm of Ideological Issues in Translation?', in Janet Cotterill and Anne Ife (eds), *Language across Boundaries: Selected Papers from the Annual Meeting of the British Association for Applied Linguistics held at Anglia Polytechnic University, Cambridge, September 2000*, London: Bloomsbury, 2005. She points out that in translating Poe's 'The Gold-Bug' Baudelaire rendered all three different sociolects (versions of English characteristic of different social classes) into standard French.

23 Bellos, *Is That a Fish?*, p. 199.

24 In an unpublished paper.

25 The NEB had 'all harsh cries and raucous shouts'.

26 See Revelation 1:4.

27 A rare exception is David Bentley Hart, who comments that he has deliberately tried to convey the different styles of the various New Testament books even to the extent of rendering bad Greek into bad English: 'Where the Greek of the original is maladroit, broken, or impenetrable (as it is with some consistency in Paul's letters), so is the English of my translation; where an author has written bad Greek (such as one finds throughout the book of Revelation), I have written bad English' (Hart, *New Testament*, p. 18).

28 See William Radice, 'Introduction', in William Radice and Barbara Reynolds (eds), *The Translator's Art: Essays in Honour of Betty Radice*, Harmondsworth: Penguin, 1987, pp. 9–30, p. 24.

29 See Gary A. Rendsburg, *Linguistic Evidence for the Northern Origin of Selected Psalms*, Atlanta, GA: Scholars Press, 1990; *Israelian Hebrew in the Book of Kings*, Bethesda, MD: CDL Press, 2002; 'A Comprehensive

Guide to Israelian Hebrew: Grammar and Lexicon', *Orient* 38, 2003, pp. 5–35.

30 The translation is by William Lorimer, sometime Professor of Greek at St Andrews University. It was completed by his son Robin, and published as *The New Testament in Scots*, Edinburgh: Canongate, 1983.

CHAPTER 6

1 C. S. Lewis, *Reflections on the Psalms*, London: Geoffrey Bles, 1958, pp. 113–14.

2 *Bibel in gerechter Sprache*, Gütersloh: Gütersloher Verlagshaus, 2006. *Gerecht* ('just' or 'fair') has established itself as the equivalent of 'inclusive' in German.

3 There are particularly good discussions of the *Bibel im heutigen Deutsch* and of all the issues involved in inclusive language in Siegfried Meurer (ed.), *Die vergessenen Schwestern: Frauengerechte Sprache in der Bibelübersetzung*, Stuttgart: Deutsche Bibelgesellschaft, 1993. Unfortunately this does not exist in translation, though two of the articles are in English: Paul Ellingworth, 'The Scope of Inclusive Language: Structure and Usage', pp. 53–66, and Harold P. Scanlin, 'Inclusive Language in Recent English Bible Translations', pp. 95–100.

4 Ellingworth, 'The Scope', p. 59.

5 'Humankind' is sometimes derided by those who dislike inclusive language as a politically correct and recent piece of Americana, but it was already used by T. S. Eliot (admittedly American, but not recent): 'humankind cannot bear very much reality', 'Burnt Norton I', *The Four Quartets*.

6 This is discussed very helpfully in Katharina Reiß, 'Frauengerechte Sprache?', in Meurer (ed.), *Die vergessenen Schwestern*, pp. 37–52.

7 Hart, *New Testament*, p. 552.

8 See Athalya Brenner and Jan Willem van Henten (eds), *Bible Translation on the Threshold of the Twenty-First Century: Authority, Reception, Culture and Religion*, Supplements to the Journal for the Study of the New Testament 353, Sheffield: Sheffield Academic Press, 2001.

CHAPTER 7

1 Also the case in the 1975 revision of the Luther Bible, but the most recent revision has reverted to 'soul': see Gerhard Sauter, 'Seele: geprägte Lebendigkeit', *Berliner Theologische Zeitschrift* 34:2, 2017, pp. 120–48.

2 There is an excellent discussion of modern attitudes to translating the Greek vocabulary of soul and spirit in David Bentley Hart, *New Testament*, pp, 560–67.

3 This case was argued with particular force by Oscar Cullmann, *Immortality of the Soul or Resurrection of the Dead? The Witness of the New Testament*, London: Epworth Press, 1958.

4 See the lengthy discussion in James Barr, *The Garden of Eden and the Hope of Immortality*, London: SCM Press, 1992, especially pp. 36–47.

5 A. R. Johnson, *The Vitality of the Individual in the Thought of Ancient Israel*, Cardiff: University of Wales Press, 1964, p. 84.

6 Barr, *Garden of Eden*, p. 37.

7 A detailed study of the vocabulary connected with 'soul' is provided in Katrin Müller, *Lobe den Herrn, meine 'Seele'. Eine kognitiv-linguistische Studie zur næfæs des Menschen im Alten Testament*, Beiträge zur Wissenschaft des Alten und Neuen Testament 215, Stuttgart: Kohlhammer, 2018.

8 R. Loewe, ' "Salvation" is Not of the Jews', *Journal of Theological Studies* new series 32:2, 1981, pp. 341–68.

9 For a full discussion of these points see James Barr, 'An Aspect of Salvation in the Old Testament', in E. J. Sharpe and J. L. Hinnells (eds), *Man and his Salvation: Studies in Memory of S. G. Brandon*, Manchester: Manchester University Press, 1973, pp. 39–52; reprinted in John Barton (ed.), *Bible and Interpretation: The Collected Essays of James Barr*, Oxford: Oxford University Press, 3 vols, 2013, vol. ii (*Biblical Studies*), pp. 127–50.

10 For the 'new perspective on Paul' there is a collection of essays by J. D. G. Dunn, *The New Perspective on Paul: Collected Essays*, Tübingen: Mohr Siebeck, 2005, in which the progress of the debate can be followed. See also Heikki Räisänen, *Paul and the Law*, Tübingen: Mohr, 1983.

11 J. Boehmer, 'Der Glaube und Jesaja – zu Jes. 7,9 und 28,16', *Zeitschrift für die Alttestamentliche Wissenschaft* 41, 1923, pp. 84–93.

12 R. Smend, 'Zur Geschichte von *he'emin*', Vetus Testamentum Supplements 16, 1967, pp. 284–90, suggested that Isaiah may have been the first to use the verb *he'emin* absolutely to mean 'trust'. See also the recent discussion in Arthur Jan Keefer, *The Book of Proverbs and Virtue Ethics: Integrating the Biblical and Philosophical Traditions*, Cambridge: Cambridge University Press, 2021, p. 169.

13 Cf. Boehmer, 'Der Glaube'.

14 Egon Pfeiffer, 'Glaube im Alten Testament', *Zeitschrift für die alttestamentliche Wissenschaft* 71, 1959, pp. 151–64. See the extended discussion by James Barr, *The Semantics of Biblical Language*, Oxford: Oxford

University Press, 1961, pp. 176–87. Barr rebuts the suggestion, popular at the time, that religious ideas about the relationship of people to God were somehow inherent in the very words used. On the contrary, he argued, they were *explicitly affirmed* in the text. The Hebrew language is not a kind of special tongue that already contains theological truths even before any actual propositions are articulated in it. It remains true, however, that some of the words used to make theological affirmations had a different sense from that of their English 'equivalents', and that is observably true of *he'emin*, which does not mean 'believe' in the sense(s) that term normally has in English, but something nearer to 'trust'. This is a perfectly ordinary linguistic point: two languages virtually never have terms whose meanings exactly correspond.

15 Classically argued in C. A. Keller, 'Das quietische Element in der Botschaft des Jesaja', *Theologische Literaturzeitung* 11, 1955, pp. 81–97.

16 Cf. H. Wildberger, ' "Glauben", Erwägungen zu *he'emin* ', Vetus Testamentum Supplements 16, 1967, pp. 372–86. See also idem, ' "Glauben" im Alten Testament', *Zeitschrift für Theologie und Kirche* 65, 1968, pp. 129–59.

17 There is one other relevant verb, *damah*, which normally means 'intend', sometimes 'ponder', but in one place must mean 'think [something to be so]': Psalm 50:21, where God says 'you thought (*dimmitha*) that I was one just like yourself'. Interestingly, here again the implication is 'thought wrongly'.

18 James Barr provided the classic demonstration that the word for faith in the New Testament (Greek *pistis*) is not to be understood as having the meaning of Hebrew *he'emin*, as though the New Testament authors such as Paul were having 'Hebrew thoughts' when using Greek words: see Barr, *The Semantics of Biblical Language*, pp. 161–205. For the New Testament and its Graeco-Roman background, as well as later developments, see Teresa Morgan, *Roman Faith and Christian Faith*: Pistis *and* Fides *in the Early Roman Empire and Early Churches*, Oxford: Oxford University Press, 2015.

CHAPTER 8

1 On this see also Peter Heller, 'Some Functions of the Leitmotiv in Thomas Mann's Joseph Tetralogy', *The Germanic Review: Literature, Culture, Theory* 22, 1947, pp. 126–41.

2 Buber and Rosenzweig, *Scripture and Translation*, p. 114, in a lecture delivered by Buber in 1927.

3 Discussed in ibid., pp. 123–4.

4 See the classic work of Michael Fishbane, *Biblical Interpretation in Ancient Israel*, New York and Oxford: Oxford University Press, 1985; also Richard B. Hays, *Echoes of Scripture in the Gospels*, Waco, TX: Baylor University Press, 2016; and David Allen and Steve Smith (eds), *Methodology in the Use of the Old Testament in the New: Context and Criteria*, Library of New Testament Studies 579, London: T & T Clark, 2020.

5 Robert Alter, *The Art of Biblical Narrative*, London: George Allen & Unwin, 1981, p. 51.

6 It can be found in her doctoral thesis, 'Séméiotikè: recherches pour une sémanalyse', Paris: 1969.

7 Julia Kristeva, *Desire in Language: A Semiotic Approach to Literature and Art*, New York: Columbia University Press and London: Blackwell, 1980, p. 65.

8 Ibid., p. 36.

9 Kristeva herself quickly saw that 'intertextuality' was turning into a method of identifying allusion rather than, as she had intended, a theory about culture: 'since this term has often been understood in the banal sense of "study of sources" we prefer the term *transposition* because it specifies that the passage from one signifying system to another demands a new articulation of the thetic – of enunciative and denotative positionality' (Julia Kristeva, *Revolution in Poetic Language*, New York: Columbia University Press, 1984, pp. 59–60). This suggests she would see a lot of what is called intertextuality in biblical studies as 'banal'.

10 Ibid., p. 104.

11 Harold Bloom, *A Map of Misreading*, New York: Oxford University Press, 1975, p. 3.

12 See, classically, Eliot, 'Tradition and the Individual Talent'.

13 Harold Bloom, *The Anxiety of Influence: A Theory of Poetry*, New York and Oxford: Oxford University Press, 1973, p. xxv.

14 As Bloom observes, Borges himself 'made a career out of exploiting his secondariness', often adopting (and adapting) the ancient literary tradition of pretending that his original work was really an ancient document he had discovered – thereby subverting the idea of 'originality'.

15 Johannes de Moor, 'Introduction', in J. C. de Moor (ed.), *Intertextuality in Ugarit and Israel. Papers Read at the Tenth Joint Meeting of the Society for Old Testament Study and Het Oudtestamentisch Werkgezelschap in Nederland & België, held at Oxford, 1997*, Leiden: Brill, 1998, p. ix.; cited in Stephen D. Moore and Yvonne Sherwood, *The Invention of the*

Biblical Scholar: A Critical Manifesto, Minneapolis, MN: Fortress Press, 2011, p. 34.

16 Anthony C. Thiselton, *New Horizons in Hermeneutics: The Theory and Practice of Transforming Biblical Reading*, London: HarperCollins, 1992, p. 171.

17 Richard B. Hays, *Echoes of Scripture in the Letters of Paul*, New Haven, CT and London: Yale University Press, 1989; see also Richard B. Hays, Stefan Alkier and Leroy Andrew Huizenga (eds), *Reading the Bible Intertextually*, Waco, TX: Baylor University Press, 2009.

18 Spike Draisma (ed.), *Intertextuality in Biblical Writings: Essays in Honour of Bas van Iersel*, Kampen: Kok, 1989.

19 Peter D. Miscall, 'Isaiah: New Heavens, New Earth, New Book', in Danna Nolan Fewell (ed.), *Reading between Texts: Intertextuality and the Hebrew Bible*, Louisville, KY: Westminster/John Knox Press, 1992, pp. 41–56, p. 44.

20 Buber and Rosenzweig, *Scripture and Translation*, p. 23 (from a 1927 letter of Rosenzweig).

21 Buber and Rosenzweig, *Scripture and Translation*, p. 91 (from a 1935 essay by Buber).

22 Alter, *Hebrew Bible*, vol. i., p. xlix (my italics).

23 See *The Translators to the Readers: Preface to the King James Version of 1611*, CrossReach Publications, 2016, pp. 52–4.

24 Brevard S. Childs, *Biblical Theology of the Old and New Testaments: Theological Reflections on the Christian Bible*, London: SCM Press, 1992, p. 71. See also Christopher R. Seitz, *Word without End: The Old Testament as Abiding Theological Witness*, Grand Rapids, MI and Cambridge: W. B. Eerdmans, 1998, and R. W. L. Moberly, *Old Testament Theology: Reading the Hebrew Bible as Christian Scripture*, Grand Rapids, MI: Baker Academic, 2013.

25 J and E are called after the name they typically use for God: Yahweh (in Germany, where the theory was developed, spelt Jahwe) or Elohim. D is the book of Deuteronomy and passages elsewhere in the Pentateuch inspired by it. P is the source that contains all the laws about ritual, thought to be typical of priests. Identifying which passages in the Pentateuch derive from which source has long been a major concern for scholars of the Hebrew Bible. Recently there has been a tendency to simplify the hypothesis by speaking simply of P and non-P: the priestly material is certainly the easiest to identify. There are many scholars who defend alternative explanations for the complexity of the Pentateuchal narrative and laws, while among some evangelical Christians and some Orthodox Jews the pursuit

of sources is controversial, deplored by the former as heretical, and by the latter as potentially or even actually antisemitic – so the stakes are high. But anyone studying the Hebrew Bible seriously needs to know about the 'Documentary Hypothesis', as it is called. For more detail see my discussion in *History of the Bible*, pp. 48–51.

26 Coverdale sought to unify the Bible in his translation by a consistent Christianizing of the text – see Iona Hine, 'Translator as Theologian: The Praxis of Miles Coverdale, 1488–1569', forthcoming.

CHAPTER 9

1 The *Bibel in gerechter Sprache* says: 'Saul was quite old (*ziemlich alt*) when he began to reign.' I assume that this rests on the idea that the Hebrew 'son of year' is to be taken as 'son of years', that is, in Hebrew idiom, 'old', with 'quite' added to avoid the idea that the text is suggesting Saul was really aged.

2 James Barr, *Escaping from Fundamentalism*, London: SCM Press, 1984, p. 146. Overlooking a short passage by going from a word to the same word a few lines below and missing out what is in between, familiar to anyone who has ever copied anything, is known technically as parablepsis. It should be explained here that *thummim* on its own can mean 'perfection', hence the AV rendering 'perfect', with *lot* in italics because it does not occur explicitly in the original text – normal KJV practice, as we have seen.

3 In this I am following S. C. Daley, *The Textual Basis of English Translations of the Hebrew Bible*, Supplements to the Textual History of the Bible 2, Leiden: Brill, 2019.

4 Bart Ehrman, *The Orthodox Corruption of Scripture: The Effect of Early Christological Controversies on the Text of the New Testament*, New York and Oxford: Oxford University Press, 1993, second edition, 2011. For this example see pp. 69 and 115.

5 Ibid., p. xi.

6 Tertullian alleges that the singular reading was corrupted into a plural by the Valentinians, a gnostic sect he opposed (*De carne Christi* 24), while Irenaeus (*Against Heresies*, vol. iii, 16:2 and 19:2) argues from the singular verb that Jesus was no ordinary man but born miraculously, which is certainly what the change in the text was designed to affirm. As Ehrman says, what we have here is 'not a heretical tampering with the text, but an orthodox one' (*Orthodox Corruption*, p. 70).

7 See Jan Joosten, *The Verbal System of Biblical Hebrew: A New Synthesis Elaborated on the Basis of Classical Prose*, Jerusalem: Simor, 2012,

pp. 171–3. A pluperfect sense is more usually conveyed by using the *qatal* form of the verb.

CHAPTER 10

1 See the discussion in Adrian Schenker, 'L'Ecriture Sainte subsiste en plusieurs formes canoniques simultanées', in *L'interpretazione della Bibbia nelle chiesa. Atti del Simposio promosso dalla Congregazione per la Dottrina della Fede*, Vatican city: Libreria Editrice Vaticana, 2001, pp. 178–86; German transl. 'Die Heilige Schrift subsistiert gleichzeitig in mehreren kanonischen Formen', in A. Schenker, *Studien zu Propheten und Religionsgeschichte*, SBA 36, Stuttgart: Katholisches Bibelwerk, 2003, pp. 192–200.

2 Though note the case for a 'Septuagintal piety' made by G. Bertram, 'Septuaginta-Frömmigkeit', *Die Religion in Geschichte und Gegenwart* (third edition), 1961, Tübingen: Mohr, vol. v, pp. 1707–9, and the important discussion by Mogens Müller, 'Theology in the Septuagint?', in Salvesen and Law (eds), *Oxford Handbook of the Septuagint*, pp. 105–19, and in Hans Ausloos and Bénédicte Lemmelijn (eds), *Die Theologie der Septuaginta/The Theology of the Septuagint*, Handbuch zur Septuaginta/Handbook of the Septuagint LXX.H., vol. v, Gütersloh: Gütersloher Verlagshaus, 2020.

3 Philip Jenkins, *Crucible of Faith: The Ancient Revolution that made our Modern Religious World*, New York: Basic Books, 2017.

4 Joachim Schaper, *Eschatology in the Greek Bible*, Wissenschaftliche Untersuchungen zum Neuen Testament 2:76, Tübingen: Mohr Siebeck, 1995.

5 Ibid., pp. 93 and 140. The numbering of Psalms in the Greek Bible is often slightly different from the Hebrew.

6 Cf. Joachim Schaper, 'Messianism in the Septuagint of Isaiah and Messianic Intertextuality in the Greek Bible', in M. Knibb (ed.), *The Septuagint and Messianism*, Bibliotheca Ephemeridum Theologicarum Lovaniensium 195, Leuven: Peeters, 2006, pp. 371–80.

7 Law, *When God Spoke Greek*, pp. 104–5.

8 Ibid., p. 134. Ross Wagner similarly argues that there is more about the Torah in Greek Isaiah than in the Hebrew original: see J. Ross Wagner, 'The Septuagint and the "Search for the Christian Bible"', in M. Bockmuehl and A. J. Torrance (eds), *Scripture's Doctrine and Theology's Bible*, Grand Rapids, MI: Baker Academic Press, 2008, pp. 17–28.

9 Thus in Geza Vermes, *Christian Beginnings: From Nazareth to Nicaea, AD 30–325*, London: Allen Lane, 2012, pp. 186–7.

10 Law, *When God Spoke Greek*, pp. 96–7.

11 Cf. Wagner, 'The Septuagint', p. 20.

12 An exception is the Syriac translation, which was made from the Hebrew: see Chapter 1.

13 See my discussion of this phenomenon in *History of the Bible*, p. 467.

14 See Hartmut Gese, *Vom Sinai zum Zion*, Munich: Chr. Kaiser, 1974, and *Zur biblischen Theologie*, Munich: Chr. Kaiser, 1977, transl. as *Essays in Biblical Theology*, Minneapolis, MN: Augsburg, 1981; also idem, 'Tradition and Biblical Theology', in D. A. Knight (ed.), *Tradition and Theology in the Old Testament*, Philadelphia, PA: Fortress Press, 1977, pp. 301–26.

15 James Barr, *The Concept of Biblical Theology: An Old Testament Perspective*, London: SCM Press, 1999, pp. 362–77.

16 Ibid., p. 373.

17 The preceding discussion of Gese is reworked (with permission from Oxford University Press) from my contribution to Salvesen and Law (eds), *Oxford Handbook of the Septuagint*, pp. 737–8: the whole essay is John Barton, 'Christian Theology', ibid., pp. 731–44.

18 This was called for by Albert C. Sundberg Jr, a great expert in the history of the biblical canon, in the 1960s: see his 'The Protestant Old Testament Canon: Should it be Re-examined?', *Catholic Biblical Quarterly* 28, 1966, pp. 194–203. The case was argued more recently by Mogens Müller, *The First Bible of the Church: A Plea for the Septuagint*, Sheffield: Sheffield Academic Press, 1996.

19 Hans Hübner, *Biblische Theologie des Neuen Testaments*, Göttingen: Vandenhoeck & Ruprecht, vol. i, 1990.

20 Nicholas King, *The Old Testament: A New, Cutting-Edge Translation of the Septuagint*, Buxhall, Stowmarket: Kevin Mayhew, 2008–.

21 Albert Pietersma and Benjamin G. Wright (eds), *A New Translation of the Septuagint*, Oxford and New York: Oxford University Press, 2007.

22 *La Bible d'Alexandrie*, Paris: Éditions du Cerf, 1986–.

23 *Septuaginta Deutsch*, Stuttgart: Deutsche Bibelgesellschaft, 1999–2008.

24 *La biblia griega Septuaginta*, Salamanca: Ediciones Sígueme, 2008.

25 *The Orthodox Study Bible*, Nashville, TN: Thomas Nelson, 2008.

26 See also Eberhard Bons, 'Modern Translations of the Septuagint', in Salvesen and Law (eds), *Oxford Handbook to the Septuagint*, pp. 691–705, where there is a comprehensive list.

CONCLUSION

1 Reiß had already laid the foundations in her book *Möglichkeiten und Grenzen der Übersetzungskritik. Kategorien und Kriterien für eine sachgerechte Beurteilung von Übersetzungen*, Munich: Hueber, 1971, where she argued that different kinds of text required different types of translation: for example, 'informative' texts called for literal (formal-equivalence) renderings, 'expressive' texts functional-equivalence ones. Using these terms, we could say that the dispute between Nida and Alter (in this chapter I take them as representative of the two main tendencies) is over whether the Bible is informative or expressive.

2 'Text-type' can be used for a high-level classification such as 'novel' and 'genre' for subtypes such as 'romantic novel', 'detective novel', 'epistolary novel', and so on.

3 Reiß and Vermeer, *Towards a General Theory*, p. 83.

4 Ibid., p. 170.

5 Ibid., p. 49.

6 Ibid., p. 124.

Bibliography

Aejmelaeus, Anneli, *Parataxis in the Septuagint: A Study of the Renderings of the Hebrew Coordinate Clauses in the Greek Pentateuch*, Helsinki: Suomalainen Tiedeakatemia, 1982.

Allen, David and Steve Smith (eds), *Methodology in the Use of the Old Testament in the New: Context and Criteria*, Library of New Testament Studies 579, London: T & T Clark, 2020.

Alter, Robert, *The Art of Bible Translation*, Princeton, NJ and Oxford: Princeton University Press, 2019.

Alter, Robert, *The Hebrew Bible*, 3 vols, New York: W. W. Norton and Co., 2018.

Alter, Robert, *The Art of Biblical Narrative*, London: George Allen & Unwin, 1981.

Amos, Flora Ross, *Early Theories of Translation*, New York: Columbia University Press, 1920, reprinted Octagon Books, 1973.

Ballard, M., *De Cicéron à Benjamin: traducteurs, traductions, réflexions*, Lille: Presses universitaires de Lille, 1992.

Barr, James, 'After Five Years: A Retrospect on Two Major Translations of the Bible', *Heythrop Journal* 15, 1974, pp. 381–405; reprinted in John Barton (ed.), *Bible and Interpretation: The Collected Essays of James Barr*, 3 vols, Oxford: Oxford University Press, 2014, vol. iii, pp. 231–52.

Barr, James, 'An Aspect of Salvation in the Old Testament', in E. J. Sharpe and J. L. Hinnells (eds), *Man and his Salvation: Studies in Memory of S. G. Brandon*, Manchester: Manchester University Press, 1973, pp. 39–52; reprinted in John Barton (ed.), *Bible and Interpretation: The Collected Essays of James Barr*, Oxford: Oxford University Press, 3 vols, 2013, vol. ii, pp. 127–50.

Barr, James, 'Modern English Bible Versions as a Problem for the Church', *Quarterly Review* (United Methodist Church, Nashville, TN) 14/3, 1994, pp. 263–78; reprinted in John Barton (ed.), *Bible and Interpretation: The Collected Essays of James Barr*, 3 vols, Oxford: Oxford University Press, 2014, vol. iii, pp. 253–65.

Barr, James, *Escaping from Fundamentalism*, London: SCM Press, 1984.

Barr, James, *The Concept of Biblical Theology: An Old Testament Perspective*, London: SCM Press, 1999.

Barr, James, *The Garden of Eden and the Hope of Immortality*, London: SCM Press, 1992.

Barr, James, *The Semantics of Biblical Language*, Oxford: Oxford University Press, 1961.

Barr, James, *The Typology of Literalism in Ancient Biblical Translations*, Göttingen: Vandenhoeck & Ruprecht, 1979.

Barton, John, 'Christian Theology', in Alison Salvesen and Timothy Michael Law (eds), *The Oxford Handbook of the Septuagint*, Oxford: Oxford University Press, 2021, pp. 731–44.

Barton, John, *A History of the Bible: The Book and Its Faiths*, London: Allen Lane, 2019; American edition *A History of the Bible: The Story of the World's Most Influential Book*, New York: Viking, 2019.

Bassnett, Susan, *Translation Studies*, London: Routledge, fourth edition, 2014.

Batnitzky, Leora, 'Translation as Transcendence: A Glimpse into the Workshop of the Buber-Rosenzweig Bible Translation', *New German Critique* 70, 1997, pp. 87–116.

Belloc, Hilaire, 'On Translation', *The Bookman: A Review of Books and Life* 74:1, 1931.

Bellos, David, *Is That a Fish in Your Ear? Translation and the Meaning of Everything*, London: Penguin, 2011.

Benjamin, Walter, 'The Translator's Task', in Lawrence Venuti (ed.), *The Translation Studies Reader*, New York and Abingdon: Routledge, second edition, 2004, pp. 75–83; transl. by Stephen Rendall from German original, 'Die Aufgabe des Übersetzers', 1923.

Berlin, Adele and Marc Zvi Brettler (eds), *The Jewish Study Bible*, New York: Oxford University Press, second edition, 2014.

Berman, Antoine, 'La traduction comme épreuve de l'étranger', *Texte* 4, 1985, pp. 67–81, transl. by Lawrence Venuti as 'Translation and the Trials of the Foreign', in Lawrence Venuti (ed.), *The Translation Studies Reader*, New York and Abingdon: Routledge, second edition, 2004, pp. 240–53.

Bertram, G., 'Septuaginta-Frömmigkeit', *Die Religion in Geschichte und Gegenwart* (third edition), 1961, Tübingen: Mohr, vol. v, pp. 1707–9.

Bibel in gerechter Sprache, Gütersloh: Gütersloher Verlagshaus, 2006.

Black, Matthew, *An Aramaic Approach to the Gospels and Acts*, Oxford: Clarendon Press, third edition, 1967 (first edition 1946).

Bloom, Harold, *A Map of Misreading*, New York: Oxford University Press, 1975.

Bloom, Harold, *The Anxiety of Influence: A Theory of Poetry*, New York and Oxford: Oxford University Press, 1973.

Boehmer, J., 'Der Glaube und Jesaja – zu Jes. 7,9 und 28,16', *Zeitschrift für die Alttestamentliche Wissenschaft* 41, 1923, pp. 84–93.

Boer, Roland, 'The Dynamic Equivalence Caper', in S. S. Elliott and R. Boer (eds), *Ideology, Culture, and Translation*, Atlanta, GA: SBL Press, 2012.

Bons, Eberhard, 'Modern Translations of the Septuagint', in Alison Salvesen and Timothy Michael Law (eds), *The Oxford Handbook of the Septuagint*, Oxford: Oxford University Press, 2021, pp. 691–705.

Brenner, Athalya and Jan Willem van Henten (eds), *Bible Translation on the Threshold of the Twenty-First Century: Authority, Reception, Culture and Religion*, Supplements to the Journal for the Study of the New Testament 353, Sheffield: Sheffield Academic Press, 2001.

Brunn, Dave, *One Bible, Many Versions: Are All Translations Created Equal?*, Nottingham: Inter-Varsity Press, 2013.

Buber, Martin, 'Zu einer neuen Verdeutschung der Schrift', 1954, transl. by D. Robinson as 'Martin Buber: On the Diction of a German Translation of the Scripture', *Translation and Literature* 2, 1993, pp. 105–10.

Buber, Martin and Franz Rosenzweig, *Die Schrift und ihre Verdeutschung*, Berlin: Schocken, 1936.

Buber, Martin and Franz Rosenzweig, *Scripture and Translation*, transl. Lawrence Rosenwald and Everett Fox, Bloomington and Indianapolis: Indiana University Press, 1994.

Cadwallader, Alan H., *The Politics of the Revised Version: A Tale of Two New Testament Revision Companies*, Scriptural Traces 14, Library of Hebrew Bible/Old Testament Studies 637, London: T & T Clark, 2019.

Campbell, George, *The Four Gospels Translated from the Greek, with Preliminary Dissertations and Notes Critical and Explanatory*, four vols, Boston, MA: Thomas B. Watt and Co., 1811 (first edition two vols, Edinburgh, 1789).

Chan, Lucienne, 'La traduction littérale dans l'histoire de la traduction', unpublished dissertation, Ottawa 1987.

Chesterman, Andrew, *Memes of Translation: The Spread of Ideas in Translation Theory*, revised edition, Amsterdam and Philadelphia, John Benjamin's Publishing Company, 2016.

Chesterton, G. K., *The Collected Poems of G. K. Chesterton*, London: Methuen, seventh edition, 1939.

Childs, Brevard S., *Biblical Theology of the Old and New Testaments: Theological Reflections on the Christian Bible*, London: SCM Press, 1992.

Chouraqui, André, *La Bible*, Paris: Desclee de Brouwer, 2003.

Crystal, Ben and David Crystal, *Shakespeare's Words: A Glossary and Language Companion*, London: Penguin, 2004.

Cullmann, Oscar, *Immortality of the Soul or Resurrection of the Dead? The Witness of the New Testament*, London: Epworth Press, 1958.

Daley, S. C., *The Textual Basis of English Translations of the Hebrew Bible*, Supplements to the Textual History of the Bible 2, Leiden: Brill, 2019.

Damrosch, David, 'Translation and World Literature: Love in the Necropolis', Chapter 4 of David Damrosch, *What is World Literature?*, Princeton, NJ: Princeton University Press, 2003, pp. 147–69; reprinted in Lawrence Venuti (ed.), *The Translation Studies Reader*, New York and Abingdon: Routledge, second edition 2004, pp. 411–28.

Daniell, David, *The Bible in English: Its History and Influence*, New Haven, CT: Yale University Press, 2003.

De Crom, Dries, 'The *Letter of Aristeas*', in Alison Salvesen and Timothy Michael Law (eds), *The Oxford Handbook of the Septuagint*, Oxford: Oxford University Press, 2021, pp. 121–34.

De Moor, Johannes, 'Introduction', in J. C. de Moor (ed.), *Intertextuality in Ugarit and Israel: Papers Read at the Tenth Joint Meeting of the Society for Old Testament Study and Het Oudtestamentisch Werkgezelschap in Nederland & België, held at Oxford, 1997*, Leiden: Brill, 1998.

Draisma, Spike (ed.), *Intertextuality in Biblical Writings: Essays in Honour of Bas van Iersel*, Kampen: Kok, 1989.

Dryden, John, 'Preface to Ovid's Epistles', in W. P. Ker (ed.), *Essays of John Dryden*, vol. i, Oxford: Clarendon Press, 1900.

Dunn, J. D. G., *The New Perspective on Paul: Collected Essays*, Tübingen: Mohr Siebeck, 2005.

Ehrman, Bart, *Heaven and Hell: A History of the Afterlife*, London: Oneworld, 2020.

Ehrman, Bart, *The Orthodox Corruption of Scripture: The Effect of Early Christological Controversies on the Text of the New Testament*, New York and Oxford: Oxford University Press, 1993, second edition, 2011.

Eilenberger, Wolfram, *Time of the Magicians: The Invention of Modern Thought, 1919–1929*, London: Allen Lane, 2020.

Eliot, T. S., 'Tradition and the Individual Talent' (1919), in *Selected Essays, 1917–1932*, London: Faber and Faber, 1932, second edition, 1934.

Ellingworth, Paul, 'The Scope of Inclusive Language: Structure and Usage', in Siegfried Meurer (ed.), *Die vergessenen Schwestern: Frauengerechte Sprache in der Bibelübersetzung*, Stuttgart: Deutsche Bibelgesellschaft, 1993, pp. 53–66.

Fishbane, Michael, *Biblical Interpretation in Ancient Israel*, New York and Oxford: Oxford University Press, 1985.

Foucault, Michel, 'Les mots qui saignent', *L'Express* 688, 1964, pp. 21–2.

Fowler, H. W. and F. G. Fowler, *The King's English*, third edition, Oxford: Oxford University Press, 1990 (first edition 1906).

Fox, Everett, 'The Book and Its Context', in Martin Buber and Franz Rosenzweig, *Scripture and Translation*, transl. by Lawrence Rosenwald and Everett Fox, Bloomington and Indianapolis: Indiana University Press, pp. xiii–xxvii.

Fox, Everett, *Give Us a King!: A New English Translation of the Book of Samuel*, New York: Schocken Books, 1995.

Fox, Everett, *The Five Books of Moses*, New York: Schocken Books, 1983.

Gadamer, Hans-Georg, *Gadamer on Celan: 'Who Am I and Who Are You?' and Other Essays*, New York: State of New York Press, 1997.

Gese, Hartmut, 'Tradition and Biblical Theology', in D. A. Knight (ed.), *Tradition and Theology in the Old Testament*, Philadelphia, PA: Fortress Press, 1977, pp. 301–26.

Gese, Hartmut, *Vom Sinai zum Zion*, Munich: Chr. Kaiser, 1974.

Gese, Hartmut, *Zur biblischen Theologie*, Munich: Chr. Kaiser, 1977, transl. as *Essays in Biblical Theology*, Minneapolis, MN: Augsburg, 1981.

Goldingay, John and Tom Wright, *The Bible for Everyone: A New Translation*, London: SPCK, 2018.

Gordon, R. P., '"Converse Translation" in the Targums and Beyond', *Journal for the Study of the Pseudepigrapha* 19, 1999, pp. 3–21.

Greenspoon, Leonard J., 'Jewish Bible Translation', in John Barton (ed.), *The Biblical World*, London: Routledge, 2002, pp. 397–412.

Greenstein, Edward L., 'What Might Make a Bible Translation Jewish?', in David M. Goldenberg (ed.), *Translation of Scripture*, Philadelphia: Annenberg Research Institute, 1990.

Greenstein, Edward L., *Job: A New Translation*, New Haven, CT: Yale University Press, 2019.

Hammond, Gerald, 'English Translations of the Bible', in Robert Alter and Frank Kermode (eds), *The Literary Guide to the Bible*, London: Collins, 1987.

Hammond, Gerald, *The Making of the English Bible*, New York: Philosophical Library, 1983.

Hart, David Bentley, *The New Testament: A Translation*, New Haven, CT and London: Yale University Press, 2017.

Hays, Richard B, *Echoes of Scripture in the Letters of Paul*, New Haven, CT and London: Yale University Press, 1989.

Hays, Richard B., *Echoes of Scripture in the Gospels*, Waco, TX: Baylor University Press, 2016.

Hays, Richard B., Stefan Alkier and Leroy Andrew Huizenga (eds), *Reading the Bible Intertextually*, Waco, TX: Baylor University Press, 2009.

Heller, Peter, 'Some Functions of the Leitmotiv in Thomas Mann's Joseph Tetralogy', *The Germanic Review: Literature, Culture, Theory* 22, 1947, pp. 126–41.

Hine, Iona, 'Translator as Theologian: The Praxis of Miles Coverdale, 1488–1569', forthcoming.

Hübner, Hans, *Biblische Theologie des Neuen Testaments*, Göttingen: Vandenhoeck & Ruprecht, vol. i, 1990.

Jenkins, Philip. *Crucible of Faith: The Ancient Revolution that Made our Modern Religious World*, New York: Basic Books, 2017.

Jerome, *Liber de optimo genere interpretandi (Epistula 57)*, ed. G. J. M. Bartelink, Leiden: Brill, 1980.

Johnson, A. R., *The Vitality of the Individual in the Thought of Ancient Israel*, Cardiff: University of Wales Press, 1964.

Joosten, Jan, *The Verbal System of Biblical Hebrew: A New Synthesis Elaborated on the Basis of Classical Prose*, Jerusalem: Simor, 2012.

Keefer, Arthur Jan, *The Book of Proverbs and Virtue Ethics: Integrating the Biblical and Philosophical Traditions*, Cambridge: Cambridge University Press, 2021.

Keller, C. A., 'Das quietische Element in der Botschaft des Jesaja', *Theologische Literaturzeitung* 11, 1955, pp. 81–97.

Kelly, L. G., *The True Interpreter: A History of Translation Theory and Practice in the West*, New York: St. Martin's Press, 1979.

King, Nicholas, *The Old Testament: A New, Cutting-Edge Translation of the Septuagint*, Buxhall, Stowmarket: Kevin Mayhew, 2008–.

Klein, M. L., 'Converse Translation: A Targumic Technique', *Biblica* 57, 1976, pp. 515–37.

Kraebel, Andrew, *Biblical Commentary and Translation in Late Medieval England: Experiments in Interpretation*, Cambridge: Cambridge University Press, 2020.

Kristal, Efraín, *Invisible Work: Borges and Translation*, Nashville, TN: Vanderbilt University Press, 2002.

Kristeva, Julia, *Revolution in Poetic Language*, New York: Columbia University Press, 1984.

Kristeva, Julia, *Σημειωτιχὴ: recherches pour une sémanalyse*, Paris: Seuil, 1969; transl. in Julia Kristeva, *Desire in Language: A Semiotic Approach to Literature and Art*, New York: Columbia University Press and London: Blackwell, 1980.

La Bible d'Alexandrie, Paris: Éditions du Cerf, 1986–.

La biblia griega Septuaginta, Salamanca: Ediciones Sígueme, 2008.

Ladmiral, J.-R., *Traduire. Théorèmes pour la traduction*, Paris: Payot, second edition, 1994.

Law, Timothy Michael, *When God Spoke Greek: The Septuagint and the Making of the Christian Bible*, Oxford: Oxford University Press, 2013.

Lewis, C. S., 'The Literary Impact of the Authorized Version', The Ethel M. Wood Lecture delivered before the University of London on 20 March 1950, London, 1950; reprinted in *They Asked for a Paper*, London: Geoffrey Bles, 1962, pp. 26–50.

Lewis, C. S., *Reflections on the Psalms*, London: Geoffrey Bles, 1958.

Lianeri, A. and V. Zajko (eds), *Translation and the Classic: Identity as Change in the History of Culture*, Oxford: Oxford University Press, 2008.

Loewe, R., '"Salvation" is Not of the Jews', *Journal of Theological Studies* new series 32:2, 1981, pp. 341–68.

Lorimer, William, *The New Testament in Scots*, Edinburgh: Canongate, 1983.

MacCulloch, Diarmaid, *Reformation: Europe's House Divided, 1419–1700*, London: Allen Lane, 2003.

Macdonald, Bruce Robert, *Translation as Transcendence: Walter Benjamin and the German Tradition of Translation Theory*, Ann Arbor, MI: ProQuest Dissertation Publishing, 1984.

MacGregor, Neil, *Germany: Memories of a Nation*, London: Allen Lane, 2014.

Mason, Ian, 'Text Parameters in Translation: Transitivity and Institutional Cultures', in Eva Hajicova, Peter Sgall, Zuzanna Jettmarova, Annely Rothkegel, Dorothee Rothfuß-Bastian and Heldrun Gerzymisch-Arbogast (eds), *Textologie und Translation*, Tübingen: Narr, 2003, pp. 175–88; reprinted in Lawrence Venuti (ed.), *The Translation Studies Reader*, New York and Abingdon: Routledge, second edition, 2004, pp. 399–410.

McBride Jr, S. Dean, 'Interpretive Reception of the Book of Exodus in the English Geneva Bible of 1560', in Barry R. Huff and Patricia Vesely (eds), *Seeking Wisdom's Depths and Torah's Heights: Essays in Honor of Samuel E. Balentine*, Macon, GA: Smith and Helwys, 2021, pp. 89–125.

Meschonnic, Henri, *Les cinq rouleaux*, revised edition, Paris: Gallimard, 1986.

Metzger, Bruce M., *The Bible in Translation: Ancient and English Versions*, Grand Rapids, MI: Baker Academic, 2001.

Meurer, Siegfried (ed.), *Die vergessenen Schwestern: Frauengerechte Sprache in der Bibelübersetzung*, Stuttgart: Deutsche Bibelgesellschaft, 1993.

Miscall, Peter D., 'Isaiah: New Heavens, New Earth, New Book', in Danna Nolan Fewell (ed.), *Reading between Texts: Intertextuality and the Hebrew Bible*, Louisville, KY: Westminster/John Knox Press, 1992, pp. 41–56.

Moberly, R. W. L., *Old Testament Theology: Reading the Hebrew Bible as Christian Scripture*, Grand Rapids, MI: Baker Academic, 2013.

Moore, Stephen D. and Yvonne Sherwood, *The Invention of the Biblical Scholar: A Critical Manifesto*, Minneapolis, MN: Fortress Press, 2011.

Morgan, Teresa, *Roman Faith and Christian Faith:* Pistis *and* Fides *in the Early Roman Empire and Early Churches*, Oxford: Oxford University Press, 2015.

Mounin, G., *Les problèmes théoriques de la traduction*, Paris: Gallimard, 1963.

Müller, Katrin, *Lobe den Herrn, meine 'Seele'. Eine kognitiv-linguistische Studie zur* næfæs *des Menschen im Alten Testament*, Beiträge zur Wissenschaft des Alten und Neuen Testament 215, Stuttgart: Kohlhammer, 2018.

Müller, Mogens, 'Theology in the Septuagint?', in Alison Salvesen and Timothy Michael Law (eds), *Oxford Handbook of the Septuagint*, Oxford: Oxford University Press, 2021, pp. 105–19; also in Hans Ausloos and Bénédicte Lemmelijn (eds), *Die Theologie der Septuaginta/The Theology of the Septuagint*, Handbuch zur Septuaginta/Handbook of the Septuagint LXX.H., vol. v, Gütersloh: Gütersloher Verlagshaus, 2020.

Müller, Mogens, *The First Bible of the Church: A Plea for the Septuagint*, Sheffield: Sheffield Academic Press, 1996.

Nabokov, Vladimir, 'Problems of Translation: *Onegin* in English', *Partisan Review* 22, 1955, pp. 496–512; reprinted in Lawrence Venuti (ed.), *The Translation Studies Reader*, New York and Abingdon: Routledge, second edition, 2004, pp. 113–25.

Najman, Hindy and Benjamin J. Wright, 'Perfecting Translation: The Greek Scriptures in Philo of Alexandria', in J. Baden, H. Najman and E. Tigchelaar (eds), *Sibyls, Scriptures, and Scrolls: John Collins at Seventy*, Leiden and Boston, MA: Brill, 2017, vol. ii, pp. 897–915.

Newman, Francis, *The Iliad of Homer*, London: Walton & Maberly, 1856.

Nida, Eugene, 'Principles of Correspondence', in Eugene Nida, *Toward a Science of Translating*, Leiden: E. J. Brill, 1964, pp. 156–71; reprinted in Lawrence Venuti (ed.), *The Translation Studies Reader*, New York and Abingdon: Routledge, second edition, 2004, pp. 141–55.

Nida, Eugene, *Bible Translating: An Analysis of Principles and Procedures, with Special Reference to Aboriginal Languages*, New York: American Bible Society, 1947.

Nida, Eugene, *Good News for Everyone: How to Use the Good News Bible (Today's English Version)*, London: Fount, 1977.

Nida, Eugene, *Language, Structure and Translation*, Stanford, CA: Stanford University Press, 1975.

Nida, Eugene, *Message and Mission: The Communication of the Christian Faith*, New York: Harper & Brothers, 1960.

Nida, Eugene, *On Translation: An Expanded Edition*, Hong Kong: City University of Hong Kong, 2006.

Nida, Eugene and C. Taber, *The Theory and Practice of Translation*, Leiden: Brill, 1969.

Nida, Eugene, *Toward a Science of Translating*, Leiden: E. J. Brill, 1964.

Pearson, Brook W. R., 'Remainderless Translation? Implications of the Tradition concerning the Translation of the LXX for Modern Translational Theory', in Stanley E. Porter and Richard S. Hess (eds), *Translating the Bible: Problems and Prospects*, London and New York: Bloomsbury, 1999, pp. 64–84.

Pfeiffer, Egon, 'Glaube im Alten Testament', *Zeitschrift für die alttestamentliche Wissenschaft* 71, 1959, pp. 151–64.

Phillips, J. B., *The New Testament in Modern English*, 1958, revised edition New York and London, Macmillan, 1972.

Pietersma, Albert, and Benjamin G. Wright (eds), *A New Translation of the Septuagint*, Oxford and New York: Oxford University Press, 2007.

Polizzotti, Mark, *Sympathy for the Traitor: A Translation Manifesto*, Cambridge, MA and London: The MIT Press, 2018.

Porter, Stanley E. and Richard S. Hess (eds), *Translating the Bible: Problems and Prospects*, London and New York: Bloomsbury, 1999.

Prickett, Stephen, *Words and the Word: Language, Poetics and Biblical Interpretation*, Cambridge: Cambridge University Press, 1986.

Radice, William, 'Introduction', in William Radice and Barbara Reynolds (eds), *The Translator's Art: Essays in Honour of Betty Radice*, Harmondsworth: Penguin, 1987, pp. 9–30.

Räisänen, Heikki, *Paul and the Law*, Tübingen: Mohr, 1983.

Reiß, Katharina, 'Frauengerechte Sprache?', in Siegfried Meurer (ed.), *Die vergessenen Schwestern: Frauengerechte Sprache in der Bibelübersetzung*, Stuttgart: Deutsche Bibelgesellschaft, 1993, pp. 37–52.

Reiß, Katharina, *Möglichkeiten und Grenzen der Übersetzungskritik. Kategorien und Kriterien für eine sachgerechte Beurteilung von Übersetzungen*, Munich: Hueber, 1971.

Reiß, Katharina and Hans Josef Vermeer, *Grundlegung einer allgemeinen Translationstheorie*, Tübingen: Niemeyer, 1984; English version *Towards a General Theory of Translational Action: Skopos Theory Explained*, Manchester: St Jerome Publishing, 2013.

Rendsburg, Gary A., 'A Comprehensive Guide to Israelian Hebrew: Grammar and Lexicon', *Orient* 38, 2003, pp. 5–35.

Rendsburg, Gary A., *Israelian Hebrew in the Book of Kings*, Bethesda, MD: CDL Press, 2002.

Rendsburg, Gary A., *Linguistic Evidence for the Northern Origin of Selected Psalms*, Atlanta, GA: Scholars Press, 1990.

Reynolds, Matthew, *Translation: A Very Short Introduction*, Oxford: Oxford University Press, 2016.

Rieu, E. V., *The Four Gospels: A New Translation*, London: Penguin, 1953.

Rochette, Bruno, review of Astrid Seele, *Römische Übersetzer* [see Seele below], *Revue belge de Philologie et de l'Histoire* 74, 1996, pp. 186–8.

Rogerson, J. W., 'The Old Testament Translator's Translation – A Personal Reflection', in Stanley E. Porter and Richard S. Hess (eds), *Translating the Bible: Problems and Prospects*, London and New York: Bloomsbury, 1999, pp. 116–24.

Rosenwald, Lawrence, 'Buber and Rosenzweig's Challenge to Translation Theory', in Martin Buber and Franz Rosenzweig, *Scripture and Translation*, transl. by Lawrence Rosenwald and Everett Fox, Bloomington and Indianapolis: Indiana University Press, 1994, pp. xxix–liv.

Rosenzweig, Franz, 'Scripture and Luther', in Martin Buber and Franz Rosenzweig, *Scripture and Translation*, transl. by Lawrence Rosenwald and Everett Fox, Bloomington and Indianapolis: Indiana University Press, 1994, pp. 47–69.

Ruden, Sarah, *The Face of Water: A Translator on Beauty and Meaning in the Bible*, New York: Vintage Books, 2018.

Ruden, Sarah, *The Gospels: A New Translation*, New York: Modern Library/ Penguin Random House, 2021.

Salvesen, Alison and Timothy Michael Law (eds), *The Oxford Handbook of the Septuagint*, Oxford: Oxford University Press, 2021.

Sauter, Gerhard, 'Seele: geprägte Lebendigkeit', *Berliner Theologische Zeitschrift* 34:2, 2017, pp. 120–148.

Scanlin, Harold P., 'Inclusive Language in Recent English Bible Translations', in Siegfried Meurer (ed.), *Die vergessenen Schwestern: Frauengerechte Sprache in der Bibelübersetzung*, Stuttgart: Deutsche Bibelgesellschaft, 1993, pp. 95–100.

Schaper, Joachim, 'Messianism in the Septuagint of Isaiah and Messianic Intertextuality in the Greek Bible', in M. Knibb (ed.), *The Septuagint and Messianism*, Bibliotheca Ephemeridum Theologicarum Lovaniensium 195, Leuven: Peeters, 2006, pp. 371–80.

Schaper, Joachim, *Eschatology in the Greek Bible*, Wissenschaftliche Untersuchungen zum Neuen Testament 2:76, Tübingen: Mohr Siebeck, 1995.

Schenker, Adrian, 'L'Ecriture Sainte subsiste en plusieurs formes canoniques simultanées', in *L'interpretazione della Bibbia nelle chiesa. Atti del Simposio promosso dalla Congregazione per la Dottrina della Fede*, Vatican city: Libreria Editrice Vaticana, 2001, pp. 178–86; German transl. 'Die Heilige Schrift subsistiert gleichzeitig in mehreren kanonischen Formen', in A.

Schenker, *Studien zu Propheten und Religionsgeschichte*, SBA 36, Stuttgart: Katholisches Bibelwerk, 2003, pp. 192–200.

Schleiermacher, F. D. E., 'Über die verschiedenen Methoden des Übersetzens', transl. by Susan Bernofsky as 'On the Different Methods of Translating', in Lawrence Venuti (ed.), *The Translation Studies Reader*, New York and Abingdon: Routledge, second edition, 2004, pp. 43–63.

Seele, Astrid, *Römische Übersetzer. Nöte, Freiheiten, Absichten, Verfahren des literarischen Übersetzens in der griechisch-römischen Antike*, Darmstadt: Wissenschaftliche Buchgesellschaft, 1995.

Seidman, Naomi, *Faithful Renderings: Jewish-Christian Difference and the Politics of Translation*, Chicago and London: University of Chicago Press, 2006.

Seitz, Christopher R., *Word without End: The Old Testament as Abiding Theological Witness*, Grand Rapids, MI and Cambridge: W. B. Eerdmans, 1998.

Septuaginta Deutsch, Stuttgart: Deutsche Bibelgesellschaft, 1999–2008.

Smend, R., 'Zur Geschichte von *he'emin*', Supplements to Vetus Testamentum 16, 1967, pp. 284–90.

Speed Hill, W. (ed.), *The Folger Library Edition of the Works of Richard Hooker*, six vols, Cambridge, MA and London: 1977.

Steiner, George, *After Babel: Aspects of Language and Translation*, third edition, Oxford: Oxford University Press, 1998 (first edition 1975).

Sundberg Jr, Albert C., 'The Protestant Old Testament Canon: Should it be Re-examined?', *Catholic Biblical Quarterly* 28, 1966, pp. 194–203.

The Orthodox Study Bible, Nashville, TN: Thomas Nelson, 2008.

The Translators to the Readers: Preface to the King James Version of 1611, CrossReach Publications, 2016.

Thiselton, Anthony C., *New Horizons in Hermeneutics: The Theory and Practice of Transforming Biblical Reading*, London: HarperCollins, 1992.

Toury, Gideon, *Descriptive Translation Studies and Beyond*, Amsterdam and Philadelphia: John Benjamin's Publishing Company, revised edition, 2012.

Valéry, Paul, *The Art of Poetry*, transl. by Denise Folliot, New York: Vintage Books, 1961.

Venuti, Lawrence, 'Genealogies of Translation Theory: Jerome', *Boundary* 2 37/3, 2010, pp. 5–28; reprinted in Lawrence Venuti (ed.), *The Translation Studies Reader*, New York and Abingdon: Routledge, second edition, 2004, pp. 483–502.

Venuti, Lawrence, *The Translator's Invisibility: A History of Translation*, London: Routledge, revised edition, 2018.

Venuti, Lawrence (ed.), *The Translation Studies Reader*, New York and Abingdon: Routledge, second edition, 2004.

Vermeer, Hans J., 'Skopos and Commission in Translation Theory', in Andrew Chesterman (ed.), *Readings in Translation Theory*, Helsinki: Oy Finn Lectura Ob, 1989, pp. 173–87; also in Lawrence Venuti (ed.), *The Translation Studies Reader*, New York and Abingdon: Routledge, second edition, 2004, pp. 191–202.

Vermes, Geza, *Christian Beginnings: From Nazareth to Nicaea, AD 30–325*, London: Allen Lane, 2012.

Waddell, Helen, *Mediaeval Latin Lyrics*, Harmondsworth: Penguin, 1964 (first edition 1929).

Wagner, J. Ross, 'The Septuagint and the "Search for the Christian Bible"', in M. Bockmuehl and A. J. Torrance (eds), *Scripture's Doctrine and Theology's Bible*, Grand Rapids, MI: Baker Academic Press, 2008, pp. 17–28.

Wallaert, Ineke, 'The Translation of Sociolects: A Paradigm of Ideological Issues in Translation?', in Janet Cotterill and Anne Ife (eds), *Language across Boundaries: Selected Papers from the Annual Meeting of the British Association for Applied Linguistics held at Anglia Polytechnic University, Cambridge, September 2000*, London: Bloomsbury, 2005.

Wansbrough, Henry, 'Christian Bible Translation', in John Barton (ed.), *The Biblical World*, London: Routledge, 2002, pp. 413–26.

Warnke, Georgia, 'Hermeneutics and Critical Theory', in Michael N. Forster and Kristin Gjesdal (eds), *The Cambridge Companion to Hermeneutics*, Cambridge: Cambridge University Press, 2019, pp. 237–59.

Wasserstein, Abraham and David J. Wasserstein, *The Legend of the Septuagint: From Classical Antiquity to Today*, Cambridge: Cambridge University Press, 2006.

Weissbort, Daniel and Astradur Eysteinsson (eds), *Translation – Theory and Practice: A Historical Reader*, Oxford: Oxford University Press, 2006.

Whang, Y. C., 'To Whom is a Translator Responsible – Reader or Author?', in Stanley E. Porter and Richard S. Hess (eds), *Translating the Bible: Problems and Prospects*, London and New York: Bloomsbury, 1999, pp. 46–63.

Wierzbicka, Anna, *What Christians Believe: The Story of God and People in Minimal English*, New York: Oxford University Press, 2019.

Wildberger, H., '"Glauben" im Alten Testament', *Zeitschrift für Theologie und Kirche* 65, 1968, pp. 129–59.

Wildberger, H., '"Glauben", Erwägungen zu he'emin', Vetus Testamentum Supplements 16, 1967, pp. 372–86.

Wilt, Timothy (ed.), *Bible Translation: Frames of Reference*, Manchester: St Jerome, 2003.

Wright, Benjamin J., *The Letter of Aristeas: 'Aristeas to Philocrates' or 'On the Translation of the Laws of the Jews'*, Commentaries on Early Jewish Literature, Berlin: W. de Gruyter, 2015.

Index

Index of Biblical References